THE
BRIEFING
SEAN SPICER

POLITICS, THE PRESS AND THE PRESIDENT

Biteback Publishing

This edition published in Great Britain in 2018 by
Biteback Publishing Ltd
Westminster Tower
3 Albert Embankment
London SE1 7SP
Copyright © Sean Spicer 2018

ISBN 978-1-78590-380-9

10 9 8 7 6 5 4 3 2 1

A CIP catalogue record for this book is available from the British Library.

Set in Sabon

Printed and bound in Great Britain by
CPI Group (UK) Ltd, Croydon CR0 4YY

MIX
Paper from
responsible sources
FSC
www.fsc.org
FSC® C020471

THE BRIEFING

To Mike Spicer

CONTENTS

CHAPTER ONE

IT'S OVER

The president wanted to see me.

The call came at four o'clock on a Thursday afternoon in late July in the White House, a time when most staffers were grabbing a cup coffee in hope of a second wind that would sustain them until the evening. My wife, Rebecca, had taken our two children with her on a business trip to Colorado. I was looking forward to working late and catching up on a backlog of calls.

As always, I felt a twinge of anxiety whenever summoned to see the president.

The press secretary's office is roughly halfway between the Oval Office and the James S. Brady Press Briefing Room, but the walk to the Oval Office always seemed longer. Typically, if you are called into the Oval Office, it isn't for an "attaboy." More likely, the president was upset by something in the press, or wanted to get ahead of a story, or identified a problem in our communications strategy, or wanted to know more about a reporter.

Madeleine Westerhout, the president's executive assistant who sits right outside the Oval Office, directed me to the private dining room that adjoins the Oval Office. Off the Oval Office is a hallway with a bathroom, a private study, and a small, but elegant, dining room.

President Donald J. Trump was sitting at the end of the dining room table—a rectangular table made of polished, dark-brown wood, surrounded by six chairs. The windows at one end of the room overlooked a patio. At the other end of the room was a large, flat-screen television, mounted to the wall, which had a cable news station on it. He was facing the TV, stone-faced, with two columns of papers on either side of him on the tabletop—memos, documents to be signed, and printouts of news stories and blogs. My deputy, Sarah Huckabee Sanders, joined me. Stephen Miller, speechwriter and senior policy adviser, was also in the room, wrapping up a separate discussion with the president.

President Trump said, "Sean, we're getting killed in the media. No matter what we do, we're getting killed. I know it's not your fault. I know you guys are trying. I think we need to change some things. We need to get some new people in here."

Sarah and I nodded; we were understaffed and needed help.

"We need to get Anthony in here."

"Anthony?" I thought.

Keith Schiller, Donald Trump's long-time bodyguard, then director of Oval Office Operations, walked into the dining room. "Scaramucci," he piped in.

Immediately, the picture became much clearer for me.

"We need him in here. We need him part of the operation, because what we're doing now isn't working," the president continued.

If this had been a script, the stage directions would have said, *Long and pregnant pause.*

The president doubled down.

"Sean, we're getting killed in the media, and we need more people. We need to find a role for Anthony. We need to get him involved. He's coming in tomorrow morning at ten; we'll all meet then."

It's true that we needed to add staff, and we needed some fresh thinking, but Anthony Scaramucci wasn't suited for a position in communications.

I knew Anthony. His background on paper was impressive. A degree from Harvard Law School, a career at Goldman Sachs, and then financial success at his own firm. Anthony had initially supported Wisconsin Governor Scott Walker for president. When Walker faded, he supported Jeb Bush. On Fox Business in August 2015, acting as a Bush spokesman, Anthony had called Trump "a hack politician," "anti-American," president of the "Queens County bullies association," and dared him to "bring it, Donald. Bring it."[1]

Anthony Scaramucci may not have been an original Trump supporter, but he was now fully on board the Trump train. In the final months of the campaign, he was often deployed as a spokesman on cable talk shows. Trump appreciated Anthony's aggressiveness in defending him and attacking Hillary Clinton. Anthony had been considered for other administration jobs, from White House public liaison to ambassador to the Organization for Economic Co-operation and Development in Paris, France. He was temporarily parked as "chief strategy officer" of the Export-Import Bank of the United States, but the president thought he might have a magic touch with the media.

One reason was because of how Anthony had handled CNN. The cable news network had wrongly accused Anthony of being the target of an alleged congressional investigation into an investment fund with ties to Russia. An internal investigation showed that the story was false and had been rushed through CNN's news division without the usual editorial checks. Anthony threatened a defamation lawsuit. As a result, three journalists were forced to resign.[2]

CNN retracted the story and publicly apologized.

"@CNN did the right thing," Scaramucci tweeted the next day. "Classy move. Apology accepted. Everyone makes mistakes. Moving on."

Anthony had slayed the media dragon, and the president noticed. The president had long said, "We need a fighter." He thought Anthony was just that person.

The president also hoped that Scaramucci's apparent toughness might stop the incessant White House leaks to the press. The president was furious about his conversations and internal deliberations turning up in the media, spun by leakers that played into a narrative about a "chaotic" White House. The knife-turn in his gut was the realization that these leaks could only come from people he trusted, from members of his own staff.

Could the man who had humbled CNN get control of White House leaks?

We learned that Anthony Scaramucci had told the president, "I can get it done."

I shared the president's frustrations, but plugging all the leaks in *any* White House is a tall order. That's how Washington works, and I didn't see Anthony Scaramucci as the antidote to leaks or anything else that might be wrong with our communications.

Despite his financial successes, Anthony had no political background, no experience in government, no knowledge of running a large communications operation, and no idea of what a difficult job it is to manage communications in the White House. It might seem turnkey and easy to the casual observer—but the reality is very different. You need great understanding of how the federal government works (and each of the agencies). You have to create a message, maintain that message, and recognize that your audience is not only the press and the general public but also the administration itself, Congress, lobbyists, businesses, workers, special interest groups, and even foreign governments. You have to manage a large staff and balance the needs of a wide range of White House offices. And a communications aide to the president needs to understand the culture of the media—what drives reporters; when to call them out on a wrong report, and when to let it slide; how to negotiate deals on press embargoes; how to keep some information "on background" and off the record.

Anthony might have delivered energetic and passionate interviews on camera during the campaign, but bringing him into the White House communications office with so little experience was like asking a student pilot with one lesson to take the stick of an F-22 in mid-flight.

The president repeated, "Anthony will be here ten tomorrow morning, and we need to have him involved."

"Yes, sir." I immediately began thinking about how we could fit Anthony into our work.

I had been press secretary from the first day of the administration. I also was the on-again, off-again communications director. The press secretary's office handles the day-to-day interaction with the media. The communications office shapes long-term strategy to promote the president's agenda. Communications strategy in itself is a high-wire act, trying to balance all the competing interests within the administration and outside of it. Trying to do that while dealing with the press, agitated by the controversy of the day, is like being Nik Wallenda walking a tightrope while bricks are being thrown at you. It was nearly impossible to do both jobs well, and my preference was to promote Sarah to the press secretary job so that I could focus on strategy.

I had talked to White House Chief of Staff Reince Priebus and Chief Strategist Steve Bannon about me stepping away from the podium and taking a more strategic role, which I thought better suited my talents. And I was already in that role anyway, working closely with Chief Economic Advisor Gary Cohn and others from his shop at the National Economic Council, the Treasury Department, the White House Office of Legislative Affairs, and the White House Office of Public Liaison to develop a message to sell the president's tax plan.

Given the intense demands of the job, I definitely could have used more help.

But Anthony Scaramucci?

※   ※   ※

I wrapped up my work for the night and headed home. No sooner did I close the door to my house than friends and White House colleagues began calling me. The calls all had the same message. Anthony wasn't just joining the team. He was going to be named communications director.

Reince and Steve agreed with me that he didn't have the demeanor and experience that the job demanded, but it appeared to be a done deal.

Soon reporters were calling as well, asking if I could confirm the rumor that Anthony Scaramucci had been hired. Their source was Anthony himself.

Before going to bed that night, I made two calls—one to Rebecca in Colorado, and the other to my mother, Kathy, in Rhode Island. I told them that if the president made the changes I thought he was going to make in the communications office, I would resign.

"You do what you have to do," my mom said. "But be sure you're doing the right thing for your future."

My wife was more direct.

Rebecca, who had served in the communications office of the George W. Bush White House and who had spent years in television news, knew from her front-row seat that my constant struggle to balance press and communications duties was unsustainable. Behind the scenes, her everyday reality had changed dramatically over the past several months, too. We agreed that stepping down from the wire at the right time and in the right way was one of the few things I could control.

"I support your decision. Just call me if you do resign—I want to know before a news alert pops up on my phone," she said.

We had thought this would last a bit longer, but when it's time, it's time.

■   ■   ■

The next morning at 8:56, I was sitting in my office and heard the little buzz announcing a text message.

It was from Scaramucci.

"Hey give me a buzz," it read.

I stood there in the morning light and stared at the message.

I didn't make that call.

As 10:00 a.m. approached, I walked over to the Oval Office. The president was hunched over the Resolute desk (carved from the oak timbers of HMS *Resolute*, and a gift from Queen Victoria to President Rutherford B. Hayes). He had an almost glowering expression, which some mistake for hostility, but I knew it reflected intense concentration.

Sitting in one of the chairs positioned in front of the desk was Anthony Scaramucci, compact, well-groomed, dressed like a slick Wall Street banker, and smiling. Reince was there too, standing next to Hope Hicks, a long-time Trump aide who was now White House director of strategic communications. Steve Bannon and Sarah had taken places on the couches.

"Anthony, as I was telling the team yesterday, we need new blood," the president said. "We're getting killed in the press. We've got to do anything we can to get back on track."

Scaramucci said he was honored to serve.

"Sean, we need to make this work. Reince, are we clear?"

In my experience, you had to pick and choose your battles with Donald Trump. This was not a time to confront him.

The previous night Steve Bannon had told me that a communications appointment for Scaramucci was an impending disaster. But there was no longer any room for debate, not with "the Mooch" accepting his appointment in the Oval Office. Steve sat quietly on the couch.

"This will be great," Hope said. "This will all work out."

"This is what we need. You guys will be great together," the president said, closing the discussion. Anthony Scaramucci was to be the new White House director of communications.

Reince, Steve, Sarah, and I retreated to Reince's office to discuss next steps. The chief of staff's office is on the first floor of the West Wing, down the hall from the Oval Office. In the confined space of the West Wing, space matters. Most offices are small and cramped. Reince's office had a long conference table and a patio out back. Only the president and vice president had larger offices.

As the discussion began about how this transition would work, I didn't make eye contact. I didn't take in much of what was said. I do remember Reince suggesting that he and Anthony go see White House Counsel Don McGahn because there would be a lot of issues to clear up internally and with the press before Anthony Scaramucci could take over.

Just a few months before, hoping he would get a White House position, Anthony had put his stake in SkyBridge Capital up for sale for an estimated $180 million to the Chinese HNA Group, which some business journalists reported was twice the normal value for such a deal.[3] There were rumors about China trying to buy influence in the administration, but there were rumors about everything in Washington.

Additionally, there was the issue of Anthony's position as vice president and chief strategy officer at the Export-Import Bank. He would need to resign that post before he could take another government position.

While Reince was going over the details, I interrupted him.

"Why don't you guys handle this? I've got something I need to do now."

I walked back to my office. I sent two copies of a letter to the printer. It was a document I had first drafted in mid-May.

I changed the date to July 21, 2017.

> *Dear Mr. President,*
>
> *It has been an honor to serve in your administration as White House press secretary.*
>
> *After considerable reflection and discussion with my family, I have decided to pursue other opportunities. To ensure a smooth transition, I will work through the end of next month.*
>
> *I will continue to support your efforts to strengthen the U.S. economy, create American jobs, and fight the evils of terrorism.*
>
> *Thank you for keeping our country safe, defending the foundation of our great democracy, and Making America Great Again.*

It was now 11:00 a.m. While the letter finished printing, I quickly called Rebecca and my mother. After I signed it, I walked to the area known as the "Outer Oval." Madeleine Westerhout was sitting at her desk. I asked her, "Is the president available?"

She nodded and motioned me into the Oval Office.

As I walked in, I nearly collided with Reince.

I asked the president if we could talk and told Reince he could stay if he wanted. The president asked me what was up.

"Sir, I've been thinking about our conversation this morning. And I agree, we need a fresh start in communications."

The president smiled and nodded.

"So, for that reason," I continued, "I think it is in your best interest and my best interest for me to resign and let Anthony have a clean slate."

I held out a copy of my resignation letter.

The president first sat back in his chair, as if trying to gain perspective on the paper in my hands. Then he leaned forward for emphasis.

"No, Sean, no, no, no. We need you here to help make this work. You are part of this team."

"Mr. President, the press secretary is supposed to tell the president's story. But from my first day on the job, I have become the story." I knew I had become a lightning rod for press criticism. Right or wrong, I had been defined. There was no potential for a do-over.

"Look, I get it, Sean, but I think we can work this out together as a team."

The president knew and appreciated that for six months on a daily basis I had taken punishment to protect him and promote his agenda. I had my share of self-inflicted wounds, but the president knew I did my best to promote his agenda, and Donald Trump has a fierce code of loyalty. He will stand by those who fight for him, just as he is ruthless with people who take advantage of his trust and betray him.

"Sean, you're an important part of this team."

"Mr. President, I'll stay on until the end of August to ensure a smooth transition. But this is the change you need and deserve."

The president paused a moment before saying, "Okay, if that's what you think."

I thanked the president and calmly walked out of the Oval Office knowing that I had made one of the biggest decisions of my life. I have seen a lot of sides of Donald Trump—tough talking negotiator, political pitchman—but that day I saw another. He was caring, kind, and gracious.

As I walked back through the Outer Oval, I picked up my pace and rushed down the stairs to the lower level of the West Wing, racing to Staff Secretary Rob Porter's office. The staff secretary is the president's gatekeeper for briefings, memos, speeches—the entire presidential paper flow. The staff secretary makes sure that the right papers get to him in a timely way, that they are all tracked and recorded, and that superfluous paperwork doesn't land on his desk.

While the White House itself is rather expansive, the West Wing is rather small. The lower level has only a handful of offices, including the Navy Mess where senior staff can dine and get takeout. Before its latest renovations were done, the West Wing was tired with carpet that had not been replaced in over a decade and paint that showed the test of time.

The staff secretary position is by no means a clerical job, and the role requires personal neutrality and a depth of experience to know what is essential for the president and what isn't. Policies, appointments, and programs can live or die according to what the staff secretary decides is important.

Rob Porter, acting in that role, was a seasoned, political professional. Until the story broke about domestic abuse allegations against him, very few people in America knew about this key position in the White House. A graduate of Harvard University and a Rhodes Scholar, Rob is the son of Roger Porter, also a Harvard grad and a Rhodes Scholar, who was the domestic policy adviser to President George H. W. Bush.

Rob's assistant told me he was not in his office. He was in a meeting.

"Could you please call him out?"

She did. Rob came down the cramped, dimly lit hallway, expecting a crisis.

"Do you have a folder?"

Rob gave me a sidewise look—*did you truly call me out of a meeting for a folder?* He reached into a nearby office and grabbed a folder from a shelf.

I handed him the second copy of my letter.

"Can you timestamp this for me?"

Rob gave me another funny look.

"What's going on?"

"This is my resignation letter. I've told the president it is time for me to leave."

I wanted my resignation recorded properly so that it would be clear I was in fact resigning. With all of the media reports on White House palace intrigue, one in which back-stabbing daggers are fashioned from leaks, somebody would surely try to sell the story that I had been pushed out.

Rob went back to his meeting. I stood there alone in the West Wing of the White House for a moment trying to absorb the magnitude and impact of what had just happened in the last few minutes.

I was not gone, not yet. I was still White House press secretary. I had tasks to complete and responsibilities to fulfill. Above all, I had a staff that needed to know what was going on. Given the way that closed-door discussions in the Oval Office were seemingly secretly live-streamed to the media, my staff would certainly have heard something about Scaramucci.

They needed to hear straight from me why I was leaving and how much I appreciated and valued their work and support. I had worked with many of them in the trenches during the campaign and at the Republican National Committee (RNC). Some of them I had known for years.

As I walked back to my office, I had a strange feeling—one we get only a few times in our lives.

It's over.

It's that feeling you get when you end a relationship. Or when you move from a home you've lived in for years. Or when you graduate from a school. It's that feeling you get when you know that a rich, significant part of your life has come to a definitive end and there is no turning back. Great and interesting things may await you in the future, but what you had known was gone for good. And the future—be it good or ill—would not be the same.

Working in the White House and speaking for the president had been a dream of mine. That dream was now over.

CHAPTER TWO

AGAINST THE ODDS

I n the days leading up to the election, the media sketched the outline of Donald Trump's political obituary: he was a fluke candidate who would be trounced by Hillary Clinton, many proclaimed.

Statistician, ABC correspondent, and editor of the influential FiveThirtyEight.com website, Nate Silver gave Hillary Clinton a 71 percent chance of winning the presidency.[1]

The *New York Times* gave Donald Trump a 15 percent chance of winning.[2]

Newsweek even printed a special edition all about Hillary Clinton's historic election as the first woman president, because that magazine, like almost every other media outlet and pundit, dismissed the possibility of a Trump victory.[3]

Or in the unvarnished opinion of *Deadspin* columnist Drew Magary, "Donald Trump is going to get his ass kicked."[4]

On Tuesday, November 8, election day, I saw Donald Trump and he looked nothing like a man who was about to get kicked.

Around 11:00 p.m., when the polls in all the pivotal states had closed, I turned to Donald Trump and said, "Congratulations, Mr. President-elect."

"Not yet," he replied without taking his eyes off the incoming results on several screens. Wisconsin was looking very good, but it wasn't confirmed. And Pennsylvania was not yet official.

He didn't want to jinx it.

Donald Trump was very focused, filled with anticipation, as we all were. He was optimistic from the word go, but he grew more excited as one critical county after another swung his way. Melania Trump's face expressed the suspense that we all felt while anxiously waiting for the results of the long, hard-fought campaign. As precincts in key states started reporting their results, she remained pensive, likely beginning to realize the awesome responsibilities her husband would soon have.

The man who was not expected to break 270 electoral votes—veteran-poll-watcher and political-analyst Larry Sabato of the University of Virginia's Center for Politics predicted Donald Trump would win only 216 electoral votes[5]—was on track to rack up 306 of them, with blue state after blue state going for him. When I saw him at the magic moment, Donald Trump's trademark grin filled his face.

■   ■   ■

If you've ever been involved in an election, from student council to U.S. president, you always think, no matter the odds, you can swing a win somehow. On election night four years earlier, the Romney campaign in Boston had convinced us that we had a clear path to victory. By then, I was a veteran of close elections.

In my first paid job, I served as a campaign aide in a congressional race in Connecticut's second district (the New London and Groton area). I was a "field operative" for the challenger, and we as a team had given it our all. The polls had us down—and down big. On election night, we were glued to the returns. The results weren't nearly as bleak and dreary as the polls had suggested. Throughout most of the night, the results were neck and neck. But at the end of the night, after every single vote had been counted, we lost by two votes. Not two thousand. Not two hundred. Two.

Every vote matters.

I experienced the same anxiety several years later while I was working for Representative Clay Shaw's re-election campaign in Florida. Clay was a beloved grandfather figure in South Florida who had served several terms, but his district was changing. His district was home to an aging population, and about a third of his constituents died between each election. But this year wasn't like the others for Clay—it was 2000. It was the year that the word "hanging chad" became a household name during the Bush vs. Gore recount in Florida. And here I was working on a congressional race that was too close to call on election day. Once again, on election night, I found myself glued to the returns. Would we pull it out? We wouldn't know until every single vote had been counted. Fortunately, this cliffhanger had a much better ending than my Connecticut experience. Clay Shaw won—even if by a narrow margin of 300 votes.

Every vote matters.

So, it shouldn't come as a surprise that I never accepted the media's certainty that Donald Trump couldn't win. I thought it would be close, and we were campaigning until the very end in places like Grand Rapids, Michigan; Raleigh, North Carolina; Scranton, Pennsylvania; and other key cities in critical states.

As all-consuming as the election was, I also had something very personal going on.

In the last weeks of the campaign, my father, Michael Spicer, was valiantly fighting pancreatic cancer. Emotionally, I was pulled in two directions—excitement at the possibility of a great professional achievement and deep anxiety over my father's illness.

There were other pressures as well. The more I was drawn into the Trump orbit, the more I heard that "long-time" Trump "loyalists" were sniping against Republican National Committee Chairman Reince Priebus and myself as RNC outsiders who weren't "Trump guys." To some degree, they were right. My priorities have always been very clear: God, family, country, Navy, Republican Party, candidate. I was a Republican operative and strategist who had worked at the RNC, the National Republican Congressional Committee, and the National Republican

Senatorial Committee. So, yes, I worked for the Republican Party, but, *of course*, I wanted Trump to win. I hadn't spent this much time and effort—and put so much of my personal reputation on the line—to lose, and I didn't remember many of these so-called loyalists campaigning for Donald Trump in May, June, and July. Many of them didn't show up until October. Yet they couldn't wrap their minds around the idea of a party operative who could be just as loyal to the candidate as they were while perhaps offering perspective and knowledge they lacked.

There was one more thing working on me. Donald Trump had come to know me at the RNC and through the campaign. He was beginning to accept me as a trusted adviser and spokesman. I hoped I would have a significant role in his White House, and I knew that working with the new president would be an extraordinary experience—a man who is calculating and mercurial, charismatic but erratic, and now a politician capable of defeating anyone, including himself.

■   ■   ■

I was raised in a Roman Catholic family that had dinner together every night, with very few exceptions. TV never supplemented this nightly ritual. Instead, we enjoyed robust dinner conversations about school or our friends, but never about national politics. When politics was mentioned at all, it was usually my father complaining about some "idiot" in local or state government who screwed something up or said something stupid. It was never ideological or based on party.

I grew up in a tiny town in a small state, Barrington, Rhode Island, down the street from the Barrington River just before it flows into the Narragansett Bay. It's the kind of place where everyone knows everyone else. As a boy, I'd simply tell my mother, "I'm going to the neighbor's," without specifying which one, and she knew I would be in a safe place. We played four square in the street, rode our bicycles everywhere, and played tag with flashlights when it was dark. If we weren't home by din-nertime, my mother would call the neighbors to find out where we were.

But there were no real worries. Everyone looks out for you in Barrington. Everyone on Oak Manor Drive was part of your family.

Oak Manor Drive was also where I learned the very basics of business. I was a neighborhood entrepreneur, doing everything from selling stationery, to delivering birthday cakes, to creating my own ski-sharpening business. In college, I sold sailing apparel and gear.

Barrington has a reputation for being one of Rhode Island's most prestigious towns, with its yacht club, country club, large homes on the bay, and good schools. But like affluent towns everywhere, Barrington had a section for middle-class homes and working-class families. We lived in the Hampden Meadows neighborhood in a comfortable, two-story, four-bedroom home with a large lawn, and we were decidedly in the middle-class category.

Both of my parents attended college, though neither graduated. Mike Spicer grew up loving the water in nearby Newport. Sailing was in his blood. His father, Harry, had worked at the naval station in Newport. His grandfather, William Spicer, had been a gunner's mate in the Spanish-American War and was awarded the Medal of Honor for bravery. A natural sailor, Mike Spicer was more industrious than studious, and at thirteen he had already joined the boat business rebuilding outboard motors.

Whenever he earned a pocketful of money, he'd get out on the water. Newport had two yacht clubs, the Ida Lewis Yacht Club, where the America's Cup trophy had been showcased (on behalf of the New York Yacht Club), and the Newport Yacht Club, which sounds impressive but was really the working man's club. It became my father's second home. He once sailed on one of the trail boats for the America's Cup competition. And after a succession of jobs working for boat builders, he launched his own yacht brokerage company.

Yacht broker sounds fancier than it was. Our family income depended solely on how many people were buying boats. Some years weren't so bad. But there were others you knew would be a struggle by the beginning of January. I still have no idea how my parents made ends meet during certain stretches, though I do know my dad took out credit cards to pay off other credit cards.

When I was a kid, my family's income fluctuated depending on the year and the market for yachts.

While the market and the economy fluctuated, my dad's work ethic never did. He was an entrepreneur by nature, a hardworking man, a disciplinarian, and a stickler for principle. He was also the kind of person who made time for others, looked you in the eye, and kept his word. No matter how tough of a day he had or how hard he had worked, he always had time to throw a ball, attend a practice, or review homework. And he always let you know he loved you.

He was also the kind of father who led by example. If someone needed something, he gave it to them, whether it was advice or a helping hand. He often reminded me that life's about taking care of people, being a good friend, and, above all, doing the right thing.

Kathy Spicer, my mother, was the caregiver, the one who held everything together. She made sure every kid got to practice with the right uniform, every meal was prepared, and every elderly relative or close friend who needed help got it.

In short, my parents were the kind of people you didn't want to disappoint. If you did something wrong, they would give you that "let-down" look, which was much worse than any other kind of punishment. When I served as chief strategist of the RNC, I went on a cable show for a discussion that escalated into a battle of harsh words and insults. Later, when I was catching up with my dad, he said, "You're better than that."

That soft rebuke hit me harder than anything the press has ever said.

■   ■   ■

Father John Hugh Diman was an Episcopal priest who founded what is today St. George's School in Rhode Island, a Middletown academy (although they like to use a Newport address) thick with many of America's elite families—Astors, Biddles, Bushes, and Pells. Father Diman then converted to Roman Catholicism at age sixty-three and founded another preparatory school, Portsmouth Abbey School, run by Benedictine monks, just down the road on the other end of Aquidneck Island.

When Portsmouth Abbey was smaller, it was named the Portsmouth Priory. And as I grew up, my grandmother would say, "All the really smart boys go to the Priory." So, the idea of going to a rigorous, elite school stuck with me. As I prepared to go to high school, I started bugging my parents to send me to Portsmouth Abbey. I had no concept of the financial burden I was asking them to shoulder. To their credit, they said nothing about money, just, "Why don't you look into it?"

I did. Portsmouth Abbey's tuition was as expensive as college, which was out of my family's financial reach. But not all the boarding school's students lived on campus. I discovered that I could live at home and attend as a day student. I put together a plan. From my home on Oak Manor Drive, I could walk a mile down the main road to "downtown" Barrington, buy a bus token, take a forty-minute bus ride to Portsmouth, and walk down Cory's Lane to the school to begin my day. And I could do the reverse commute home after school in the afternoons. Realizing that I could make it all work, I went to Portsmouth Abbey's open houses, sought financial aid, and got in at age thirteen.

We went to school six days a week to obtain a Benedictine education that included a class in Christian doctrine taught by one of the institution's monks. As I progressed through Portsmouth Abbey, I grew steadier in my faith and prayer life. Students went to Mass once a week and prayed every day in a morning assembly.

The press occasionally describes me as a "devout Catholic." I have never liked that designation. It sounds "holier-than-thou." I would just say I am a practicing Catholic who strives to be better every day and to listen to that still, small voice I find in prayer. I regularly ask the Lord for forgiveness and for the grace and strength to be a better follower.

Throughout my father's terminal illness and all the ups and downs I faced in Donald Trump's White House, the two things that sustained me were my strong, loving family and the deep faith my parents instilled in me in Jesus and His Church with its steadfast catechism.

After faith and family, the next most important thing to me as a young man was sports. Growing up, I played in Barrington's town soccer league. Despite being five foot six (and a half, but who's counting), I became the starting goalie on Portsmouth Abbey's soccer team. And, like my father, I grew up sailing and became an avid and competitive sailor.

The Abbey had a sailing team that competed in interscholastic regattas. We sailed in international 420 class dinghies, less than 14 feet in length, with a beam of just over 5 feet. Each 420 has a two-man crew for short, fast courses. I was on the Narragansett Bay almost every day in the spring, jibing, leaning over the water with my crew, and enjoying the sensation of cutting across the bay.

The school's academics were demanding, and order and discipline were expected in every class. Male students (while now coed, Portsmouth Abbey only admitted boys then) had to wear a coat and tie every day, though the school let us pare down to collared shirts in the late spring and early fall. And all students arrived on time for class, stood when a teacher entered the classroom, and started each class with a prayer.

One teacher still stands out in my memory, and in the memory of everyone who attended Portsmouth Abbey—J. Clifford Hobbins. When the movie *Dead Poets Society* came out in 1989, the year I graduated from the Abbey, I couldn't shake the feeling that the movie had been about Cliff, his Socratic challenges, and his unorthodox, disruptive style of teaching. He taught history, economics, and foreign affairs with animated storytelling that electrified us, making us look forward to his next class.

Sporting a mustache and often sucking on a pipe, Cliff Hobbins always came to class in his trademark, three-piece suit. A bachelor at the time, Cliff lived on campus. He was relaxed, fluid, and ready to pounce on the unprepared like a panther. A fan of Ronald Reagan and a conservative intellectual in his own right, Cliff would regale us with Washington lore and endless stories about politics. He once told us the story of a summer, spiritual retreat hosted by William F. Buckley Jr. at Portsmouth Abbey. The retreat was supposed to help attendees escape from the normal routine of daily life and focus on eternal things. So, the head of the Priory was perplexed when he spotted Buckley reading a newspaper.

"Mr. Buckley, why are you reading the *New York Times*?"

Buckley looked up at the prior and replied, "I am looking for heresies."

It was a classic Buckley quip, but it was also a classic Hobbins story.

Cliff was unusually well connected in Washington and New York, mostly with former students who ended up on Capitol Hill or Wall Street. Noticing that I had an early interest in politics, Cliff called in a favor with the office manager of the Democratic majority leader in the U.S. Senate, George Mitchell of Maine, and set me up with a Washington internship over spring break. Mitchell was to bedevil and stymie the administration of future President George H. W. Bush. While it was an odd pairing for a young, budding conservative like me, Cliff understood that what I needed more than anything else was to experience Washington.

In between sealing envelopes and operating the autopen, I rode the Senate subway, watched proceedings from the galley, and delivered papers to the cloakroom. I remember Senator Mitchell was gracious to a fault.

At age seventeen, I found the Washington scene intoxicating, but I soon learned—along with the rest of the Spicer family—a lesson about the impact Washington's policies can have on families like mine.

Shortly after my internship, Senator Mitchell and the Democrats forced the George H. W. Bush White House to accept a measure in its budget deal that enacted a 10 percent tax on luxury items above $100,000. Popularly known as the "yacht tax," it went into effect in 1991. Cliff Hobbins could have told Mitchell and the Democrats what would happen to any industry if Washington singled it out for punishment. He was a big believer in the axiom "You get less of what you tax and more of what you don't."

U.S. production of $100,000-plus yachts had peaked at 16,000 in 1987. By 1992, it had fallen to 4,250. North Carolina's largest luxury-boat manufacturer fired more than 1,000 people. But Rhode Island was hit the hardest with 12,000 direct and indirect jobs lost. The "yacht tax" that eliminated these jobs generated a measly $12,655,000 for the U.S. Treasury.[6] "That's enough to run the Agriculture Department for a little over two hours," observed James K. Glassman in the *Washington Post*. "Meanwhile, the tax has contributed to the general devastation of the American boating industry – as well as the jewelers, furriers and private-plane manufacturers that were also targets of the excise tax that was part of the 1990 budget deal."[7]

The rich spent their money on other things. And instead of buying new boats, they started buying used boats. The luxury tax was a classic case of Washington stupidity that allegedly targets the rich but actually hurts working men and women.

While this had a direct impact on my father's livelihood, it also directly affected me. I spent my teenage years working in a boatyard prepping, maintaining, and cleaning boats. Because the rich were not buying boats, there were fewer boats to work on. And that meant fewer opportunities for me and people like me to earn a paycheck. Liberals always complain that tax cuts never "trickle down" to the working man— something that has been disproven for the umpteenth time by President Trump's own massive tax cuts. And they never seem to understand that tax hikes trickle down to hardworking Americans trying to earn a living.

The timing of this new tax couldn't have been worse for my family. While my parents were excited to open my acceptance letter to Portsmouth Abbey, it came with a hefty price tag. Never revealing what a huge financial burden this was, my mother, who had raised three kids and served as the CEO of our family, entered the workforce. She was hired to manage Brown University's Department of East Asian Studies.

While I didn't realize it at the time, the experiences of my adolescence were shaping me into the conservative I am today.

■   ■   ■

During my senior year at the Abbey, Cliff Hobbins took several students—including myself—to New York City. He introduced us to some successful Wall Street executives who were Abbey alums. The biggest takeaway from our conversations was the rising importance of Asia in the global economy. More than one executive (and Hobbins concurred) made it clear that students who spoke Japanese and understood economics would be on the fast track to success. Many alarmist books at the time insisted Japan would soon surpass the United States economically, and everyone would live in a Japanese-dominated world. So, learning Japanese was, I reasoned, a smart investment for my future.

As soon as I was admitted to Connecticut College—a small, liberal arts institution with a campus that has that classic, gray-brick, New England look—I immediately set my sights on being a Japanese language major. (Imagine that on *Saturday Night Live*. I wonder how good Melissa McCarthy's Japanese is.) Then I encountered Japanese, with its subject-object-verb sentences, its three scripts, and the most complex grammatical structure of any language. It wasn't long before I received a letter from the dean suggesting that my talents should be invested elsewhere. Apparently a "D minus" in any language is still a "D minus." I didn't have to think long or hard about where I belonged. I switched to "government," Connecticut College's version of political science.

There were no larger-than-life figures like Cliff Hobbins among the Connecticut College faculty, but my professors certainly stimulated my thoughts. Almost universally liberal, they were so diametrically opposed to what I believed about God, the United States, and economics, that they forced me to re-examine, deepen, and argue in favor of my beliefs. By the time I was asked to join the government honors class, I knew I was a conservative who belonged to the party of Lincoln and Reagan.

I was painfully aware there was another side to our classroom discussions that was never acknowledged. Today, we are used to seeing "political correctness" on campuses across the country, but I was shocked when I first witnessed it as a college student.

Connecticut College had invited Dr. Louis Sullivan, then the secretary of Health and Human Services in the George H. W. Bush administration, to be our commencement speaker. But the college disinvited him when it learned the prominent black Republican did not hew to the liberal orthodoxy on abortion. The "open-minded, inclusive, and toler-ant" liberal student body and faculty couldn't tolerate that, which I thought (and still think) was the height of hypocrisy. Listening respect-fully to alternative viewpoints is the very foundation of being open-minded, inclusive, and tolerant. In 2000, I had a chance to meet Dr. Sullivan at a Susan G. Komen Race for the Cure in Florida. I went up to him, introduced myself, shook his hand, and apologized for how my class had treated him.

When I wasn't studying, I was sailing with the Connecticut Col-lege sailing team on the Thames River. By my sophomore year, I had been elected as the team captain. The truth is, I went to college to sail, have fun, and learn, in that order. I was lucky I managed to do all three, especially since my early brush with politics often inspired other pursuits.

I ran for freshman class president (and failed miserably), interned for a state legislator, and volunteered for a congressional race in Connecti-cut's second district. As a volunteer, I wrote letters to the editor and drafted talking points for a Republican candidate who used a campaign budget of no more than $50,000 to challenge a well-known incumbent. We lost that election by roughly 5,000 votes—not a bad showing for an underfunded Republican running against a longtime, well-funded incum-bent in a Democratic-leaning district.

Most Connecticut College students spent part of their junior year abroad. My financial aid would not transfer to the overseas programs I was interested in attending, but there were opportunities in Washington, D.C., that seemed interesting. So, after my sophomore year, I attended a semester-long program at American University (AU). AU won me over for two reasons: I wanted to see politics up-close again, and the univer-sity accepted all of my financial aid and scholarships.

During that semester, I started to love Capitol Hill, with its campus-like environment filled with bustling lawmakers and congressional aides as well as journalists and lobbyists who walked swiftly—and with their own distinct purpose—between the Capitol and the House and Senate office buildings. I had been bitten by the Washington bug. I loved every day I was working in D.C. even as I criticized how it functioned.

At AU, I lived in a dorm with politically-minded students who spanned the ideological spectrum. My liberal friends loved to debate with me while my conservative friends confirmed that I, in fact, had a point and made sense. Somehow, we all got along, and many of those friendships have endured the test of time...and the test of politics.

While in D.C. that semester, I applied for internships and received several offers. One was from a Rhode Island member of the House of Representatives, Ronald Machtley, which I should have taken. Instead, I interned at an office within the Office of Personnel Management that trained federal government executives to testify before Congress. Another Connecticut College student had enjoyed that internship and recommended it to me, but it revolved around research, not politics. I quickly realized I was not meant to sit behind a screen all day researching issues on LexisNexis.

When I wrote my end-of-the-semester paper on the internship, I described the office, its purpose and operations, its triumphs and failures, and questioned why it existed at all. I even explained why I had hated it so much.

I got an "A" on the paper and learned something valuable. I had followed someone else's passion instead of feeding my own. So, during the winter break of my senior year, I went back to Washington, determined not to make the same mistake. This time, I accepted an internship with Senator John Chafee, former governor of Rhode Island. And working in D.C. had never been more exciting.

Bill Clinton of Arkansas was heading to Washington as our forty-second president. The city was electric with anticipation. I sat at the front desk of Senator Chaffee's office answering phones, welcoming guests, and helping arrange courtesy meetings for the senator with Clinton cabinet nominees. I took calls from luminaries like George Stephanopoulos, the new president's communications director—the kind of political operative I could only hope to become someday (albeit as a Republican). I also got acquainted with Senator Chafee, a moderate Republican who was always impeccably dressed, courteous, and a gentleman of the old school.

Senator Chafee had a soft demeanor that only the foolish mistook for weakness. After Pearl Harbor, he left Yale University to join the U.S. Marine Corps, fighting at Guadalcanal and Okinawa. When the Korean War broke out only a few years later, the U.S. military was desperate for seasoned leaders. But most World War II veterans—especially those who had endured and survived the long, hard slog up the island chains toward Japan under General Douglas MacArthur—were understandably reluctant to re-up for hard fighting in Asia again, this time on the Korean Peninsula.

But not John Chafee.

He returned to the U.S. Marine Corps as a rifle company commander. After being surrounded by 120,000 troops of the Chinese People's Liberation Army, he and his fellow marines executed a masterful retreat at the Chosin Reservoir.

I am not a William Spicer or a John Chafee, but I have always had a deep respect for those who have served in combat. I am in awe of their service as well as their courage in the face of danger and the unknown. Their incredible example inspired me to support the noble cause they lived and died to defend.

At age twenty-nine, I earned a commission in the U.S. Navy Reserve as a public affairs officer. During my nineteen years in the Navy, I have traveled the world, including McMurdo Station in Antarctica; Guantanamo Bay, Cuba; Stuttgart, Germany; and Enköping, Sweden. I have served with outstanding Americans. They are selfless, dedicated, and talented patriots. I am proud to have served with them, and our country is fortunate that they wear the uniform. Joining the United States Navy was one of the best decisions I ever made.

■   ■   ■

I confess, I never felt like I belonged in places with marble floors, high ceilings, and rare books in burnished bookcases—places like

Portsmouth Abbey, Connecticut College, the Capitol, and the White House. And I never felt as prepared or polished as the people I met in those places who came from money, prep schools, and the Ivy League. Somehow, though, I always managed to "get in" and pursue my dreams.

CHAPTER THREE

LESSONS LEARNED

Donald Trump was holding court. That's the only way I can put it. Most politicians work the room, but this was something different. As Trump spoke with one major Republican donor after another, it seemed as if he was letting the room work him, as if these wealthy donors were getting a moment to present themselves one by one.

The "room" was an outdoor patio at the Boca Beach Club in spring 2015. As he shook hands and patted shoulders, Donald Trump had the demeanor of a man running for office; he also had very definite ideas about what a Republican candidate needed to do to win the presidency after Mitt Romney's failed campaign. But no one I knew took the idea of a Trump candidacy seriously. The tycoon had publicly toyed with running for president before, giving speeches in key primary states and making an issue out of President Obama's birth certificate in 2011. As a private citizen, Donald Trump had attended the annual White House Correspondents' Association dinner in 2011 (as a guest of the *Washington Post*, no less). He had to sit there while Obama—who had just released the long-form of his birth certificate—and comedian Seth Meyers trolled him with one jibe after another.[1]

Soon after that dinner, some pundits speculated that Donald Trump would run for president. The next month, *Politico* and George Washington University conducted a national survey asking if Trump had a chance of becoming president. The results showed that 71 percent of Americans believed Trump had "no chance" of ever winning the presidency.[2]

Standing at the donor reception in Florida that night, I thought back to that poll number and suspected it wouldn't be too far off the mark if the same question were asked again. I looked over my glass and out at the donors still eager to talk with "The Donald," as many of them seemed more excited to meet a celebrity than a potential future president. After all, he had never held political office before, and this country has only elected politicians and military heroes to serve as commander in chief. The odds of someone with a different background winning a major-party nomination for president were slim to none. The odds of winning a general election were even lower.

Furthermore, we were in Florida. Sure, Trump has multiple properties there. But that state was already home to two powerhouse Republican figures: former Governor Jeb Bush and U.S. Senator Marco Rubio. They were both presumed presidential candidates and had strong name ID among Republican voters. They both had well-established, national donor bases and national networks of support for robust get-out-the-vote campaigns.

Donald Trump had name ID, but it wasn't as an experienced politician. While toying with the idea of running for president in 2011, he had an unfavorable rating of 64 percent—which by all political standards is glow-in-the-dark radioactive.[3] And yet, the donors lined up and jostled each other for their moment or photo with the star of *The Celebrity Apprentice.*

As I normally did at political events, I stood off to the side, sipping a glass of wine and making small talk with some of the donors. But at this event, I kept an eye on the man holding court. I marveled at the dynamics at play among the sea of donors and wondered if the polling numbers could be wrong—and if maybe, just maybe, a political outsider really could run for president of the United States. And I also marveled at the fact that the two of us, both from such different backgrounds, ended up in the same room.

■   ■   ■

Sailing has always been in my blood, which isn't much of a surprise to anyone. It's easy to fall in love with sailing if you grow up in Rhode Island. But sailing was more to me than just a challenging—yet enjoyable—sport. It was a love that my father instilled in me at a young age. Perhaps more importantly, he showed me how to navigate the waters— whether smooth or choppy—and how to maneuver the sails and read the wind while going upwind or downwind.

Sailing was in my father's blood, too. Mike Spicer had grown up in Newport, Rhode Island. It's a beautiful coastal town that boasts some of the most talented sailors and breathtaking yachts in the world. It's also known for its famous estates and ornate mansions. Although my dad was raised in Newport, he grew up a world away from the lavish parties at the New York Yacht Club and other magnificent venues on the island. The Spicers were part of Rhode Island's working class, like most residents of the state. But my dad knew how to find honest work—and he knew how to find the joys in life that everyone, regardless of wealth or social status, can obtain. Sailing became a bedrock in our relationship. Out on the open water is where I learned how to work, how to play, and how to have quality time with my dad.

Sailing was special to me, and I found time—and places—to sail anytime I could.

During college, I was on the sailing team, and I spent two college summers working at a yacht club in New Orleans, Louisiana, which allowed me to get out on the water of Lake Pontchartrain every day. After graduation, I moved to Stamford, Connecticut, where I coached a sailing team. One of my students was a bright and energetic young woman named Lindley Kratovil. At one point, I mentioned to Lindley that I planned to go to D.C. at the end of the summer in search of my first "real" political job.

Lindley informed me that her father worked in Washington.

"Why don't you go see him?" she said.

Her father was Ted Kratovil, one of the biggest lobbyists of the day. At that time, he was the head of government relations for U.S. Tobacco. When I got to D.C., I took Lindley up on her offer and scheduled a day to have lunch with her father. I met him at Mr. K's, a posh Chinese restaurant that used to be a high-end lunch spot frequented by lobbyists in Washington. It was conveniently located for the lunching crowd, right on K Street, famously home to many of the top lobbying firms in the nation's capital. I walked in and asked the hostess for Mr. Kratovil's table. She led me through a sea of tables covered with white linens and surrounded by men (and a few women) in dark power suits. Somehow, I felt underdressed in my navy blazer and khaki pants.

He was already seated—I presumed at his "usual" spot. He graciously welcomed me, and I took a seat. After we made some small talk, we started discussing my career aspirations. I told Mr. Kratovil about all the work I had done trying to get a job in D.C. I had made countless phone calls (from landlines). I had mailed dozens and dozens of resumes and cover letters. (Remember, this was in the days before email.) And I had been busy networking.

"But what do you want to do?"

"I'll do *anything*," I said.

"There are no jobs for anything. You need to figure out what you want to do, and then I can I help you."

Ted was a well-connected Washington player, not a guidance counselor. His time was valuable. I needed to figure out quickly what I wanted to do. And by quickly, I meant then and there.

"I want to get into Republican politics," I blurted out.

He nodded affirmatively, and a polite smile crossed his face as if to say, "I approve of your decision."

After we left Mr. K's, he tasked one his deputies, Chris Swonger, to help me. Chris was up for the challenge. He made calls around Washington on my behalf.

While I waited for some political position to find me, I picked up some work at a temp agency called Career Blazers. I was sent to answer phones at the Organization for Economic Co-operation and Development (better known as just "OECD") bookstore in downtown D.C. I was making minimum wage, and I was thrilled to be earning a paycheck. I made just enough money to cover my share of the rent in a group house where I lived with other political hopefuls.

And then my dream job landed in my lap! Thanks to Chris Swonger's efforts, I got my first job offer in the D.C. political world. It was a position with the National Republican Senatorial Committee (NRSC), which had informed me it had no openings just weeks earlier. At the time, the NRSC was chaired by Senator Alfonse D'Amato from New York. Every day, I looked forward to walking into the NRSC building on Capitol Hill and proceeding to my desk, which actually was a shared workspace located in the windowless basement.

The NRSC exists to provide resources to senatorial candidates and win seats in the Senate. My specific job was to type quotes from Democratic senators who were up for re-election into a database; I later learned that is called opposition research. I showed up each day at 4:00 p.m. and worked until midnight, which meant there was still time to grab a beer with other young, aspiring political operatives after work. I made some of the best friends of my life in that job—people like Joe Grogan, who is still one of my closest and most loyal friends.

Not long after my start date, Joe and I joined some other guys from the NRSC and moved into a house on Capitol Hill. As Christmas time approached, the higher-ups at the committee decided that every staffer would be asked to pay ten dollars for the holiday party to help defray costs. For those of us who were making four dollars an hour, we looked at the ten-dollar "cover charge" as two-and-half beers we wouldn't be able to afford at a local bar.

Joe is one of the most gifted writers I've ever met, and he also has never been known for being short on opinion. He took to the internal "cc mail" system (remember, this was before email existed) to express his frustration over the ten-dollar fee. In some of the funniest language I've ever read, he described the audacity of having to pay ten dollars to attend an office holiday party that he considered to be "forced fun." It's no surprise that his rant made its way to Executive Director John Heubusch (who is now the executive director of the Ronald Reagan Presidential Foundation and Institute). He called Joe into his office to discuss the appropriateness of his note. After Joe had been read the Riot Act, Phil Smith, the finance director, was waiting right outside the door—also wanting to talk to Joe about what he had written. This time, however, the conversation was quite different.

"I want to talk to you about your writing," Phil said.

"Yes," Joe responded, anticipating a second reprimand.

"Do you always write like this? Because if you do, I want to put your talents to use. I want you to write for us. I want to promote you."

Joe was stunned—not knowing if this was some kind of revenge for his office-wide note, or if he really was getting a promotion.

"This is some of the best writing I've ever read, and we need someone like you to write compelling fundraising letters for the finance team," Phil added.

Needless to say, Joe took the promotion and started writing some of the most effective letters the NRSC has ever sent to donors. His first piece yielded the highest response rate the NRSC had seen until that point.

A lot of top operatives have walked through the NRSC over the years, and it was a huge accomplishment to call it the home of my first political job in D.C. It was also home to my first political lesson: relationships matter. It really is *who* you know that makes all the difference in Washington. I never would have gotten that job without the help of Ted Kratovil and Chris Swonger.

When I wasn't at the NRSC, I interned at the House Committee on Ways and Means. During the day, I made photocopies, answered phones, and acted as a gofer—running errands of all kinds.

It really didn't matter if I was making copies or entering quotes into a database, I was thrilled to be dipping my toe into politics. I was swept up in the excitement of the political moment—and what a moment it was. I arrived in Washington in 1994, just after Newt Gingrich's landmark Contract with America made history and Republicans had won both the House and the Senate. There was an air of hope and optimism unlike anything I would experience again until Donald Trump's win in 2016.

I had been working those two jobs for about eight months when I got a call from David Griswold, Senator Chafee's chief of staff. He wanted me to know a full-time position had opened up and it might be of interest to me. It was a staff assistant position for the Senate Committee on Environment and Public Works, which Senator Chafee chaired. The position paid $18,500 a year, and it came with benefits, including health care—which made my mother very happy. I took the job, excited that I was going to be earning a real salary—with benefits—for doing something that I wanted to do.

In our committee office, there was a pool of staff assistants, and we each got promoted based on seniority. Johnna Rozen was the young woman who was the "senior" staff assistant. She had been tapped to move up, entitling her to a better desk and a small pay raise. Johnna had been waiting patiently for a couple of weeks for her promotion and wasn't sure when it would happen. So, one day, when the administrative supervisor stepped away from her desk, I walked over to it, sat in her chair, and started typing an email. The note was addressed to Johnna, and it thanked her for her patience but informed her that she would have to wait a few more weeks to receive her pay raise and new desk. I finished the email and hit send. Off it went to Johnna, and off I went to her desk to chuckle with her. But when I got to her desk, Johnna was gone. I asked staffers sitting near her where she was. I was informed, "She's gone to lunch. We don't know when she will return."

This was in the days before BlackBerrys and iPhones, so she wouldn't see the email until she returned to her desk. I needed to be there to make sure she knew it was a joke. I was trying to linger so that I could catch her, but my supervisor told me, "You need to take your lunch now."

While I was taking my mandatory lunch hour, Johnna returned to her desk, read the email, and fired off a flurry of messages to senior staff in several Senate offices.

When I got back from lunch, Johnna informed me of the email that she had received. Exasperated, she said to me, "Can you believe I have to wait even longer?!" Clearly, she had no idea that I was the one behind the email. I thought it was probably a good time to inform her that the email was from me. As I told her about my prank, she informed me that she had fired off an angry email to several staff members of Senate offices whose members and staff were part of the committee. My joke had clearly backfired.

I spent the rest of the afternoon walking through Senate buildings, going office to office, apologizing to senior staff. I received several stern lectures about the proper use of government emails. And unlike my friend Joe Grogan, I wasn't offered a promotion for my writing capabilities.

■   ■   ■

A Hill career can mean climbing the ladder from staff assistant to legislative correspondent to legislative assistant to legislative director. I, however, let it be known that I wanted to become a press secretary.

I had been interviewing for months for press jobs in congressional offices. One interview after another, I was told, "You're a nice guy, but you don't have any communications experience." It's hard to get experience when you don't have experience.

Then, one day in 1995, I got the break I wanted.

"I hear you want to get into press, so I've got a deal for you," a Republican pollster told me over the phone. "There's a guy who's going to run for Congress in western Pennsylvania. It's a primary, and there's a good chance he'll lose the primary. Even if he wins this round, it's pretty certain he will lose the general. But you'll get a lot of good experience. You interested?"

Without any hesitation, I replied, "Absolutely!"

I packed everything I owned into the back of my two-toned Chevy Astro van (yes it had been my mom's) and moved to Washington County, Pennsylvania—in the western part of the state near Pittsburgh.

Two days after I arrived in Pennsylvania, I was driving down a four-lane highway when another vehicle crossed the median and plowed right into me. To this day, I don't know how I walked away from that accident without a scratch. But my two-toned van (and its burgundy captain's chairs) was totaled, leaving me with no car. I learned just how accommodating USAA insurance can be, and they helped me rent a car for the remainder of my time in Pennsylvania.

I worked tirelessly on that primary campaign. We had to build a campaign from the ground up—quickly. I walked from door to door, asking for signatures to get the candidate on the ballot, and I created a database of potential supporters. I gave it my all.

Ten weeks later, the candidate dropped out of the race.

I didn't get to see that campaign to election day. But I had been promised "experience," and I now had "experience" under my belt. I updated my resume; it now read, "campaign manager and press secretary."

That was just what I needed to open more doors.

A few weeks later, I got another call. Congressman Frank LoBiondo was looking for a campaign manager and press secretary "with experience." Frank represented southern New Jersey and was facing his first re-election race. I packed up everything—not in my Chevy Astro van, but instead in my new-to-me, 1991, dark-grey Honda Accord—and moved to New Jersey. He was an established candidate, so I was able to focus on running public events, speeches, debate preparations, opposition research, and returning press calls. On election day, Frank won with nearly 60 percent of the vote, a solid showing for a freshman re-election campaign.

It was then that I learned another important lesson: you can be on a winning political team one day and unemployed the day after the election.

But now I had two jobs with "experience"—even if they only amounted to several months combined. I also had been building relationships along the way.

One of the people I met during my weeks campaigning in New Jersey was another congressional candidate named Mike Pappas. He was running for the first time—and he won. After election day, he had to start building a staff to take to Washington with him. He reached out to me and asked if I would be interested in joining him as his communications director.

This was my first, full-time, political press job. It was filled with opportunities—and I seized every single one. When it was time for him to think about his first re-election, I offered to move back to New Jersey to handle the press for the campaign.

In the fall of 1994, I once again packed up my Honda Accord and drove north on I-95. I found a place to live—an RV parked in a constituent's yard. I tried to ignore the fact that it had no heat or running water because it was going to be my home for eight weeks. I also found a local gym where I could work out. An added selling point: the locker room had running water, so I could even get a shower there. And in the crisp fall nights, I just tossed an extra blanket on my bed. I never slowed down enough to worry about my less-than-ideal living conditions. I was working day in, day out, trying to pull out a victory for Mike.

We lost.

Campaign managers are like head coaches. You win some, you lose some. If you're good, you win more than you lose. After the election, I had an even record. And once again, I was out of a job.

I moved back to Washington where I started another job search. After a few desperate months, I was asked to be the communications director for Representative Mark Foley of Florida.

At the time, Mark was one of the most well-liked members in the House. He was smart and ambitious, and working for him was a great opportunity for a young press secretary. He was hungry for good press, understood how to get it, and knew how to manage the news cycle. And on top of all that, he was good to staff and fun to be around.

■   ■   ■

It was a heady time to be in Washington; the media environment was morphing. The news days of MacNeil/Lehrer on PBS, Peter Jennings on ABC, Tom Brokaw on NBC, and Dan Rather on CBS were giving way to cable networks that thrived on the lurid and sensational. Respectful debates gave way to contentious arguments as cable news networks began to adopt partisan leanings (though they were not yet as partisan as newspapers in the time of John Adams and Thomas Jefferson). Then there was this new thing, the Internet. When I started running campaigns, we had to ask a supporter to set his or her VCR to record the news so that we could watch news coverage of the race or the latest campaign commercials. If the supporter remembered to record, we would drive to his or her house, pop the VHS tape into the VCR, and hit play (if the supporter had kindly already rewound the tape before we arrived).

■   ■   ■

But there was still room for good, old-fashioned retail politics.

After working for Mark Foley for nearly two years, I was hired by Dan Burton of Indiana to be the communications director for the House Committee on Oversight and Government Reform, which had been at the forefront of investigating the Clinton administration. After only a few months in that role, I got another call. This time it was from the National Republican Congressional Committee (known across D.C. as the NRCC). It's the House counterpart to the NRSC where I had worked several years earlier.

The caller was asking me to help Representative Clay Shaw's re-election campaign. Clay was a long-serving member of Congress who was in the fight of his political life. The NRCC wanted me to head to Florida to help him hold onto his ninety-three-mile-long district— stretching from Fort Lauderdale to Miami-Dade County. Clay was a great gentleman and a good congressman, but he was in deep trouble.

He suffered from a problem common among many members of congress who have served for years—political atrophy. Clay hadn't exercised his political muscles in so long that he had almost forgotten what to do. I discussed this with him as we were driving down I-95 towards Miami, Florida, several weeks before the 2000 election.

"See that federal building there?" Clay said. "I got the funding to build that."

"Great, but most people who know that are dead now," I retorted.

I was serious about that. Clay's South Florida district had a significant number of elderly voters, but for the younger ones, federal construction projects were not exactly a priority at the time. The night before election day, I glanced at Clay's schedule and saw that he was planning to go shopping for a new car. When I saw that, I did two things. I called our campaign scheduler, Suzann Guimond, and asked her for a list of every diner—along with addresses—in the Fort Lauderdale area. Then his campaign manager, Eric Eikenberg, and I told Clay that he could buy a new car any day after election day. "Tomorrow, we will be visiting diners across your district and meeting your voters," I informed him.

"Sean, I won my first election before you were born. This isn't how I campaign."

"Try it my way," I said. "We'll do it once, and if you don't like it, we'll stop."

"I don't want to bother people while they're eating."

"Just once, okay?"

"Fine," he agreed.

I had won the battle and didn't feel it was appropriate to also note that, actually, I had been one year old when he had won his first election.

The next morning, we went to the first diner. Clay walked up to a couple eating breakfast and introduced himself. Their faces lit up, and they had a great conversation. Clay went from table to table and got the same reaction.

"When's the next one?" he asked.

That afternoon I got a call from Richard Hunt, a top operative at the NRCC in Washington. The team there thought we were going to lose.

"Thanks man, you did your best. We appreciate everything you did," he said. "We know you worked really hard, and it's really appreciated."

"It's not over," I said. "We're going to pull this out."

"Whatever. Next beer is on me when you get back to Washington."

Clay and I watched the returns that night along with his gracious and supportive wife, Emilie. Every politician should be so lucky as to have a spouse as dedicated she was. The three of us watched as every precinct came in. The polls closed at 7:00 p.m., but the race was still too close to call at 10:00 p.m. Eleven o'clock in the evening came and went. Then the stroke of midnight filled the air. By the wee hours of the following morning, with our eyes still wide open with anticipation, we heard a TV anchor report, "the race in the twenty-second is too close to call." Clay Shaw was clinging to a 380-vote lead—the tightest race of his career. Convinced that those 380 voters were hands he had shaken at diners, I was ready to pop the champagne and celebrate this hard-earned victory. And then my festivities got put on hold. "Just because the news declared us as being in the lead," Clay said, "*we* can't declare victory. There will probably be a recount."

"You win by *saying* you already won," I said. "Winners declare victory."

Clay trusted me and declared his victory.

The recount eventually confirmed our win...but then there was a much bigger recount. It was the historic Florida recount of the 2000 presidential election.

The media had declared Al Gore the winner of the election and the next president, only to have to retract the announcement. We got caught up in the whirlwind called *Bush v. Gore* because Clay's district consisted of the three counties—Palm Beach, Broward, and Miami-Dade—that were at the heart of the electoral dispute. I had a ringside seat for it, attending recounts and watching auditors scrutinize hanging chads under magnifying glasses until the state and the presidency were finally awarded to George W. Bush, and Clay Shaw got to return to Congress for his tenth term.

Clay went on to do great things in Congress. He deserved a longer career, and Washington needed people like Clay. He served until he lost his re-election bid in 2006. That was a bad year for Republicans—the Democrats picked up five Senate seats and thirty-one

House seats. As President Bush said memorably afterwards, "If you look at it race by race, it was close. The cumulative effect, however, was...a thumping."[4]

■   ■   ■

I was done with being in constant campaign-mode, living out of a suitcase and cleaning my clothes in hotel laundry rooms—or laundromats. I thought it was time to find "experience" of a different kind. But my work on Clay Shaw's campaign had drawn the notice of the top folks at the NRCC, then chaired by Virginia Congressman Tom Davis. The committee's executive director, John Hishta, offered me the job of director of incumbent retention, which meant I oversaw the re-election campaigns of more than 200 Republican members of Congress. It was my job to spot their vulnerabilities, advise them, as I had with Clay Shaw, on how to shore up voter support, and lead them to victory in their re-elections.

The hardest part of my job was saying "no" to powerful members of Congress who were secure in their re-election bids but still wanted the NRCC's resources—money and campaign help. They didn't need our help to survive. They needed it to win by a larger margin, and that wasn't the role of the NRCC. As a young and eager staffer, I had a lot responsibility and power because of my position. I had started to get over my skis (and some might say "cocky") when John Hishta shared a very important piece of advice with me: "Your mail can always be addressed to 'occupant.'" People weren't sucking up to me; they wanted resources from whomever held that job.

After I spent two years at the NRCC, the chief of staff for the House Budget Committee, Rich Meade, reached out to me because the committee chairman, Representative Jim Nussle of Iowa, needed a communications director. I spent three amazing years working for Jim and creating projects and strategies that highlighted our efforts to curb federal spending. After that, I worked for the House Republican Conference, which was under the leadership of Representative Deborah Pryce of Ohio. My job was to shape communications for the House GOP caucus. Managing such high-profile communications, I felt I had finally arrived. I was also, for the first time in my life, making decent money…enough that I only needed *one* roommate, not several "housemates."

While at the House Republican Conference, I helped prepare our message for promoting the House Republican budget. Getting a budget passed through Congress is as tedious as carving a grain of rice. At the time, a congressman from Indiana named Mike Pence was the chairman of the Republican Study Committee, a large caucus of conservative members who were often critical of the party's leadership. They wanted House Republicans to argue for a much smaller federal government. They had a point—one that had my personal sympathies. But as a leadership staffer, I could also see the point of the House leadership—politics is the art of making the impossible possible. The budget proposed by the Republican Study Committee had little chance of passing the House. While I was trying to coordinate the budget message ideas coming from our committees and leadership offices, an aide for Pence, Matt Lloyd, told us that the Republican Study Committee was going to announce its budget as an alternative. In other words, he was going to blow up our messaging and present two House Republican budgets to the American people.

I'd like to say I handled this coolly. I didn't, and my eruption got back to Pence. Most people in politics don't worry about things like that. I do. While Melissa McCarthy later made fun of me as the angry press secretary, the truth is that I hate to lose my cool. I have too much Catholic guilt to berate people and feel good about it. I later apologized to Matt. And years later, when I was at the RNC, I took then-Governor Mike Pence aside at an event and told him I was sorry for how I had handled the budget controversy.

He looked surprised.

"Don't worry about it," he said. "You're doing a great job."

That is classic Mike Pence.

Life wasn't all work. On St. Patrick's Day in 2001, I showed up at the Eighteenth Street Lounge in DuPont Circle dressed in jeans and a button-down shirt, planning to meet up with a girl I was casually dating.

The bouncer took a close look at me, and his eyes did a visual survey of my attire. I was digging for my wallet to pull out my ID. But before I could show it to him, his deep voice bellowed, "No jeans."

Dejected, I walked across the street to a place without a dress code called the Lucky Bar. (I would learn later just how aptly named the Lucky Bar is.) I showed my ID to the bouncer who motioned me in. As I ordered a beer, I saw a young woman sitting alone at the end of the bar. I struck up a conversation with her. Her name was Elizabeth Manresa, and she had just moved to Washington for a new job at the local ABC station, WJLA-TV (channel 7). Elizabeth and I quickly became fast friends, two people who enjoyed Washington's culture, social scene, and gossip. After a few months, she mentioned that there was a colleague of hers she wanted to introduce me to. She suggested we all meet at the Virginia Gold Cup steeplechase. This was pre-app America—you actually had to go outside to meet people and have a face-to-face conversation with them.

The Gold Cup is held in a scenic meadow in the hills not far from the farm estates of Middleburg, Virginia. It's the kind of event where people dress up in their "Sunday best" to sample delicacies and champagne in tents sponsored by luxury car companies and other corporate sponsors. Many spectators, including myself and my friends, used it as an excuse to drink in the middle of a Saturday.

You know, a real Sean Spicer kind of place.

In 2001, the Gold Cup took place a few weeks after the terrorist attacks of September 11. That tragic day united our country in sorrow, but it also united us in our pride for our country and compassion for our fellow citizens. It seemed like everyone started looking at life a little differently. The Gold Cup races, like many other events around the country, proceeded as planned so that America could begin its long healing process.

A woman of her word, Elizabeth brought her mysterious friend to the Gold Cup and made sure to run into my buddy John Sankovich and me. It was a perfectly planned "accidental" meeting. I have to admit that I really noticed Elizabeth's friend, taking in with one glance her chestnut hair and green-blue eyes. (We debate the color of her eyes to this day—she claims it depends on the weather.) She worked with Elizabeth at WJLA, and her name was Rebecca Miller. I did not forget it. We had a great afternoon, getting to know each other while having a drink...or two...and sharing a few laughs. We may have even seen a horse run around the track, too.

On Monday, Elizabeth asked me if I could meet for drinks that Thursday night at Cafe Deluxe on Wisconsin Avenue, not far from where the WJLA studios were at the time. "Rebecca and I are going for drinks after the 6:00 p.m. newscast. Wanna join us?"

Thursday night finally arrived, and I made sure I left work with plenty of time to cross town and make it to Cafe Deluxe. As promised, the three of us met and ordered a round of drinks. After twenty minutes of nonstop conversation between Rebecca and myself, Rebecca leaned over to Elizabeth and said, "I thought you had to go." Elizabeth was quick on the uptake and vanished into thin air.

The next week, I sent Rebecca an email asking if I could cook her dinner at my townhouse in Old Town Alexandria the following Sunday night. I gave her precise directions (again, this was pre-app America). When she arrived, our conversation picked up where it had left off at Cafe Deluxe. I cooked a surprisingly decent meal—steak (cooked to a perfect medium rare), potatoes, and salad. She devoured it, which impressed me considering her petite frame. I didn't know until years later that Rebecca doesn't like black pepper, yet she graciously ate every bite of the rib-eye that I had doused in cracked black pepper, thinking that I was making it extra special.

I continued to see Rebecca. And in 2004, we married at St. Alban's Episcopal Church in the shadows of the Washington National Cathedral. She had taught fifth and sixth grade Sunday school there in her single years, and it was a very special place to her. We had three priests officiating at our wedding—including a Catholic priest from St. Anselm's Abbey in D.C. We partied the night away with our family and friends aboard the *Cherry Blossom* riverboat while it cruised the Potomac River. (We have since learned that some of our guests never realized that the boat set sail. Evidently, they stayed by the bar all night!) We have changed addresses in Alexandria a couple of times and are now raising two amazing children—a darling, blue-eyed, blond boy who loves Legos, soccer, baseball and football, and a spunky, brunette, brown-eyed, little princess who enjoys soccer, lacrosse, cooking, and ballet. They are the light of our lives and the greatest blessings we could imagine.

Rebecca, a proud graduate of the University of the South (a.k.a. Sewanee), moved to Washington for her career. She worked in local news and had hopped from local market to local market, as many broadcast journalists do. She told me that she always had her dreams set on being a news producer in Washington, D.C.—much like Holly Hunter's character in the 1980s movie *Broadcast News*. After twelve years in the news business, Rebecca was asked to serve in the George W. Bush White House communications office. And, after twelve years as chief communications officer for the National Beer Wholesalers Association, she recently joined Airlines for America as the senior vice president for communications.

Throughout my time in politics, Rebecca has provided keen focus and shrewd counsel, and she has kept our family firmly rooted. During my six years at the RNC, the emotional rollercoaster of the presidential primary, the nail-biter of the Trump election, and my White House tour, Rebecca was my rock.

She still is.

■   ■   ■

To many in Washington, I was a congressional aide on the rise. Inside, I was still a kid from an Irish Catholic family in Rhode Island, where the biggest celebrity I had ever met was the local weatherman. (I'll never forget you, John Ghiorse.) Now I was on a first-name basis with the Speaker of the House of Representatives, regularly in the company of the most famous politicians in America, and had opportunities to meet the nation's leading thinkers, actors, and athletes. Sometimes these opportunities overlapped. I once spent four days doing media for Clint Eastwood to highlight how lawsuits harm small businesses. On another occasion, the Bush White House invited me to the Rose Garden to celebrate the New England Patriots win of the Super Bowl, where I got to meet Tom Brady, Bill Belichick, and other greats from my favorite football team.

My opportunity to work in the executive branch came when former Representative Rob Portman, then the U.S. trade representative (USTR), was asked to become President George W. Bush's director of the Office of Management and Budget. Portman's deputy, Susan Schwab, was selected as his successor by President Bush, and Portman's aide, Christin Baker, asked me to help her find someone to handle media and public affairs. I sent them several candidates, but in the end I went from sending them job candidates to becoming a candidate. As much as the USTR job appealed to me, I didn't know anything about trade at the time. I might have even lost a bet as to what NAFTA stood for.

Two things happened next, almost simultaneously. I got the job, and I broke my jaw.

It was July 2006, and the congressional softball league was in full swing. On my last day at the House Republican Conference, a Wednesday, I went to play what I thought would be my last congressional softball game.

We were in Anacostia, a neighborhood in D.C., playing on a rough soccer field. I was asked to pitch.

I took twenty paces to where I thought the mound should be. I turned to face a broad-shouldered, six-foot-three batter from the House Committee on Energy and Commerce. My first pitch was to the outside. I threw again, and he whacked a line drive straight into my mouth.

The next thing I remembered was lying on the ground with a cluster of staffers looking down at me. I drew "GW" in the bloody sand. I knew how well the emergency room at George Washington University

Hospital had taken care of President Reagan when he had been shot in 1981. That's where I wanted to go.

My teammates Josh Hartman and John Sankovich got me in the back of a car and drove me across town to the hospital. As we were driving, another teammate, Amy Lorinzini, tracked down Rebecca who was working late that night, preparing for a special Little League game that would be played on the South Lawn of the White House the next day. Working at the White House, Rebecca was a few blocks away from the hospital and walked over to be with me.

As Josh and John were pulling up at the hospital, they handed me a towel, and I put it over my face before walking into the ER. Since I couldn't talk, John told the admitting nurse that I had been hit in face during a softball game. Once I was in the triage area and the towel was off my face, the nurses tried to hide their shock. John looked at them with a lot of concern and a dose of his trademark humor and said, "Take care of him. He's a spokesman for a living. He needs his mouth to work."

I went into surgery and woke up in the ICU missing six teeth, three up, three down. The blow had crushed my face, breaking my jaw in two places and requiring a plate and screws to be set in place. My jaw had to be wired shut for what they said would be at least six weeks. While many people would want to have my jaw wired shut in the coming years (and probably in years prior), this was not how I planned to start a new job as a spokesman. Thankfully, Rebecca was there, holding my hand. I spent the next several days in the hospital, missing my first few days of work and our first foreign trip to Geneva, Switzerland, the headquarters of the World Trade Organization.

Then I got out and went to work for Susan as the USTR spokesman, unable to actually talk. A few weeks later, with my mouth still wired shut, we flew to Rio de Janeiro, Brazil, for the G20 Trade Ministers Meeting. When we arrived, the U.S. delegation headed to a local steakhouse. While my colleagues raved about the steak, I ordered soup. That was the only thing on the menu that I could eat. I sat at the end of the table, sipping soup through a straw.

Susan Schwab looked after me with a mix of good humor, concern, and a grateful empathy for how hard it was to travel and work while being in such discomfort. She is a brilliant woman and was a fantastic boss with a small, cohesive team of political appointees and career trade negotiators who epitomized the work hard, play hard philosophy.

Toward the end of the Bush administration, we were in Geneva working nearly around the clock for seventeen straight days on a world trade agreement. At the end of another long day, we walked back to our hotel. Every cell in my body was crying out for sleep, but I was still wound up. I couldn't stop thinking about work. So, I did something I don't do often. I popped an Ambien. Then I took a relaxing, warm shower and planned to head to bed. Then there was a knock on the door.

I cracked the door and peeked into the hallway. It was a Secret Service agent.

"Hey, you didn't answer your phone," he said. "There's a meeting downstairs."

We were in a critical phase of negotiations, and the team wanted to huddle before the morning.

I nodded and shut the door.

I quickly got dressed and went down to the meeting, which was in the posh, boutique restaurant of our hotel that we had all to ourselves.

Then the Ambien kicked in. I don't remember anything about what happened next. But that didn't matter, everyone else was happy to remember it for me, in detail. I got reports the next day from my colleagues Tim Keeler and Gretchen Reiter that when I was asked a question, I was passionately illogical.

Such events stand out in my memory. But it was a glorious time in my life and career. Before going to the USTR's office, I had been to Canada, Mexico (Tijuana), Iraq, and Ireland. I spent the last three years of the Bush administration doing press events on six continents, attending summits and ministerial meetings in Brazil, India, China, Japan, Australia, and in over thirty cities around the world. In between work, we snuck in a little culture. Private tours were arranged for us in the Vatican and the State Hermitage Museum in St. Petersburg, Russia.

I also got to work with some of the most interesting people in the world. One of them was Peter Mandelson, a British politician who had helped Tony Blair brand "New Labour." When I worked with Peter, he had been the European commissioner for trade. Well-tailored, well-spoken, Oxford-educated, Peter once hammered out a statement with me, giving me a chance to see how a master of the English language weighs the impact of every word.

I got the chance to work closely with other impressive people, many of them trade ministers, from Peru to Panama and South Korea.

Later, when I worked for Donald Trump, his critique of U.S. trade policy reminded me that the Republican Party might have strayed from Ronald Reagan's balanced wisdom on free trade. Reagan was definitely in favor of free trade and unafraid of economic competition, but he always insisted that trade be "fair as well as free" and that American workers not get shortchanged, stating flatly: "I will not stand by and watch American businesses fail because of unfair trading practices abroad. I will not stand by and watch American workers lose their jobs because other nations do not play by the rules."[5] Somewhere along the way, Reagan's sense of balance got lost, and free trade became an ideological commitment rather than a pragmatic political and economic decision.

American workers in industries slaughtered by foreign competition were too often treated as expendable by the Democrat and Republican establishments, and they noticed. While the vast majority of Americans have benefited from free trade agreements, Donald Trump gave a voice to those who did not, and they were electrified that a national politician finally noticed them and recognized their sense of abandonment.

Tied into this was U.S. policy with China. There was a bipartisan effort during the Clinton years to promote China's admission to the World Trade Organization (WTO). It was believed this would normalize China's trade practices and build a basis for the country to become more democratic. After China joined the WTO, the United States trade deficit with China mushroomed, and the Communist Party of China became even more powerful. The Chinese state was also involved in the rampant theft of Western industrial secrets and intellectual property, discriminatory tariffs, and restrictive internal policies.

Lenin famously said that capitalists would sell the rope that would hang them. In order to do business in China, the Chinese government forced U.S. companies to give away their most valuable intellectual property. Many took the deal in exchange for what would likely be a few good years in China. Now China has by some indices the world's largest economy, but until the election of Donald Trump, we were still allowing it to be treated in trade and other international agreements as if it were a weak, developing country.

So, while I remain convinced that trade deals, including the North American Free Trade Agreement, can be hugely beneficial for the United States, Republicans need to do a better job of articulating the benefits of trade and making it clear that we're watching out for American workers.

■   ■   ■

After the Bush administration ended, I became the cofounder of a small, successful public affairs firm in Old Town Alexandria with two of my former Hill colleagues, Gretchen Reiter and Nathan Imperiale. Our firm focused on helping companies communicate with the federal government, pointing out how their businesses might be harmed by unnecessary regulation and how they benefited consumers, workers, and the country. Executives of major companies and trade associations told me directly that the Obama administration was the most explicitly anti-business administration in U.S. history and was prolonging the great recession. I enjoyed helping these companies with strategy and communications, but the business side of it—like attracting new clients—was not really for me. While I was wondering what to do next, I was recalled for active duty in the U.S. Navy. My commission had come through the Direct Commission Officer program for people with specialized skill sets, including public affairs. I was sworn in as an ensign in September 1999 in the U.S. Capitol and sent to Pensacola for two weeks of training.

From the get-go, Marine "gunnies" who helped run the program saluted me. That took some getting used to. We had physical training and classroom study. Despite many reservists being called "weekend warriors," we knew getting called up for war was always a possibility. The axiom of the old commercial, "one weekend a month, two weeks a year," is not the reality of today's reserve or National Guard. If anyone doubts their sacrifices, just consider the high cost they have paid in Iraq and Afghanistan.

■   ■   ■

In July 2009, I was recalled by the Navy to serve at the Criminal Investigation Task Force and had an opportunity to go to Guantanamo Bay in Cuba. I was struck by the way our country treated suspected terrorists, accused of some of the most heinous crimes. They enjoyed twenty-first century comforts such as satellite television, a full library of DVD selections, healthcare, sporting gear, and a soccer field. These accused terrorists were receiving better treatment than many Americans will ever experience—and their accommodations were being footed by the American taxpayer. There are American veterans—who wore our country's uniform and deployed to lands far away, leaving families behind, to fight on the front lines of wars—who are living on the streets, wondering where their next meal will come from or how they will receive healthcare. Yet here were these suspected terrorists—the most heinous of them all—living in very comfortable conditions.

When my tour of duty ended, I was presented with another opportunity—would I want to take a "follow-on" position in the Pentagon? I gave it some serious thought, but Rebecca—who grew up in a Navy family—said, "You need to get back into the mix of things." She meant back into the mix of Washington and politics. And she was right. Day-to-day military life is not for me. I take pride in wearing the uniform and serving this great country, but there's a reason why I am a reservist—I

was meant to work in politics. I love the excitement of winning and losing, the fight for conservative policies I believe in, the idea of making our
country even better, and helping my fellow citizens.

Around that time, I got a phone call out of the blue from Ed Gillespie.
I had known Ed for years and always respected his work as chairman of
the RNC, a Hill staffer, and counselor to President George W. Bush.

"Sean, would you be interested in meeting with Reince Priebus?"
Ed said.

I knew that Reince was the newly-elected chairman of the RNC, but
I didn't know much about him other than he was highly respected by the
GOP in Wisconsin.

"I'm certainly willing to meet with him," I responded, not wanting
to act too interested but also expressing some interest at the same time.

I had worked inside the RNC building on Capitol Hill years earlier
when I was director of incumbent retention at the NRCC. Outside, the
white, brick building still looked like a four-story wedding cake. But
inside, it had become an empty shell filled with unoccupied offices and
an uncomfortable level of silence in the halls. The RNC had been reduced
to a skeleton staff because it had no money. I literally mean no money.
The Grand Old Party was over $23 million dollars in debt.

I took Ed up on his offer and scheduled a meeting at the RNC in
January 2011. After I checked in at the security desk in the RNC lobby,
I was escorted up to the fourth floor, where the chairman's office is. I
was introduced to Reince and his chief of staff, Jeff Larson. Reince was
a polite, professional, well-spoken Wisconsin lawyer, neat and impec-
cable in his dress, barely forty. A master of organization, Reince had
served as chairman for the Republican Party of Wisconsin, building the
state party that helped Scott Walker become such a transformative governor of Wisconsin. He also was a long-time friend of his hometown
congressman, Representative Paul Ryan, who at the time was chairman
of the influential House Ways and Means Committee.

It was well known throughout the Washington political circles, as
well as in the Republican folds, that the RNC had a lot of work to do
on many fronts in order to rebuild. The RNC was no longer trusted by

many grassroots Republicans, and it didn't have the talent, resources, or media savvy to compete against President Obama's re-election campaign machine. Before my meeting with Reince, I had prepared a strategic plan with two goals: to rebuild the RNC communications operation and to make it competitive for the next presidential campaign. In organizational charts and planning documents, I laid out specific action items aimed at regaining Republican trust and modernizing the RNC's communications strategy, especially when it came to social media and digital communications.

Reince and Jeff liked what they heard, and in short order I was sitting in my first-floor, corner office leading a communications team. When I started, the team had fewer than ten people on it. I had my communications playbook in hand, but there was a big hiccup. We didn't have any money to implement the plan. The RNC was so broke that we could barely afford the postage for our next direct-mail fundraising piece. Reince, Jeff, and I crouched around a table in the chairman's office and went through every line in the communications budget, cutting every cost we could, right down to newspaper and magazine subscriptions.

We cut what we could live without and even pared down the basic essentials. We had to make some tough decisions, but we didn't have a choice.

Our national finance chairman, Ron Weiser, and Reince challenged each other to see whose travel expenses would be cheaper—from dining off a piece of fruit from a hotel breakfast bar to making a lunch out of free pretzels saved from an airplane ride—as they traveled around the country hitting up big donors.

As RNC chairman, Reince presented a calm and reassuring face for the national party on *Meet the Press, Face the Nation*, and other Sunday talk shows. But his greatest skill was fundraising, the lifeblood of politics. He actually enjoyed gathering people together and persuading them to donate their time and money to the party.

My job was to give the communications shop a makeover. Instead of just sending out traditional press releases, we hired a social media coordinator and a Hispanic media coordinator to cut into the big Democratic lead in both of those markets. I considered these moves strategic "investments" that would get big returns and show donors we were worthy of their support.

During my first few months at the RNC, it felt more like working in a startup company than at a national, established political party's headquarters. We were on a tight timeline to get out of debt and up to speed in time for the 2012 election cycle. We ran lean and mean, and our small but growing communications staff worked seven days a week, doing multiple jobs from operating the RNC's own TV studio, to booking Republican officials on shows, to working with regional media and social media. We kept at it because we knew how much was at stake. Our purpose was simple: raise the money and build the team necessary to get Republicans elected and re-elected.

Our pump-priming investments worked. Led by Angela Meyers and the finance team, donor support for the RNC grew, and we went from a barebones RNC staff of just over eighty to more than 250 at headquarters by election day in 2012.

We were still not where we needed to be—the timeline was too short for us to match what the Democrats had—but we had built and cemented a strong team that could offer significant help to the next Republican presidential candidate.

■   ■   ■

The Republican primary debates in 2012 were an ordeal—too many debates and too many candidates, many of them marginal.

Many tried to blame the RNC for this, but the truth is that the national party had relinquished any say in the process years earlier. It was the news media that ran the debates, working with universities and civic groups to hold one primary debate after another, whenever it wished, and no candidate wanted to forgo free, national air time.

There were some sterling moments. Newt Gingrich dazzled audiences with his witty intellectualism and snappy comebacks to media moderators. Herman Cain entertained us all with his "9-9-9" tax plan.

And Rick Santorum identified the blue-collar conservatives that Donald Trump would later energize to such great effect. But it was clear, almost from the start, that there was one candidate who was more viable than the others—former Massachusetts Governor Mitt Romney. The two most important things for a candidate's success are time and money, and our best candidate was forced to fly around the country and spend both time and money at the media's behest instead of in the service of his own strategy.

We at the RNC were, unfortunately, spectators with no involvement in choosing the format, moderators, timing, or anything else. We often had to beg the state parties for tickets to the debates. But whenever anything went wrong, the RNC was blamed. And a lot went wrong.

One sore point was the moderators who often seemed to prefer pontificating instead of asking the candidates fair and relevant questions. The ABC debate that year offered an especially egregious example. Rather than illuminate the differences between the candidates, moderator George Stephanopoulos tried to lure the Republican candidates into saying something that hardly reflected the main topics of concern to Republican primary voters.

"Governor Romney, do you believe that states have the right to ban contraception? Or is that trumped by a constitutional right to privacy?"

Romney was quick on the uptake.

"George, this is an unusual topic that you're raising. Do states have a right to ban contraception? I can't imagine a state banning contraception. I can't imagine the circumstances where a state would want to do so..."

Stephanopoulos pressed on: "Do you believe states have that right or not?"

"George, I don't know if the state has a right to ban contraception, no state wants to! The idea of you putting forward things that states *might* want to do, that no state wants to do, and then asking me whether they can do it or not is kind of a silly thing."[6] That was a hard punch back at the moderator by conventional standards.

Debates aside, by April, the delegate math had solidified, and Mitt Romney was destined to be the Republican nominee. But after spending so much time and money putting away Newt Gingrich, Michele Bachmann, Ron Paul, Herman Cain, Rick Santorum, and all the rest, Romney now took one body blow after another from the well-rested, well-funded Obama campaign.

The Obama campaign had mastered the art of using social media for donations, volunteer recruitment, and votes—things I wished we could have done at the RNC. Though we lacked the time and money to fully catch up, the Romney campaign was full of former RNC staffers who understood and valued the help we could provide. I became a regular commuter between Washington, D.C., and Boston, Massachusetts. The Obama campaign targeted conservatives with front groups that railed against Mitt Romney as undeserving of any true conservative's vote. It was fake news—aimed at discouraging Republican voters—but many fell for it and stayed at home.

Romney did the best he could. He was masterful in his first debate with Obama. By September, though, opinion had congealed against Romney. Our analysis showed that however well Romney did in substantive debate, it had little impact on the voters who thought he was wealthy and out of touch—an image that didn't fade when he offered to make a $10,000 bet in one primary debate and when he was recorded saying that 47 percent of Americans would vote for Obama no matter what because they paid no federal income tax and were dependent on the government.

I liked and admired Romney, but he had run before in 2008. He knew that questions about his personal taxes and finances would come up, and he needed to have better answers. The Romney ad campaigns were equally lacking, almost from another era. They failed to include sports advertising and did not focus enough on reaching Hispanics. Four years later, Donald Trump would enormously outperform Romney, not only in chutzpah and in dominating media coverage but also in voicing the concerns of working-class voters.

■   ■   ■

"So waddya think happened?"

Donald Trump sat behind his desk, hands resting on its surface. A bank of large windows overlooked Fifth Avenue, with a view down the street to a nice green corner of Central Park.

Inside, Donald Trump's office was a mélange of helmets, boxers' belts, trophies, plaques, and awards. The walls were covered, floor to ceiling, with framed pictures, most of them magazine covers featuring the visage of Trump himself. Trump had run out of room on the walls, so more framed pictures populated the space around the floorboard. His desk housed columns of memos and blueprints.

After the election, Reince had agreed to run for a second term as chairman, and I had agreed to stay on as communications director. Now Reince and I and the staff from the RNC finance department were in New York to meet with big, loyal Republican donors, one of whom resided in a tower that bore his name. We went to Trump Tower for constructive criticism and, we hoped, a large donation. Trump had been a big Romney supporter and was disappointed by his loss.

I told him that the Democrats had huge advantages in voter data and online messaging. He nodded and shot back an analysis of his own.

"Romney blew it," Trump said. "He should have had me speak at the convention. He could have used me more."

CHAPTER FOUR

MEETING TRUMP

One cool day in May 2016, I was summoned to the tarmac of Ronald Reagan Washington National Airport to catch a ride to New York City with the presumptive Republican nominee for president.

I had seen the plane dubbed "Trump Force One" many times on television. But it was something else to see the famous Trump name in strong letters and imperial gold paint shining in the sun. I couldn't help but notice each letter one by one. I started climbing the back stairs of the Boeing 757-200 leading to the exclusive world of Donald J. Trump, presidential candidate. Reality television had become reality for me, and I was finding it a little disorienting.

I was the first to arrive, ahead of the motorcade. As I continued my climb, a flight attendant greeted me and showed me the area where I would be sitting.

After a few moments of settling in, I relaxed in my chair and looked around. Donald Trump gets a lot of ribbing in the press for the over-the-top decor of his homes, but I found the interior of his jet to be tastefully appointed—high-back seats of cream-colored leather, polished panels of cherry wood with spotless brass accents.

Within a minute, the doors were sealed and the Rolls-Royce engines roared to life. We lifted upward in the air, five thousand, ten thousand, twenty thousand feet—bouncing through turbulence on our way to our cruising altitude. I was seated with other staff—I must have made small talk with some of them, but I don't remember it because my focus settled forward, on the candidate's head, bobbing as he spoke energetically to someone in the seat facing him.

Once the plane leveled off, the staffer talking to Trump departed, and Corey Lewandowski turned to me and said, "Let's go talk to Mr. Trump."

Corey had asked me to go to New York to help plan media strategy and staffing. The candidate was sprawled out in his seat wearing his trademark blue suit, white shirt, and red tie, relaxed a few notches—a human flag, which of course was the idea. Donald Trump looked up at me and smiled warmly, though whether he remembered our previous encounters throughout the primary debates, I couldn't be sure. Twice during the campaign, as the spokesperson for the RNC, I had criticized comments Trump had made about Mexican immigrants and John McCain's status as an American war hero.

Had he noticed? Did he hold a grudge? I later learned that if you didn't criticize Trump personally—and I had not—he didn't take it personally. Whether he remembered me or had been prompted by Corey, he called me by name.

"Hey, Sean," he said. "Take a seat."

I did and for the next ten minutes we had an easy conversation about the state of the race, the stories of the day, and what the media was up to. By the time we landed in New York, I was feeling better about the candidate, the campaign, and where I stood with the likely nominee and possible future president.

As we landed, Keith Schiller, Trump's longtime bodyguard, took me to the cockpit to watch the landing as the plane approached LaGuardia Airport.

■   ■   ■

Starting in 2012, I had helped craft a major RNC initiative called the Growth and Opportunity Project. It was based on the premise that we had to meet the changing demographics of the United States if the Republican Party was to remain viable as a national party. GOP governors—from Scott Walker in Wisconsin, to John Kasich in Ohio, to Rick Scott in Florida—were making deep inroads with millennials and independent women as well as with Hispanics, Asians, and Latinos. Walker in particular resonated with blue-collar workers and union members, alienated by a Democratic Party that was dominated by identity politics and appeared remotely elite to working men and women.

The party of Lincoln and Reagan has an inclusive message of opportunity for all, but many Republican politicians had little interest and saw little benefit in expanding the message beyond our base of middle-class, suburban, white voters. Too many expected that African Americans, Hispanics, and Asians would naturally come our way because they shared our Republican values and stood to benefit from Republican policies. But that's not how politics works. You have to make the ask—and too many of our candidates weren't doing that. We weren't in their neighborhoods, churches, and businesses, and the vote totals showed it.

The RNC aimed to change that by going into minority communities and union strongholds and explaining how Republican policies would greatly improve their economic prospects.

In the RNC's Growth and Opportunity Project report (many would call it an "autopsy," a term that I have never liked) of the 2012 campaign, the RNC concluded that Hispanic voters were especially ripe for Republican appeals. They were far more conservative than the liberal politicians they supported in the Democratic Party. Millions of church-going, Hispanic small business owners were particularly amenable to hearing Republican arguments about lower taxes, less regulation, respect for life, and school reform that focused on hard academics and employable skills rather than liberal social engineering. Our failure to reach Hispanics and engage with them on their top issues would have a major impact on our ability to win national elections if we did not make significant structural changes. We needed to create a system akin to those used by missionaries, one that would spread conservative values.

So, political alarm bells went off at the RNC in mid-June 2015 when Donald Trump, in his announcement that he was running for the Republican nomination for president, declared, "The U.S. has become a dumping ground for everybody else's problems....When Mexico sends its people, they're not sending their best. They're not sending you....They're sending people that have lots of problems, and they're bringing those problems with us. They're bringing drugs. They're bringing crime. They're rapists. And some, I assume, are good people."[1]

That was so far from our message that it was almost a parody—and not a funny one. Reince and I agreed that we needed to make sure we communicated about where the party was on this. When CNN asked me about Trump's statement, I said, "[A]s far as painting Mexican Americans with that kind of a brush, I think that's probably something that is not helpful to the cause."[2] I criticized the message but not the messenger.

Just a month later, I saw Donald Trump being interviewed by pollster Frank Luntz at a Family Leadership Summit in Iowa. The pollster asked the candidate if it was appropriate to call Senator John McCain of Arizona a "dummy," as Trump had done at a recent rally, in retaliation for McCain calling some Trump supporters "crazies."

Luntz said, "He's a war hero."

Trump shot back, "He's not a war hero....He's a war hero because he was captured. I like people that weren't captured....I believe, perhaps, he's a war hero. But right now he said some very bad things about a lot of people...."[3]

Criticizing John McCain's position on the issues is fair game, and it is true that McCain sometimes seems like the *Washington Post*'s favorite go-to critic of whatever his fellow conservatives and Republicans are trying to do. At the same time, John McCain is a man who wore our country's uniform—and wore it proudly—and never wavered during the arduous years he was held captive as a POW. At one point while he was in solitary confinement, his brutal North Vietnamese captors offered to release him because his father was an admiral and they wanted to score propaganda points. But he refused any special treatment and rejected any parole unless every other American prisoner of war captured before him was released as well. The North Vietnamese responded by torturing McCain even more. His actions were unmistakably heroic and honorable. Most Americans, including myself, felt that John McCain has endured more pain and suffering for our nation than most of us can ever fathom.

I did not want to get involved in a political feud between Senator McCain and Donald Trump, and I did not want the RNC to take the side of one Republican presidential candidate over another. But I did think that it was important to affirm that McCain, a longtime Republican senator and our former presidential nominee, was a genuine American hero.

I felt the RNC needed to make a statement. Beyond my own feelings, we were getting flooded with calls from reporters and dismayed Republicans—but what should the statement say, and who should issue it?

Reince was speaking at the Bohemian Grove in Northern California, a gathering of business and political elites, where no phones or electronic devices are allowed. I consulted Katie Walsh, Reince's chief of staff. We made an executive decision and issued a statement and a tweet under my name.

@SenJohnMcCain is an American hero because he served his country and sacrificed more than most can imagine. Period.[4]

(See, I have a tendency to end statements with "period.")

Once again, I was careful not to criticize Donald Trump personally, and I let Trump's campaign manager, Corey Lewandowski, know what we were going to do. Later, there was a lot of speculation about "fissures" between the Trump campaign and the RNC, but Corey understood our concerns and, I think, shared them.

The press saw the political damage from Trump's remarks in stark terms. In reporting on the McCain comments, *Politico* concluded: "Donald Trump might have finally crossed the line."

I hope *Politico* coded that sentence with a single keystroke because it would have reason to use it again and again. If "crossing the line" was the concern, candidate Trump would cross the line, jump over the line, and dance merrily back and forth over the line. But he never paid the price any other candidate would have paid.

Why? In a word, relatability. There was group of voters who believed neither party understood their concerns or was speaking to them. They view Trump, despite his wealth, as being one of them.

I slowly came to realize that for all his roughness of speech and manner, Donald Trump was a Growth and Opportunity Project all to himself. He was doing personally what the RNC was only beginning to do nationally, but he was doing it in a very different way to a somewhat different group of voters. While he was not reaching out to black, Hispanic, and Asian voters in the way that the RNC had prescribed, he was reaching out to many of these voters and others in a way that we could never have imagined—what he called the "forgotten men and women."

His ability to do this came from his lifetime career as a contractor and hotelier.

Donald Trump had taken the time to get to know the people employed on his projects—the electricians, plumbers, carpenters, boilermakers, ironworkers, masons, and roofers. He also got to know hotel housekeeping teams as well as cooks, bellmen, and cashiers.

The media wants to believe that Trump's base is all white. The people Trump took pains to know represented a diverse cross section of our country—white, black, Hispanic, Asian American, and immigrants from a wide range of countries. He asked them about their dreams, their fears, and their complaints about job security and upward mobility. Even though he was their boss, there was something about him that prompted people to open up. Franklin Delano Roosevelt had come to know the lives of rural Southerners during his stays in Georgia, joining them on the porch and following them by car on hunts. Trump went to the trouble to get to know "working-class people" and recognize that his businesses wouldn't survive without their hard work and dedication. He valued their work, and he listened when they opened up about a relative who was worried about keeping a job or a small business while living from paycheck to paycheck. He knew that many of these people felt ignored during the Obama administration, which was passionate about reassigning bathrooms and combating climate change while apparently dismissing the interests of small business owners and working-class Americans. The Obama administration was very keen on "globalism" and seemingly unconcerned about job losses among coal miners and steelworkers and people who worked in struggling small towns. Many Americans felt that neither party really spoke for them—the Republicans focused on business owners rather than workers; the Democrats obsessed with progressive crusades rather than jobs.

But now the forgotten men and women of America finally had a candidate who heard their concerns and whom they could support.

The RNC had spent several years analyzing the 2012 election results and trying to figure out how to win a national election. We invested over $150 million and worked diligently to build a data system that effectively identified the voters we needed to get to the polls. But Donald Trump knew how to win by instinct. He had a populist message that no Republican messaging laboratory could have ever devised. He motivated conservative and working-class voters, some who had sat out previous elections because they felt that neither party's candidate truly represented their views or cared about them. He was taken seriously because he was willing to discard the clichéd, boilerplate conservative message and replace it with something that resonated with blue-collar workers' experiences and observations. He attacked Republican orthodoxy on free trade and the Iraq War. He made fun of the party's barons. He was so politically incorrect that pundits assumed, over and over again, that his campaign was finished, that no candidate could survive such controversy and media condemnation. But Trump stayed in the game because he spoke to the dreams and ambitions of millions of Americans of all races who felt they were the heart and soul of this country but were being ignored. My father put it this way: "Many candidates say something like, 'I will fight for policies that will create a better economy,' while Trump says, 'I'm going to get your job back.'" It was a very personal message that was vastly different from what people were used to hearing.

Donald Trump could sell his message to working-class people of all backgrounds and colors because they knew he was more comfortable among them than he ever would be at the annual Gridiron Club dinner or the Council on Foreign Relations. And if he sometimes spoke crudely or bluntly, they forgave him because they believed that they or their friends or their relatives spoke that way, too. Despite his glamorous lifestyle, Trump had developed his image as a man of the people who spoke his mind and not a typical politician who only reiterated what he had been told to say by handlers, pollsters, and strategists. For people who thought America was headed in the wrong direction, Donald Trump seemed to offer real hope and change, despite any inappropriate language.

As ridiculous as it sounds, the RNC had little role in the overall nominating process or primary debates. After losing the 2012 election, we made several structural reforms to improve our future chances. We shortened the primary season but involved more states, slowed down the potential of a runaway candidate, moved up the convention, and took control of the primary debates.

I told Reince that our debate and presidential nominating process was backwards with too many debates that forced our candidates to be led around the nose by media sponsors.

After the 2012 elections, the Growth and Opportunity Project, with a sophisticated data and technology operation, was well underway. The 2014 midterm elections were very successful for Republicans, and I offered to stay at the RNC for the 2016 presidential cycle, provided Reince gave me a chance to lead the sort of major initiatives I thought we needed. Reince agreed and added chief strategist to my title.

Along the way, we also had to manage the party's internal ideological tensions and cultural divides. Small donors—people who give between twenty and one hundred dollars per year and also put up yard signs and make get-out-the-vote calls—tend to be social conservatives who want their issues at the forefront of the party's agenda. High-dollar donors, drawn from the top ranks of business, finance, and technology, tend to be more socially moderate and focused on fiscal responsibility. They wanted us to lean into issues of regulation and taxation. The party's bigger donors naturally felt their libertarian take on social and economic issues should be paramount.

Managing these disparate and sometimes fractious constituencies was a task for which Reince Priebus was well suited. A consensus-builder by nature, his calming, businesslike demeanor got everyone pulling their oars in the same direction.

In the 2014 midterm elections, the Republican Party gained control of the Senate, increased our hold on the House, and added two governors. We had the largest majority in the House and state legislatures since 1928. As the presidential campaign got underway, the RNC was finally able to compete at the Democrats' level when communicating our message and getting people to the polls. I truly believe that if Mitt Romney had gone into the 2012 race with the capabilities the RNC had in 2016, he would have won the election.

The RNC had gotten up to speed, but we weren't pushing the cruise-control button. We still had our foot on the accelerator. We didn't want just to *compete* against the Democrats—we wanted to *beat* the Democrats in the 2016 election. Inside the RNC building and among donors, we could feel even greater success building. There was an energy like I had never experienced in more than two decades in political circles. At the time, none of us had any idea that energy would result in the election of one of our donors—one of our celebrity donors.

■   ■   ■

Becoming the nominee of the Republican Party in 2016 required getting 1,237 delegates from the primaries and caucuses. Delegates from the states are awarded in different ways: winner take all, proportional, and hybrid. In order to get more voters and states involved in the process of selecting the nominee, the RNC had reformed the way delegates were apportioned and had limited the ability of early states to be "winner take all." This reduced the ability of a well-funded candidate, or one with high national name ID, to come out of the gate and rack up delegates without being "tested" in the political arena.

In recent cycles, the presidential primary season started in January and wrapped up in June. A candidate would generally become the presumptive nominee about halfway through the process, limiting the number of states and voters whose votes mattered and forcing the eventual nominee to spend valuable time and resources fending off lingering opponents. The 2016 rules of the RNC shortened the season, but they also involved more states and voters and helped more states award their delegates "proportional" earlier in the process. No states were allowed to be "winner take all" until after the second week in March, which was two weeks longer than the 2012 timeline. Further, only four "carve-out" states—Iowa, New Hampshire, South Carolina, and Nevada—were allowed to hold contests before March 1, further reducing the chances of a runaway candidate. While states had ignored the rules and jumped the queue in previous cycles, the new system worked—no state broke the rules. For states that violated the rules, higher penalties were put in place that would strip them of their delegates. A state like Florida, which had ignored the rules in the previous cycle, didn't want to risk losing delegates because leaders in the state assumed one of their own, Bush or Rubio, would need those delegates in the race to 1,237. Ironically, Florida was a "winner take all" state, and Donald Trump took all ninety-nine delegates.

Another strategic step we took after the 2012 cycle was to move up the convention date by a few weeks. Conventions used to be held much earlier in the cycle, but after Watergate and the advent of public financing, conventions were moved back to late August and early September. As it is with most things, money was the motivating factor. Candidates who agree to public financing also agree to forgo raising money for their campaign in return for a lump sum from the government. The conventions were pushed back to maximize the money during the final weeks of the campaign. In 2008, Barack Obama's campaign flip-flopped on their pledge to take public financing and began raising money for the general election. That cycle will likely be the last time any major candidate takes public financing. Thus, the need to wait to access the money is gone.

Romney came into the 2012 convention dead broke (to steal a Hillary Clinton phrase) because, prior to becoming the official nominee, he could not legally tap funds he had raised for the general election. Unbeknownst to many, we actually made it possible for Romney to appear on the first night of convention just to give him a forty-eight-hour advantage.

When Reince announced his intention to move up the primary, many prominent, Democrat political operatives mocked the action as being short-sighted. Ironically, not too long afterward, the Democratic National Committee (DNC) followed our lead. No one reform was going to win us a national election, but combined they gave us an edge.

At the beginning of the 2016 presidential election, one of our first and most urgent tasks was addressing the dysfunction we had all seen in the 2012 debates that dragged on for too long, exhausting the candidates and draining voter interest.

We came up with a new plan to streamline the debate process, and I outlined it in the editorial pages of the *Wall Street Journal*. There was a debate about the debates, I wrote, because the 2012 debate schedule had kept candidates off the campaign trail, robbing them of time they wanted to spend meeting voters and listening to their concerns. There was also, I noted, "frustration about debate hosts and moderators, some of whom had concocted bizarre and irrelevant questions." This was a reference not just to George Stephanopoulos's question from the previous cycle, but also to Candy Crowley's during the general election. Candy had interjected to rebut Governor Romney's assertion that President Obama had failed to call the attack on the U.S. consulate in Benghazi "an act of terror." President Obama, basking in her apparent support, treated her as his de facto debate partner and said, "Can you say that a little louder, Candy?"[5] Romney later told radio host Hugh Hewitt:

Well, I don't think it's the role of the moderator in a debate to insert themselves into the debate and to declare a winner or a loser on a particular point. And I must admit that at that stage, I was getting a little upset at Candy, because in a prior setting where I was to have had the last word, she decided that Barack Obama was to get the last word despite the rules that we had.

So she obviously thought it was her job to play a more active role in the debate than was agreed upon by the two candidates, and I thought her jumping into the interaction I was having with the president was also a mistake on her part, and one I would have preferred to carry out between the two of us, because I was prepared to go after him for misrepresenting to the American people—that the nature of the attack.[6]

At the RNC, we wanted fewer and fairer debates, but it wasn't entirely up to the RNC to decide. The idea that the two parties had zero role in the debates that would decide their nominee was malpractice. The media should be able to ask questions of our candidates, but we also should ensure that issues important to primary and caucus voters be addressed and not outsourced to the mainstream media. Televised debates constitute free air time for candidates and are regulated by the Federal Election Commission. Federal election law holds that only a 501(c)(3) organization or media outlet can stage debates, determining their criteria and format. If we organized a debate, the Federal Election Commission could consider it a financial contribution to the participating campaigns.

But the RNC was not powerless—and should never act like it is powerless. We set out to do four things.

First, we would give our candidates an advance schedule instead of forcing them to continually adjust their campaigns for pop-up debates. We accomplished this with a schedule that included one debate a month starting in August 2015 and then two a month beginning in 2016. There would ultimately be twelve debates. Never again would we have one debate on a Saturday and another on a Sunday, as had been the case in the previous election cycle.

Second, we wanted to lessen the stranglehold of liberal, mainstream media by bringing diverse voices to the debates, including conservative media outlets like Salem Radio, Fox News, and the *Washington Times*. This would not only add balance, it would also ensure that the issues of primary interest to many Republican voters would be addressed on a large stage.

Third, we wanted more geographic diversity with each debate held in a different part of the country to bring more people closer to the process. It may not be as convenient for the media to leave the coastal power centers and head to "fly-over states," but we felt it was important to include the middle of the country and connect with voters there, too.

Finally, we recognized that even a big stage wasn't large enough for all of the Republican candidates to appear at once. With so many major candidates running, the debates would have to be tiered with an objective standard to determine who fell into the upper or lower tier (the first or second round of a debate). Some argued that preference should be given to candidates who were currently holding elective office. In retrospect, that would have left out our eventual nominee and the future president of the United States. While there was no perfect answer, we ultimately found the fairest solution by dividing candidates into tiers based on their standing in the national polls. The one thing we never imagined was that we would have seventeen well-qualified candidates running at once. And remember—those are just the seventeen you've heard of. There were more than one hundred candidates on the New Hampshire ballot that November.

Publishing our debate plan in the *Wall Street Journal* and getting early buy-in from the candidates was itself a major part of our strategy—establishing ground rules right away. Another part of our strategy was requiring that debates be "sanctioned" by the RNC. If a major media organization announced it was going to have an unsanctioned debate anyway, and our candidates said "yes," there was nothing we could do about it. To give our plan teeth, we warned candidates that appearing in unsanctioned debates would disqualify them from sanctioned debates.

We were essentially drawing a line in the sand and daring candidates to step over it.

One of my personal goals, and greatest regrets since it never materialized, was to create a debate that consisted entirely of conservative media, was available to be streamed on the internet, was possible for all to carry, and had no dedicated network host. The balancing act of getting conservative media outlets to pay for such a debate and getting candidates to buy-in made reaching this goal impossible.

■   ■   ■

As neutral as we were, we couldn't help but wonder: would it be Bush? Rubio? Walker? Cruz?

Few said Trump. When Donald Trump burst on the scene, taking that famous ride down the escalator at Trump Tower, he was in the single digits. He had no real campaign infrastructure. He'd never run for any political office of any kind. Some overheated commentators even suggested he was a Hillary campaign plant, meant to disrupt the Republican primaries. But from the start, we at the RNC recognized that he had a following. Our concern was that if he lost in the primary, he'd complain that he had been robbed and finance his own third-party bid, splitting the Republican vote the way Ross Perot did against George H. W. Bush in 1992, which helped put Bill Clinton in the White House.

And this was not just a hypothetical. In the Fox News debate in Cleveland in August 2015, moderator Bret Baier posed the question we all wanted answered.

> BRET BAIER: Is there anyone on stage—can I see hands?—
> who is unwilling tonight to pledge your support to the
> eventual nominee of the Republican Party and pledge
> not to run an independent campaign against that person?

Nine of the ten candidates in attendance that night stood still as stone. Donald Trump thrust his hand up into the air.

> BRET BAIER: Mr. Trump. Mr. Trump, to be clear, you're standing on a Republican—
> DONALD TRUMP: I fully understand....
> BRET BAIER: And the experts say an independent run would almost certainly hand the race over to Democrats and likely another Clinton. You can't say tonight that you can make that pledge?
> DONALD TRUMP: I cannot say....I am discussing it with everybody. But I am talking about a lot of leverage.[7]

It was easy enough to say that Trump wanted to have his cake and eat it, too. But there was more at work here. Trump was under pressure from parts of his base. Taking the pledge was seen as a betrayal by some of the more ideological factions of the Republican Party. "The GOP has not been loyal to members of its own party during previous election cycles," Katrina Pierson, then a spokeswoman for the Tea Party Leadership Fund, told CNN. "I can't see any reason why he would give up that leverage considering a lot of his supporters like the idea that he's running against the establishment."[8]

Fortunately for the RNC—and ultimately for Donald Trump himself—we already had two reasons for him to sign the pledge. First, Donald Trump was able to run a skeleton campaign, lightly staffed and with very little advertising, because he knew that if he won the nomination, he'd be able to rely on the backbone of the RNC. Second, we had the data.

Trump's admission that he might not stay in the party if he wasn't the nominee presented the RNC with a major problem. Almost the entire Republican field was using RNC data and had signed a pledge to support whoever became the nominee. The RNC has comprehensive voter data going back to 1992. That data was available to all candidates *who signed the pledge*. As long as Donald Trump kept his options open, his competitors had an advantage he lacked. The other candidates clearly did not want anyone to have access to data that might advance the candidacy of anyone but the Republican nominee.

I explained this to Trump campaign manager Corey Lewandowski: if you want the same data the others are using, you've got to sign the pledge. When Corey protested that this was unfair, I pointed out that it would be unfair for an independent candidate to exploit resources developed and paid for by Republicans for a Republican nominee.

Right before Labor Day, I was exhausted and went to Dewey Beach in Delaware to take a few days off. I spent my entire "vacation" walking up and down the surf line on my phone, handling conference calls between Reince and Corey. Yes, we were told, Mr. Trump is going to sign the pledge. Next call: No, he cannot. Next call: Yes, we're on. In my dealings with Corey, I found him to be unwaveringly wavering.

On the other hand, Hope Hicks, who served as Trump's lead on media affairs, was steady, calm, and impressively professional during her debut in national politics. She possessed a poise that complemented another invaluable asset—she was a loyalist and had worked for Donald Trump before he was a candidate. She believed in her boss and his message, and, most importantly of all, he trusted her.

By early September, Donald Trump had decided he wanted to sign the pledge. To ratify the deal, Reince and I met with him at his twenty-sixth-floor office at Trump Tower. Corey and Hope were standing by. Reince presented two copies of the pledge and Trump immediately signed them.

"So, let's go down and show this to the press," Donald Trump said.

Reince immediately stared at me while I stared at Corey.

Corey and I had previously agreed that there would be no press conference.

Trump turned to Corey and Hope and said, "What do you think?"

Corey had an instant change of heart. They both nodded and responded, "Great idea."

The other candidates had signed the pledge without fanfare and were tired of being asked if Trump would sign. Trump's refusal had also started to cost the RNC money. Republican donors were being asked to help fund a costly data program, and one of the candidates was not pledging to stay in the party.

I knew that a press conference between Trump and Reince would elevate the displeasure of the other campaigns into high orbit.

Reince and I told Trump why we thought a joint press conference was a bad idea—the RNC couldn't look like it was taking the side of one campaign over another. He understood, and as we left, he went down to the lobby and made the announcement himself.

"The RNC has been absolutely terrific over the last two-month period, and as you know, that's what I've wanted,"[9] Donald Trump said, holding up his signed pledge.

In the most heated moments of the primary in March, Donald Trump seemed ready to renege, but he never did. He went on *Morning Joe* on MSNBC at a time when Joe Scarborough and Mika Brzezinski had become his on-air confessors. Trump was being pummeled by negative ads from his opponents, political action committees, as well as prominent Republicans like Arnold Schwarzenegger and Mitt Romney.

Donald Trump could hardly believe such hostility. "I brought in millions and millions of people to the Republican Party, and they're going to throw those people away," Trump said. "And I-I'll be honest, Joe, whether I ran as an independent or not, those people will never go out and vote" for another Republican candidate.[10] And by then, what Donald Trump said was undeniably true. How he got there was one of the most amazing ascensions in the history of politics.

■   ■   ■

Like everyone else, I was mesmerized, perplexed, and astonished by the 2016 Republican primary debates. Donald Trump was the center of every single debate, the sun around which all planets orbited.

Trump dominated the debates by making one unorthodox move after another. He voiced what many were thinking but didn't dare say, calling the Iraq War "a big, fat mistake." He denounced the Trans-Pacific

Partnership trade pact as "a horrible deal." He denounced the lack of enforcement of America's immigration laws and demanded the construction of a wall along our southern border.

Donald Trump recognized the economic stresses between Main Street and Wall Street, and his message was directed not at the titans of finance but at workers and mom-and-pop businesses. While Wall Streeters profited from corporations that achieved higher valuations by shedding unnecessary workers, many Main Streeters had family members who had been laid off from manufacturing jobs or had their jobs outsourced overseas. Trump appealed to them, in large part because he made a case for "fair trade" that few other Republicans did. Wealthy executives had long funded campaigns extolling the benefits of free trade. As one of the spokesmen, I had seen firsthand at the Office of the U.S. Trade Representative how Republicans sometimes glossed over the realities of trade. Trump indirectly posed the question that if free trade was such a wonderful, conservative thing, why was it supported by the Clintons and Barack Obama, and why weren't its benefits felt by all Americans beyond the single measure of lower consumer prices? Putting America first, in Trump's formulation, meant putting American jobs ahead of international economic efficiency—and many voters thought he had a point, which they listened to because many Americans were hurting financially. They wanted someone to hear them. And they wanted relief.

Trump was disruptive. Everyone else played by an old set of campaign rules and sounded like yesterday's candidates compared to the dynamic, dramatic, unscripted businessman. He was a master of branding and psyched out his opponents by defining them with nicknames that stuck. Jeb Bush became "low-energy Jeb." Marco Rubio was cut down with "Little Marco." Ted Cruz turned into "Lyin' Ted." And Rand Paul's eccentricities became "Truly Weird." Trump would later, and most effectively, slap a moniker on his general-election opponent, "Crooked Hillary." To the pundits, this all seemed like a joke, typical of a candidate they thought was unseemly and unserious; but to Trump's opponents, the nicknames were like caps they couldn't shake off.

I am often asked if Donald Trump permanently changed campaigning. The answer is yes, but only up to a point. I don't think we will ever again see a candidate like Donald Trump. His high-wire act is one that few could ever follow. He is a unicorn, riding a unicorn over a rainbow. His verbal bluntness involves risks that few candidates would dare take. His ability to pivot from a seemingly career-ending moment to a furious assault on his opponents is a talent few politicians can muster.

* * *

While the public saw the candidates sparring in front of the cameras in the primaries, the RNC communications team reinvented how we supported them behind the scenes. For decades, candidates had "spin rooms" where the campaign communications directors acted as post-debate analysts to deliver their message to the press.

Instead of that outdated model, the RNC communications team looked for new ways to help the candidates communicate their messages and add their own "spin" after a debate. I had established a partnership with Google so that, through the technological assistance of Google Trends and Google Analytics, we could give reporters instant data on audience reactions to debates, instant fact-checking, and instant access to movements in the polls.

Since 2014, part of my job had been making sure the RNC debates went smoothly. The first two debates—the Fox News debate in Cleveland, Ohio, on August 6, 2015, and the CNN debate at the Ronald Reagan Presidential Library and Museum in Simi Valley, California, on September 16, 2015—both went according to plan. Then came the CNBC debate at the Coors Events Center on the campus of the University of Colorado on October 28, 2015. From the start, some candidates grumbled about doing a debate at a university given the anti-conservative slant present on many college campuses. I reminded them, though, that this would be the first debate televised by a business network, surely a comfortable venue for Republicans.

I would come to regret this.

First, CNBC pulled a fast one and informed us they were going to have a live Twitter feed crawl across the bottom of the screen, adding a layer of interpretation to what the candidates had just said. I told them this was a last-minute surprise and the candidates would not like it. CNBC didn't care. Worse, CNBC angered the candidates by refusing to allow opening and closing remarks. They did agree to give the candidates an open-ended question at the beginning, but they ultimately reneged on that too, opening with pointed questions. As CNBC changed the rules, I threatened to pull our candidates out by not sanctioning the debate, but our candidates undercut any leverage I had with CNBC by saying they would turn up anyway.

The minute I arrived in Boulder, Colorado, I knew we were in trouble. Chris LaCivita, a marine and a seasoned political operative working for Rand Paul, tweeted a picture of his candidate's green room. It looked like a closet, and its most prominent feature was a door that opened to a toilet. He compared it to Donald Trump's green room, which looked, in comparison, like a five-star hotel. More tweets of other green rooms surfaced. They all looked small and depressing.

Why had this happened? Each candidate obviously had to have privacy to review notes and speak candidly with staff within a close proximity to the debate hall. There are only so many spaces in a gym that are appropriate for such uses. We allocated makeshift green rooms by the only objective standard we could think of: a candidate's standing in the polls as assigned by the network. There was no other way to do it and no better rooms to give out. I became the focus of ire for this and for every other complaint the campaigns had, including the apportionment of tickets. Every candidate thought the others were getting a better deal.

Things went from bad to worse for me when Rand Paul stepped out of the secure zone for an interview and then tried to get back in without his credentials. He jumped a gate and was chased down by a security guard. The senator was furious, and some of his campaign's fury fell on me.

At the debate itself, the candidates were asked one "gotcha" question after another by the CNBC moderators. *New York Times* columnist

John Harwood, for instance, asked Trump, "Is this a comic-book version of a presidential campaign?"[11] I had known Harwood for years but never appreciated his bias or how he could ask such an inexcusable question. Media bias, always a problem for Republican candidates, escalated whenever Trump was involved.

Afterwards, all the candidates were angry and adamant that we would never deal with NBC ever, ever, ever again.

So, Reince withdrew sponsorship for a planned NBC-Telemundo debate, and this time the candidates had our back. Reince's letter to NBC News President Andrew Lack still gives off verbal steam.

> CNBC billed the debate as one that would focus on "the key issues that matter to all voters—job growth, taxes, technology, retirement and the health of our national economy." That was not the case. Before the debate, the candidates were promised an opening question on economic or financial matters. That was not the case. Candidates were promised that speaking time would be carefully monitored to ensure fairness. That was not the case. Questions were inaccurate or downright offensive. The first question directed to one of our candidates asked if he was running a comic book version of a presidential campaign, hardly in the spirit of how the debate was billed.[12]

I came out of Boulder determined not to repeat such a painful debacle. The campaigns were incensed. They were so furious at how the RNC and I had handled the debate with CNBC that they decided to take matters into their own hands. The campaigns met to come up with a better system without us.

The Saturday night before their big meeting was Halloween. Rebecca and I took our children trick-or-treating, but I was on the phone the entire time. With my headphones firmly locked in, I trailed my wife and kids from house to house as people put candy in their buckets, and I talked with one campaign after the next, trying to minimize the fallout with the RNC. The RNC had tried to protect the best interest of the candidates and play the dual-role of negotiator and manager of logistics for the seventeen campaigns that wanted to be part of the debates. If they came up with a better system, we were happy to support it. But there had to be a consensus, and there was one possible holdout. I called Corey Lewandowski. He told me he would not be at the meeting. Trump was up in the polls. He was doing well in the debates, and since his campaign was receiving the spoils of being in first place, he didn't have any major concerns about how the debates were being run.

To my surprise, later that evening I saw Corey's name listed as one of the meeting's attendees. But I shouldn't have been surprised—being told one thing by him and finding out another was par for the course. During the Republican primary debates, he decided that Reince's chief of staff, Katie Walsh, had not afforded him the respect he deserved, and he refused to work with her. So, I became the RNC's delegated Trump campaign handler, on top of my other duties of managing logistics, communications, and strategy for the RNC as a whole. This assignment became all-consuming once Trump won the Indiana primary on May 3, effectively clinching the nomination.

I soon found out that many "Trump people," like Corey and others who had no campaign experience, viewed the RNC with suspicion. That was a sign of their political inexperience and ignorance, not a mark of loyalty to Trump. They did not appreciate that the RNC's job was to support the party's presidential candidate *and* to win races down the ballot. They did not appreciate the good work the RNC was doing to pacify nervous donors who were worried by some of Trump's statements and tweets. They blamed the RNC for every comment and criticism from local and former party officials who had no connection to the RNC. And they did not yet appreciate the whole campaign apparatus that the RNC had painstakingly assembled—over a period of several years—and that would soon be at the service of the Republican presidential candidate.

Reince had to balance the demands of supporting the nominee, promoting the long-term viability of the party, retaining a congressional majority, and fundraising. We were taking shots from donors, the media, and elected Republicans as the party divided over Trump. Reince, under these trying circumstances, did a solid job of keeping the party together and working for the congressional majority that any Republican president would need to enact his or her agenda.

One morning, when I dialed into the 9:00 conference call with the Trump campaign, only Paul Manafort, who had joined the campaign to handle the convention and was serving as its chairman, picked up.

"We can just start," he said. "Corey's in a meeting." (It would be his final "meeting.")

Since those days, Paul Manafort's image has suffered. He worked for anti-democratic politicians in Ukraine and was indicted for alleged money laundering and acting as an unregistered agent for a foreign principal. Keep in mind, these revelations and charges were yet to come and, as I write, are still being adjudicated.

With his well-tailored suits, deep voice, and gravitas, Paul was a K Street lobbyist out of central casting. It was clear that Paul wasn't going to be a modern campaign manager in the mold of Obama's David Plouffe, pulling insights from big data to execute brilliant social media strategies. But Paul brought a much-needed maturity to the Trump campaign when it needed an experienced political professional operative more than anything else.

At the time, the Trump campaign was running on bare-bones. Frugality is one thing, malpractice is another. I had seen congressional campaigns that were better staffed with significantly less funding. There was no semblance of a campaign structure, just a few, distraught, overworked people constantly barking into their phones. Paul immediately set up and staffed the political and communications operations necessary to take on the Clinton machine.

It was a relief to see all of this, but the campaign clock was ticking. It was getting very late in the game. Imagine an NFL football coach who assembles a team and scribbles a playbook while the national anthem is being sung. That is what it felt like as we prepared for the upcoming Republican National Convention in Cleveland, Ohio, and the future presidential debates with virtually no presidential campaign to work with.

The campaign had a bare-bones political and communications team, no fundraising operation or fundraising staff, and no opposition research or opposition-research staff. The RNC had expected to augment the nominee's campaign, but it essentially became the campaign.

There was chaos on the other side as well. Hillary Clinton was having trouble putting away the socialist from Vermont. Her deliberate and orchestrated plan to handle classified secrets by shifting them onto a private, unsecured server highlighted a long career of ignoring the rules. When FBI Director James Comey gave his long, unprecedented statement on July 5, 2016, both excoriating Clinton and exonerating her, we knew that our side wasn't the only one seeing things that had never happened before.

We recognized in Comey's actions the influence of an Obama administration and its attorney general, Loretta Lynch, to protect their candidate at all costs. We also saw a wounded front runner. And Donald J. Trump saw someone he was determined to beat and a swamp of political corruption he was determined to drain.

CHAPTER FIVE

THE NEVER-TRUMP CONVENTION THAT NEVER WAS

The contentious primary season was over in terms of the delegate count, but in emotional terms it was an unspent force. Donald Trump had risen as an insurgent within the Republican Party, leaving a lot of bruised egos and raw feelings in his wake. "Never-Trump" Republicans threatened to challenge his nomination and spark a contested convention, even if it was, in reality, all but impossible to replace a candidate with such an impressive majority of delegates. We still had to keep the RNC rulebook close at all times to avoid surprises that could embarrass the convention and the Republican Party.

In our worst dreams, we imagined the 2016 Republican National Convention in Cleveland, Ohio, becoming the GOP version of the notorious 1968 Democratic National Convention in Chicago, Illinois, which had been roiled by controversy within the convention hall and riots in the streets.

We leaned heavily on the professionals serving the Committee on Arrangements. That's a fancy title for the specialists who show up every four years and put the big show together for the nominee—everything from logistics and staging to lighting and confetti.

At the RNC, we understood that there is more to national party conventions than formally nominating the candidates for president and vice president. They have become media spectacles that present the party nominee to the country. Less visibly, delegates vote on and establish the party's governing rules for the next four years.

Despite Paul Manafort's last-minute efforts, the Trump campaign was still far behind the organizational curve. It didn't have a good lineup of surrogate speakers who could talk on behalf of the candidate—one of the first prerequisites of any national political campaign. What they did have were successful business associates of the candidate and celebrities from the fringes of reality TV, country music, and sports, but very few prominent Republicans had been on the "Trump train." The Trump campaign had no detailed plan for who should speak at the convention and no organization to handle the mundane, but important, tasks of assigning and managing rooms and credentials. At previous conventions, these sorts of decisions had been made weeks before the event, but the Trump campaign was almost a one-man show, lacking the large, professional campaign structure of previous candidates like Mitt Romney, John McCain, and George W. Bush.

Delegate committees generally meet a week before the convention to establish how the convention will be run. Usually, this isn't a big deal, but this year would be quite different. In 2012, I don't think the rules committee received more than a dozen requests for media credentials. This time, there were hundreds because the Never-Trump coalition wanted to establish rules that would "unbind" the delegates. And the media didn't want to miss that.

Under the RNC's existing rules, most delegates had to vote for the candidate with the majority or plurality of the delegates in their state primary or caucus. Those were the rules that had made Donald Trump the presumptive nominee. The rules also prohibited nominations of other candidates who had not received a majority of the delegates from at least five states. If these rules were adopted again by the 2016 convention, no other candidate would have been allowed to have their name placed in nomination. The Never Trumpers thought that changing these rules was their great opportunity.

As a Republican Party loyalist, I recognized that Donald Trump had won fair and square according to the RNC rules. The Never Trumpers did not want to accept that outcome. Their attempt to manipulate the rules, had it been successful, would have disenfranchised millions of voters who had voted for Trump, blown up party unity, and made it possible for them to elect Hillary. What worried me most was that Trump and his team expected the RNC to have a tight grip on this process because the Trump campaign certainly didn't. And most of his team didn't understand that when a convention kicks off, it's the delegates, not the RNC and its staff like me, who run the show and have full control. In fact, for the duration of the convention, the party is led by a temporary chairman, and, under the rules, *the RNC literally does not exist.*

As delegates gathered to discuss the rules, many signed on to support changes without fully understanding that such alterations would make nominating an alternative presidential candidate (or candidates) possible and thus create chaos on the convention floor, which might have been good for TV ratings but would have been utterly destructive to the party and our chances of winning the White House. Seeing the danger, Manafort, Reince, and key RNC members (all 168 members of the RNC party structure are delegates to the convention) engaged in old-fashioned politics—twisting arms, making promises and even the occasional threat.

The rules committee held fast, and we were moving on to the convention.

Unfortunately, that was not the end of that fight. Many Never Trumpers argued that it was a matter of principle that delegates should always be unbound, regardless of the fact that their state rules bound them to a particular candidate. They threatened to challenge the rules on the convention floor. There were tense moments when delegates assembled to vote on the rules package.

As the vote was being called, Manafort released an all-points bulletin to the leaders of each state's delegation. We were dangerously close to a convention-floor fight over the rules. The Never Trumpers had circulated a petition to vote down the rules package. It would have taken the party away from its grassroots voters and volunteers and handed it over to a faction that thought it could manipulate the convention in its favor.

But make no mistake, whatever the Never Trumpers thought, Trump would still be the nominee, and we would be single-handedly giving the media and the Democrats the sort of contentious convention of turmoil and mayhem they had all wanted.

Manafort and his lieutenants went one by one down the list of people who had signed the petition and persuaded them to remove their signatures. How Manafort and company did this was a scene out of 1950s politics—alternating between carrot and stick and sometimes bat, even, at one point, conveniently making the convention's parliamentarian unavailable to keep the opposition from formally submitting their petition. The Manafort message was clear: Trump will be our nominee and our next president, and anyone who didn't want to work to that end could spend the next four years in political Siberia. (No Russia pun intended.)

Finally, it came down to Robert Sinners, a South Carolinian who was now a member of the Washington, D.C., delegation. Sinners is a hard-charging, passionate Republican who had been told that the petition was in the best interest of the party and somehow the candidate himself. Sinners suddenly became the focus of the Manafort team, and he had an issue he wanted addressed.

He wanted Donald Trump to support gay rights.

Without missing a beat, Manafort summoned Jason Miller, the Trump campaign's senior communication adviser. Jason was an experienced, conservative operator with a background in South Carolina politics and knew Sinners.

Jason assured Sinners that Trump would be the most "inclusive" candidate the Republican Party ever had.

"This is your moment, Robert," Jason told him. "You can deliver this."

Before Jason could finish, Brian Jack, a top member of Manafort's delegate whip team, jammed a pen in front of Sinners so that he could sign a form that officially removed his name from the petition. Jason told Sinners Donald Trump's acceptance speech would acknowledge the LGBT community, which no other Republican acceptance speech had done. And it did.

The 2016 convention had its occasional, minor breakdowns, and it had the Never Trumpers who tried to derail it, but overall it ran like a well-oiled machine—thanks in large measure to the steady hands of the staff and volunteers of the Committee on Arrangements and convention veterans like Steve King, Jeff Larson, Bill Harris, Sara Armstrong, Mike Miller, Kirsten Kukowski, Phil Alongi, and John Zito.

With the delegate fight behind us, we thought the drama was over. But that would not be the case. Enter Ted Cruz. The Texas senator had been asked to speak, but no one knew what he was going to say. There were many assumptions but no agreements about the content of his address. The two candidates had sparred during the primary season, and this was an opportunity to turn a corner. At the event, he gave a speech that went on...while we waited for him to endorse Donald Trump...and went on...while we waited for the endorsement...and approached the conclusion without an endorsement of the nominee.

"Say his name!" delegates screamed at Cruz. "Say his name!"

Donald Trump had been in his holding room waiting for his son Eric to take the stage after Cruz. The plan was for Trump to wait until Cruz was done and then take his seat in the family viewing area while Eric spoke.

As Cruz continued to go on and on, and it became obvious that he wasn't going to say those magic words, Trump did what Trump does. He changed the narrative.

"Let's go," he said to his team.

Trump came tearing through the curtains and the far side of the arena across from the stage, interrupting Cruz's peroration with thunderous applause that echoed through the hall. Trump had come out and sucked the oxygen out of Cruz's speech. It appeared that Cruz's non-endorsement speech was supposed to establish him as the conservative standard-bearer for a run in 2020. If that was in fact his goal, he miscalculated badly.

Instead, it helped unite the party behind Trump, and Cruz faced backlash from his own donors and constituents. The Never-Trump movement was effectively done as a political force, and Donald Trump had won another victory.

The next stop for me was Philadelphia where the Democrats were preparing to nominate Hillary Clinton. It is expected that a presidential campaign will plant its flag in the opposing campaign's convention city for what we call "counterprogramming." While we knew the Democrats and Hillary Clinton would dominate news coverage, our goal was to be the biggest thorn in their side. So, we set up a site a mile from the convention to talk with reporters and introduce them to Republican surrogates. Our primary draw would be our nominee's campaign manager.

I asked Paul Manafort when he was coming to Philadelphia.

"I'm not," he said. "I'll be in the Hamptons."

"You're going on vacation?" I asked, incredulously. "Now?"

I finally talked Manafort into coming down to Philadelphia for a few hours on the first night of the Democratic convention. He stayed for ninety minutes, answered questions, chatted up reporters, and went straight back to the Hamptons.

Except for Manafort's brief and forced appearance, and Josh Pitcock from Mike Pence's team, not a single member of the campaign joined us in Philadelphia. The director of surrogate speakers for the campaign, normally a key player in responding to the other party's convention speakers, had gone on vacation. In contrast, in 2012, more than twenty-five members of the Romney campaign had joined a core RNC team at the Democratic convention.

Despite it all, we still managed to put together a great team to respond to the Democratic convention. Republican elected officials, pundits, and activists like Congressman Lee Zeldin, former Congressman Jason Chaffetz, Ric Grenell, Boris Epshteyn, Arkansas Attorney General Leslie Rutledge, Ashley Bell, former Mayor Rudy Giuliani, Jose Fuentes, and Kellyanne Conway (who was not with the campaign at the time) helped drive our counterprogramming message home with press conferences and media interviews. At our convention, the Democrats had hosted a modest spin room at a law firm in downtown Cleveland. We tried to do more, so we peppered the city with mobile billboards that were not intended for mass consumption but rather to annoy Democrat delegates and create a larger-than-life feeling that we had invaded their convention. We took over a mixed-martial-arts boxing facility and turned it into a Republican headquarters with surrogate speakers, a robust social media team that put out our message, and a variety of social events to attract reporters.

At our convention, we had to deal with the schismatic Never Trumpers, but the Democrats faced a schism of their own. Hillary's defeat of socialist Bernie Sanders left his supporters bitter, especially when it became apparent that the DNC and its superdelegates had squashed their grassroots efforts.

We sought to exploit this division.

Despite the partisan nature of our time in Philadelphia, there was a semblance of bipartisanship at work. In the past, the RNC and DNC each begged, borrowed, and spent countless hours doing who knows what else to acquire passes to each other's conventions. To save time, my counterpart at the DNC, Communications Director Luis Miranda, and I made a deal: we agreed to provide a handful of hall passes to each other. When his team showed up in Cleveland, we ensured they had their passes. But when we showed up in Philadelphia, DNC Chair Debbie Wasserman Schultz had been forced to resign amid the disclosure of her behind-the-scenes effort to advantage Clinton over Sanders. After Wasserman Schultz resigned, most of the DNC's senior staff followed suit, including Luis. Luis wanted to be helpful, but with him officially gone I thought I was screwed. So much for my deal.

Our surrogates were coming to Philadelphia with the understanding that I would be able to get them access to the convention center for their media interviews. I called Donna Brazile, who had been named interim chair of the party. Even though Donna would not assume control of the DNC until after the convention ended, she understood the nature of the deal and that it was made in good faith. Despite it being a tumultuous time for her and the Democratic Party, Donna was a true professional and ensured the deal was upheld.

As the conventions came to a close and the general election season swung into full gear, reporters began to ask Republican operatives and officials how we could support Trump. I told them what I tell everyone to this day: I wasn't a Rubio guy, a Bush guy, or any candidate's "guy." I am a fiscal and social conservative who will take any Republican candidate over any Democrat any day of the week. I am a party guy who believes in the system and worked hard to make the party better—and the grassroots voters of our party chose Trump.

On August 14, 2016, the *New York Times* reported that Paul Manafort's name was found on a secret ledger account, showing he had received millions of dollars from former Ukrainian President Viktor Yanukovych, a strong ally of Russian President Vladimir Putin. Within two days of that news appearing, Manafort was gone from the Trump campaign.

First Corey, then Paul. As I was wondering who would be next, my phone rang. Two people were on the line—Steve Bannon and Kellyanne Conway.

"We need to talk to you in confidence," Steve said. "We're going to be announced tomorrow."

"That's right," Kellyanne chimed in. "I'll be campaign manager. Steve will be chief strategist."

I congratulated them and thought, *this is going to be interesting.* Kellyanne had been in politics for a long time. I knew she had a deep understanding of polling and how to spot the direction of underlying currents of public opinion. Steve knew how to read the populist pulse, which he would ensure would remain the beating heart of the campaign. While I knew both fairly well, and respected them in their domains, neither had run a national campaign.

ampaign had moved most of the operation to the fourteenth floor
which was just one flight of stairs above the fifth floor). The fourteenth
loor had actual offices, conference rooms, and a large, open, war-room
rea. But many of the desks and offices were still empty, waiting for
ampaign positions to be filled.

Hope Hicks was my guide to navigating Trump World. What she
icked in political experience, she more than made up for with her knowl-
dge of our candidate—what he wanted to do and how he wanted to do
. And how Trump wanted to do things was often not what we teach in
olitical campaigning 101.

What made the Trump campaign so different was that eight times
it of ten they would break the rules and be proven right. We'd say you
in't do that, and they would do it anyway. And it would work. It was
humbling experience to give professional advice only to see it empiri-
lly refuted time and again. And it was also bracing to see a campaign
willing to act indifferently to the sort of political correctness that
hibits all but the most conservative (and safe-districted) Republican
liticians without any apparent political cost.

But I also saw a danger. If you were with Donald Trump from the
art—you believed he could be president when no one else did, you were
ld he would be slaughtered for the things he said, and you knew he
uld thrive despite these obstacles—it was easy to start feeling infallible
hen he succeeded.

One of my main goals was to make the campaign team understand
w the campaign could benefit from the massive investment the RNC
d made in data and technology. It could help us target voters, tell us
here and how we should campaign, and guide our ad strategy.

Donald Trump knew a campaign that followed the polls was apt to
led by the nose to positions and postures not of its choosing. The goal
s to shape opinion, not to be a creature of it. But to do that, you had
know where opinion was and what the best messages were to lead it
the direction you wanted.

We also had to convince the campaign that it actually needed to
...well, a campaign. To that end, Reince, Katie Walsh, RNC Political

"We need you to come up to New York on a full-t
away," Kellyanne said.

I felt a twist in my gut.

I was torn. I knew at my age, this was a chance t
role in a national campaign. With my kids growing
years—if ever—before I could or would want to ma
commitment again.

I was looking forward to some family time on Lab
were about to start kindergarten. I was already workin
the RNC, but at least I could go home every night and he
the kids. And then there was my dad. His long and brave
pancreatic cancer was clearly becoming harder.

But, if I moved to New York, I'd be closer to Rhod
father, and I could bring some (necessary) RNC expe
Trump's campaign. I thought about my time aboard Tru
that Donald Trump and I had clicked.

I asked Rebecca. She had always supported my ca
this was different. She knew it was important because
entertained the idea of moving otherwise. She saw
moment in my career and said, "Well, you'll only be g
or so. What's a few weeks?"

I still worried about leaving Reince Priebus beh
Reince had hired me six years earlier. I thought we ma
and had done important work building up the RNC. R
my position at the RNC vacated at such a crucial time
with a compromise that from a campaign point of view
point of view) would serve as a workable solution. I w
New York and work three or four days a week in Trur
return to D.C. for the rest of the week and maintain n
worked from a family point of view as well.

During the primaries, the campaign had been base
of Trump Tower, which had previously served as the p
Apprentice and was now an unused, barren storage s
port beams, and exposed wood. Now that Trump wa

Director Chris Carr, Kellyanne, Steve Bannon, Jason Miller, digital strategist Brad Parscale, Jared Kushner, Donald Trump Jr., Eric Trump, and I were all pulling our oars in the right direction, working to support the rapid building of a national campaign structure.

A final challenge was managing the general election debates. Here we had greater leverage than we had in the primaries. If either of the two candidates was unhappy with a proposed debate format, there would be no debate.

Before the debates began, NBC proposed to host a "Commander-in-Chief" forum on national security issues. It was to be held on the USS *Intrepid*, an Essex-class aircraft carrier from the Second World War, now a museum docked on Pier 86 on the Hudson River. It wasn't to be an actual debate but two separate discussions by the candidates with Matt Lauer, the now-disgraced, former host of NBC's *Today* show.

Republicans remained skeptical of NBC.

While we had concerns about NBC News, our primary concern was about the role MSNBC would be playing. NBC News shared resources and personnel with MSNBC, which leans left and provides America with the nightly wisdom of Rachel Maddow and Chris Matthews.

So, why deal with NBC in any form?

Because Donald Trump said so. He decided that this time it would be different. He was looking forward to facing Matt Lauer one-on-one and appearing on the same stage as Hillary. Looking back, I can see it was a good trial run for Trump. After all, he was the political newcomer, facing an opponent, Hillary Clinton, who had not only served in high office but also had been involved in politics virtually her entire life, including her teenage years. With the decision made, Kellyanne and Steve asked me to negotiate the logistics and lines of questioning with NBC News President Deborah Turness and her team. When we first started negotiating the terms of the forum, the NBC team clearly believed that I had been sent on behalf of the campaign with a hidden agenda of blowing up the event. After the RNC canceled NBC's Republican debate, NBC executives were clear that they would not soon forget what they perceived as a slight and an insult to their journalistic integrity. We eventually came to terms, and in the process, I learned that Donald Trump likes to manage the details when it comes to the media.

With the deal done, NBC invited me and a Clinton campaign representative to meet aboard the *Intrepid* for a coin toss to determine which candidate would be interviewed first.

"Whatever you do, Sean," Donald Trump told me, "make sure I go first."

"I'll do my best, sir."

On my way out of Trump Tower, I ran into Eric Trump.

"Should I call heads or tails?"

Eric didn't hesitate.

"Heads."

The coin toss was in an interior, below-deck office of the *Intrepid*. Knowing I would be held accountable for the outcome, I brought newly hired campaign aide David Bossie with me to serve as my witness. Waiting for us were cameras to memorialize the event. We were offered no choice of heads or tails. Deborah Turness simply announced that heads meant Hillary and tails meant Trump.

When we were done, I called Steve Bannon.

"I've got good news and bad news."

"Give me the bad news," Steve said.

"We got tails for the coin toss."

"And what's the good news?"

"We're going first."

Trump would be pleased. I had passed the first small but seemingly important test. I was relieved and ready to never do another coin toss again.

During the interview with Matt Lauer, Donald Trump seemed comfortable talking about veterans, the military, and foreign policy. Before the event, I had briefed Trump on a series of issues that affected veterans. One statistic I shared with him was that every day twenty-two veterans kill themselves.[1] Throughout my briefing, Trump listened intently, occasionally asking questions to get more details.

In his discussion with Matt Lauer, it was the host who got that statistic wrong, and Trump corrected him. I had done my job in the briefing, and Trump had nailed it. I relaxed. When Hillary's turn came, she appeared uncomfortable. She seemed resentful of Lauer's probing into her email scandal, as if her handling of national secrets as Secretary of State had no business being brought up in a national security forum.

It was not a good night for her. In the end, the Hillary camp and her media allies were reduced to blaming her bad performance on Matt Lauer. For us, it was a double victory—Trump had exceeded media expectations, and Hillary looked like a sore loser.

CHAPTER SIX

UPSHIFTING THE DOWNSHIFTERS

Donald Trump's preparation for the debates was unorthodox. He thought mock debates, with a staffer filling in for Hillary, were a waste of time. But reporters who said he just showed up at the debates and winged them were also wrong. The truth was, Trump was preparing all the time, in his rallies, in give and take with voters and journalists, and in talks with Reince, Governor Chris Christie, former Mayor Rudy Giuliani, Stephen Miller, Hope Hicks, Steve Bannon, Jason Miller, Jared Kushner, and other top aides. They would toss issues at him at the Trump National Golf Club in Bedminster, New Jersey, as if the candidate were in batting practice.

At the first formal debate at Hofstra University, Hillary Clinton was poised and on the attack. For all her rhetoric, her campaign was never about the issues. It was a relentless attack on Donald Trump's character and the character of his supporters, "the deplorables." Trump wanted to talk about his issues—tax cuts, economic nationalism, immigration reform, an America-first foreign policy—but Hillary had him playing defense much of the night. She hit Donald Trump for having a "long record of engaging in racist behavior." She accused Donald Trump of supposedly calling a Latina beauty contestant "Miss Housekeeping."

Trump, fighting a cold, tried to over-talk her and accused Hillary of lacking "stamina." She coolly replied, "When Donald Trump spends eleven hours testifying in front of a congressional committee, he can talk to me about stamina."

While she may have had a point, she reminded people why she had been testifying before Congress (about the handling of the raid on the U.S. compound in Benghazi, Libya) and her lack of candor in the aftermath of the attack. So, while she made her point against Trump, she did so at the expense of her own message.

This time, the media consensus was set by the Clinton spin room. John Podesta, chairman of the Clinton campaign, said of Trump, "He came in unprepared and what we saw was kind of a meltdown."

I could not entirely disagree. Trump seemed slightly and uncharacteristically off his game. He left several attacks unanswered and missed obvious opportunities. And things were about to get worse.

■   ■   ■

The second debate with Hillary Clinton was to take place on Sunday, October 9, 2016, at Washington University in St. Louis.

On the Friday before the debate, our digital team told me that a deal long in the making with Twitter was being scrapped by its leader, Jack Dorsey. The team had worked for months with Twitter to create a political emoji, and the plan was to create an image when people tweeted about "crooked Hillary." I never fully understood the usefulness or effectiveness of it, but the digital experts were convinced the emoji would yield results. Twitter had offered this new opportunity to both sides, but the Clinton campaign took a pass. So, Twitter worked with the RNC digital team for months to build a robust online effort that would total into millions of dollars. When word reached Jack, he abruptly canceled the buy, claiming legal concerns (lawyers had been part of the process). As I was walking down a jetway to board a flight, I was on my phone listening to Jack explain his rationale for cancelling the million-dollar deal. As I hung up, I was certain we could make a big deal out of Twitter's political bias. I had hoped that their cancelling the deal would make a big splash as another example of the tech community's bias. But just moments later, another story would overshadow it in a big way.

As I took my seat on the plane flying from Reagan National Airport to St. Louis, Missouri, my phone chimed. I had a message from Katie Walsh.

We have a problem. Look at the email I just sent you.

On the plane, as discreetly as I could, I read a transcript Katie had flagged as urgent. It was not good. But it was a transcript, and perhaps it was inaccurate. Then came a second email from Katie. There was a video that had been leaked to the *Washington Post*. The video had been recorded in 2005, and it captured a raunchy conversation between Donald Trump and Billy Bush, then host of *Access Hollywood*, in which Trump bragged that being a celebrity made it easy for him to seduce women, in rather graphic terms.

Katie called me.

"Sean, this is huge. We need you to get back now."

"Katie, if I get off this plane, I'm not getting to St. Louis. This is the last available flight before Sunday."

She didn't like it, but I stayed on the plane, stewing the whole way to St. Louis, unable to talk to anyone or do anything. And, because of a lack of Wi-Fi, I was unaware of how it was playing out. The instant the plane hit the runway in St. Louis, I turned on my phone and saw that I had missed dozens of calls. For the rest of the day I was on the phone, nonstop, till sleep overtook me.

At first, we thought we were dealing with a dump of opposition research by the Democrats, but as events unfolded, it appeared that the *Access Hollywood* recording had been leaked by someone from NBC to the *Washington Post*. TMZ reported the following:

NBC execs had a plan to time the release of the Donald Trump audio to have maximum impact on both the 2nd

presidential debate and the general election...top network
execs knew about the video long before they publicly said they
did, but wanted to hold it because it was too early in the election. The sources say many NBC execs have open disdain for
Trump and their plan was to roll out the tape 48 hours before
the debate so it would dominate the news cycle leading up to
the face-off.[1]

Every campaign has a pivotal crisis that marks either the final decline
of the candidate or the moment when the candidate transcends his or
her own shortcomings. For example, Bill Clinton won the presidency
when he and Hillary Clinton went on *60 Minutes* to explain away the
taped conversation of shared, intimate recollections between the then
governor and his mistress, Gennifer Flowers. Bill Clinton admitted to
CBS's Steve Kroft that he had caused "pain in my marriage."

Everyone at the RNC and in the Trump campaign knew that this
video was our pivotal crisis. Trump had three options at that point. One
was to curl up and die. The second was to do an apology tour, like the
Clintons. The third was to barrel through it and come out with all guns
blazing. At this moment, the media couldn't comprehend how Donald
Trump could even dare to show his face in St. Louis, much less present
a spirit of proud defiance. Most political operatives would opt for the
apology route.

Didn't Donald Trump know that it was all over?

But Trump read the national mood better than his critics. On Saturday, as I took calls from Republican committee members, donors,
reporters, pundits, and friends, I was surprised by how many women
who contacted me did not consider Trump's comments a big deal. One
prominent Republican woman told me, "You all talk like this; we know
it." (Actually, we men don't all talk like this, but I held my tongue.)
Clearly there were a lot of detractors, but many people I spoke with
didn't think Trump's vulgar remarks from eleven years ago were relevant or important.

As he often does, Trump moved forward when any other candidate would have been left for dead.

Trump succeeded by dismissing his remarks as "locker-room" talk—which many people apparently thought they were—and by pivoting against Hillary in a way that no other Republican candidate would have dared: why should I be crucified for locker room talk when you protected your husband after he faced a credible allegation of rape?

Steve Bannon supported the candidate's response by bringing a surprise to the debate. He invited Juanita Broaddrick, Kathleen Willey, Kathy Shelton, and Paula Jones—women who had accused Bill Clinton of rape, groping, and sexual harassment—as the campaign's guests. Steve tried to keep their arrival secret (though, inevitably, rumors started leaking) lest someone in the campaign or the debate organization overrule him.

Then Steve did something no one saw coming. Prior to the start of the debate, he gathered the women and held a press conference in which they appeared with Donald Trump.

If anyone was unnerved by this turn of events after the release of the *Access Hollywood* tape, it wasn't Trump. It was the Clintons. Hillary had to debate with these women staring her down from the audience. With this panel of women, Donald Trump had not only leveled the playing field, he had put Hillary on the defensive. Many people had to ask themselves: if what those women said is true, what kind of a woman would stand by a man who did such things? In the debate, Trump did not act chagrined or pull his punches. He did not even shake hands with Hillary. He was aggressive and pointed in his criticism. Hillary later said that Trump had made her "skin crawl" during the debate. The pivotal moment had arrived...and the pivot turned in Trump's direction.

The media didn't see it. David A. Graham, writing in *The Atlantic* under the headline "Donald Trump's Disastrous Debate" declared, "With Republicans abandoning Trump in droves just 29 days before the election, Trump seemed content to drive all of them off..."[2] While the *Access Hollywood* video had taken a temporary toll, the debate had provided an even bigger boost. Trump's underdog campaign was in fact regaining its momentum.

In the third and final debate, in Las Vegas, Donald Trump employed another nontraditional tactic. The format required one candidate to stay seated while the other stood and took the floor. Donald Trump refused to sit still. He paced around while Hillary spoke, always staying in the frame behind her and towering over her. It was domineering and a little strange, but it worked. Everything she said was under the scowling face of Donald J. Trump. It was not something I would have thought of or advised. But Trump showed, once again, that he is a master at emotional imagery. The political playbook for debates had been thrown out the window and burned.

Throughout the primary and general debates, Donald Trump was like an inflatable ball in a swimming pool. Hillary Clinton and the media tried hard to keep him submerged, but he always popped back up to the surface. Nothing could sink him. And that fact caused quite a few media heads to explode.

"Relax," *The Nation* assured its left-wing readers in a choice bit of graveyard whistling, "Donald Trump Can't Win."

"Trump won't win," a writer in the UK's *The Guardian* declared, "In fact, the US could be on the brink of a liberal renaissance."

Even some of our side's own political gurus were not projecting a win. Karl Rove, no stranger to presidential politics, said on Fox News, "I don't see it happening...If he plays an inside straight, he could get it, but I doubt he's going to be able to play it."[3]

In making such predictions, the media and even some Republican loyalists didn't see the power of Trump's populism and message; they also misread "outside the Capital Beltway" voters. The smugness and rhetoric of the naysayers created an echo chamber that helped amplify the over-confidence of the Clinton campaign, the worst case of choosing-the-Oval-Office-drapes-before-the-election since Thomas Dewey. Clinton headquarters in Brooklyn assumed the election was in the bag.

But then came two more October surprises.

On October 28, 2016, three of us from the RNC—Sean Cairncross, Katie Walsh, and I—were asked to attend a briefing held by the Department of Homeland Security. We met with senior officials in a conference room at their headquarters in Washington, D.C., near American University. They informed us that they were aware of and monitoring Russia involvement in our upcoming elections. The message they wanted us to convey publicly, however, was that there was no way to infiltrate or manipulate the outcome of a national election because we have a disparate voting system spread across thousands of counties, cities, towns, and precincts. Seeming to believe that Clinton would win, they implored us to publicly express confidence in the integrity of the voting process, system, and outcome.

On the same day as this briefing, FBI Director James Comey sent a new letter to Capitol Hill reopening the Clinton email scandal by revealing that more classified material had possibly been exported to an improper source, this time by Clinton aide Huma Abedin onto a computer owned by her husband and former Democrat Congressman Anthony Weiner.

Even though two days before the election Comey popped up yet again, bizarrely, to announce, "Based on our review, we have not changed our conclusions that we expressed in July,"[4] most Americans felt they had reason to doubt Hillary Clinton's honesty. If Trump was frank to a fault, openly imprecise in his language, and brashly indulgent of "truthful hyperbole" on his own behalf, many found Hillary to be skirting the truth in ways that were much more serious. For example, the Clinton staff's efforts to hide her pneumonia, revealed by her fainting episode after a 9/11 commemoration in New York, had underscored the predicate that she lacked candor. Had Hillary Clinton gone to the hospital right away, it would have been better for her. At every turn, Hillary and her overly protective staff acted as if they had something to hide. Every email and Clinton Foundation scandal, every too-clever-by-half statement by the Clintons and their team, came together to define her in that moment as the soul of duplicity.

In politics, there comes an instant when people have had enough of someone. It happened to Lyndon B. Johnson. It happened to Richard Nixon. This was Hillary Clinton's moment.

Of course, Donald Trump had huge negatives of his own. He largely got a pass because he spoke about a reality that the Clintons were not talking about—the economy—even though it was the Clinton administration years earlier that had coined the phrase, "It's the economy, stupid." And Trump wasn't just talking about corporate earnings and investments, he was talking about jobs and wages in a way that resonated with disenfranchised, unemployed Americans, all while Hillary and the Democrats played identity politics. Whatever you believe about transgendered bathrooms, they don't put meals on the table for an unemployed welder in Michigan. Bill Clinton had begun his career with a powerful connection to working Americans. Now Hillary was calling these Americans "deplorables."

Her last campaign stop was in Raleigh, North Carolina, where her campaign had said she would win. The event featured a high-energy, get-out-the-vote speech by Lady Gaga. That was Hillary Clinton's idea of populism.

Lady Gaga would play really well in many states, but she was the wrong messenger in the wrong state at the wrong time.

Hillary Clinton would go on to lose North Carolina and its fifteen electoral votes by more than 3 percent.

■   ■   ■

It was in the wee hours on Wednesday, November 9, 2016, that Donald Trump was declared the winner of the presidential election, with 306 electoral votes.

Since then, Hillary has thought a lot about why she lost—and how it could have happened. It was Comey's press conference that did it. It was Anthony Weiner. It was voter suppression or Russian interference. It was anyone and everyone…except the candidate.

It's easy to be a Monday morning quarterback in presidential elections, but in the end, the buck stops with the candidate. It's a matter of having the right message, the right campaign operation, and the right judgment. Hillary had failed on all three counts.

At the RNC, we had learned our lesson during the Romney campaign about the importance of using voter data effectively. We began what would ultimately be a $175 million investment on a system of high-tech, integrated data as part of our Growth and Opportunity Project.

Chris Carr, our political director at the time, had made an especially brilliant move to turn our data into actionable knowledge. After carefully studying what the Obama campaign had done in 2008 and 2012, Chris spearheaded a major transformation in how the Republican Party would track and get out voters. He created a system that assigned a sentiment score (using a scale of one to one hundred) on key issues for every voter in the country. Our data operation did this by vacuuming up data from magazine and digital subscriptions, voting history, membership rolls of groups ranging from the NRA to Planned Parenthood, donations, social media actions, and combining them all to give us a reliable profile of every voter.

We compiled these consumer data points on all 190 million American voters: Republicans, Democrats, and Independents across all fifty states, in each congressional district and in every single voting precinct.

We knew from our data how likely someone is to vote, whether that person is likely to vote early or absentee, and his or her views on education, gun control, national defense, and many other areas. Is he registered with one party but independent-minded? Is she willing to vote across party lines?

This strategy allowed us to follow and communicate with specific voters on a weekly basis. The regularity of our communications gave us the ability to follow and analyze trends and identify messages that persuaded undecided voters to become committed voters.

The media's pessimism about the prospects of the Trump campaign bled over into stories claiming that the RNC's internal models indicated Trump was destined to lose. Our models showed no such thing. In fact, our models didn't project a win for either candidate. But our models did highlight what we needed to do to win the election.

Winning a campaign is like building a house. If your house is going to cost $100,000 to build, and you have only $90,000 in the bank, you wouldn't throw up your hands and quit. You figure out how to scrape together another $10,000 or how to cut corners. You know what you need to acquire or change.

In a similar way, our predictive modeling, which was being spear-headed by long-time GOP strategist Bill Skelly, told us where we were short and which voters we needed to win over to win.

After a campaign targets its valued, likely voters, it must map where they are concentrated. Thanks to Chris Carr, we had a map that was broken up into "turfs"—areas with high concentrations of gettable voters. The Trump-rich "turfs" were where we put a pin in the map and placed a field office. Chris had derived these strategies from concepts that the Obama campaign had used effectively in 2008 and 2012, but he modernized them to benefit our entire party.

In 2004, the Bush campaign made two revolutionary changes to political campaigns. First, they created a seventy-two-hour task force that reached voters in the final three days before an election. The goal was to motivate potential voters to get out and cast their vote. The task force effectively activated a system that micro-targeted voters. Simply put, micro-targeting means you look at the traits at a small group of voters and apply that to a larger group. Obama's 2008 and 2012 campaigns took that to a new level: they recognized that people were voting earlier and earlier, and they utilized data to target voters on a personal level. The issue for the Democrats was that the Obama campaign had built a great model for that particular candidate, and their data was not necessarily relevant for another candidate like Hillary. Frankly, it's simple marketing.

The RNC had learned from the Obama campaign, but we were going to apply those principles to a national party and benefit our presidential campaign as well as candidates up and down the ballot.

On election day, we needed to maximize that data with a well-organized effort composed of volunteers and paid staff who, in large part, had been working in communities we had targeted for months. They had been making calls to persuade "our" voters to vote before election day, during their lunch hour or before or after going to work. More and more voters are casting ballots earlier and earlier in the election season—not waiting for election day—sometimes as early as September. Our goal was to encourage as many people as possible to vote before election day, and we followed that with a strong second push on election day to get any remaining voters to go vote. Katie Walsh had worked with Chris and Bill to oversee that effort. Here, as in so many cases, the RNC did essential tasks that most national campaigns did for themselves. I don't say that as a criticism of the Trump campaign but to highlight the fact that those who say there was a fundamental rift between the RNC and Trump are wrong; the RNC's efforts were perfectly integrated with what the Trump campaign needed to do, providing the organization, data, and ground game.

While Bill Skelly and Chris Carr are two names most Americans will never know, I am convinced that beyond Donald Trump himself, they are the two people most responsible for the victory of the forty-fifth president of the United States.

Here's how they did it.

The RNC data revealed many blue-collar workers in Pennsylvania, Ohio, Michigan, and Wisconsin were likely Trump voters. They had a history of voting Republican. We just had to bring them home. We knew how many votes we needed in key states to make the difference, so we focused our resources on where we could pick up enough outstanding voters to push us over the top.

It was a tall order, and it was getting taller. Since February, our voter scores showed that a group of likely GOP voters had moved about 15 percent away from the Republican ticket.

Chris and Bill met nightly with Steve Bannon to plan our response to this deterioration. The group expanded to include Marc Short from Mike

Pence's team; Brad Parscale, who led the campaign's digital effort; and others from the campaign like Jared Kushner, Kellyanne, Donald Trump Jr., and Eric Trump. We felt, in our guts, that the people who were slipping away were still our voters. Chris and Bill greenlit focus groups that allowed us to drive every decision about where to go, what to say, and what ads to run. What we found were voters who would never cast a ballot for Hillary Clinton. They were not what we called "a persuasion group." They were already persuaded. They were what we called a "turn-out group." They would never vote for Clinton, but they were uncomfortable voting for Trump, even as solid Republicans. If we could get them into a booth or get them face to face with a ballot, where they had a strict, binary choice, Carr and Skelly bet they would vote for Trump.

For that reason, Chris and Bill had taken to calling these voters "downshifters." After the *Access Hollywood* video, our model showed Trump dropping to 180 electoral votes, almost overnight. But even at the lowest point, we saw that our comprehensive portrait of individual voters and predictive analysis could guide Brad Parscale and his digital team, and Chris and his staff in each battleground state, to target the right ad to the right voter at the right time, millions of times.

We had to upshift the downshifters.

We also followed up with a strong ground game. The RNC had added more than 172,000 voters to the rolls than the Democrats had in the battleground states. To make the most of this advantage, our field staff had become a large and capable army. In Colorado in 2012, we had forty-six field staff members deployed. In 2016, it was 933. In Michigan, we had thirty-three people in 2012. In 2016, it was 778. Our volunteers had knocked on the doors of 14.5 million likely Trump voters nationwide against 11.5 million for the entire 2012 cycle.

We made almost 26 million phone calls to voters based on big data.

Trump himself had never wavered in his belief that Pennsylvania was gettable. The RNC political staff saw hidden opportunities in Wisconsin and Michigan. What we saw in the aftermath of the second debate and the RNC follow-up was a strong, upward trend. Michigan provided a clear illustration of the national trend.

In September, the RNC model depicted Trump with 260 electoral votes (Wisconsin was tied and Trump was even closing in on blue Minnesota and Colorado). After the release of the *Access Hollywood* video in early October, our model showed us dropping nearly 100 electoral votes as potential Trump voters "downshifted" into possibly sitting out the election in response to the saturation of negative media coverage.

The "upshifting" of this group occurred after the RNC reached these discouraged voters via social media (Brad Parscale and his team of digital ninjas) combined with old-fashioned, door-to-door politicking (under the direction of Chris Carr and his talented staff in the field). We targeted these voters one by one. We reminded them how important the election was, with big issues at stake, including the future direction of the Supreme Court, the economy, and issues of particular interest to certain voters. Then we confronted them with a binary choice between a blemished candidate (Donald Trump) and an unacceptable candidate (Hillary Clinton). That started moving the trend lines back in our direction in the battleground states. We deployed Donald Trump, Mike Pence, and our top surrogate speakers wherever the data told us we had the greatest chance of shifting voters to win a state.

In Florida, for example, our model showed us that 6 percent of the state's voters—consisting of 680,000 possible votes—were undecided. Exit polls later confirmed that this undecided 6 percent remained uncommitted until just before election day. Our data showed that most of these undecideds were likely Trump voters, and they were gettable—but we had to reach them.

Ohio, Iowa, and other battleground states were all showing the same upward trend in our direction. We felt that if one major battleground state fell our way, the trend was such that the others would as well because the demographics of the "downshifted" voters in the battleground states were similar—and they were all moving our way.

State after state, we reached our vote goal, and the Democrats did not. The media had completely bought into the idea that no one could match the Clinton machine's ground game. But, in fact, the Democrats underperformed in many places with early voting and absentee ballots.

Our model suggested a Trump win was possible, but the path to victory was narrow.

Electing a president and a congressional majority was our overriding goal, but we also had another institutional stake in the outcome. Reince had bet the farm that if we could build a superior data operation, our candidates up and down the ballot would have an advantage over their Democratic opponents. Donors had bought into the plan. We had to prove that the RNC had provided the right technology and necessary resources and that our data had been accurate and valuable. So, we created a digital presentation that showed not only the investment the RNC had made but also what the data revealed heading into the final week of the campaign, state by state. The presentation laid out the vote goals Trump needed to meet in order to win and our predictions (assembled by Bill Skelly and his team) of what each state's overall vote totals would be.

Katie Walsh, Chris Carr, and I briefed key political players, pundits, and the media. The data showed where we stood in every battleground state. More importantly, it showed how many votes we needed and where they were. Win or lose, no one could say that the RNC had not done its work, and we were increasingly confident that the trend was moving our way and that Donald Trump had a shot at becoming the forty-fifth president of the United States—even if, at the time, no one in the media seemed to believe us.

In retrospect, one of the most interesting aspects of this race was Donald Trump's rallies. Until then, political professionals considered rallies to be in the same vein as yard signs. Having a lot of them doesn't mean you're going to win. It just means you've dedicated your resources to cultivating your committed supporters.

But there was something different about the Trump rallies. A good example is the last rally Trump held before the general election. It was at the DeVos Place in Grand Rapids, Michigan. He easily filled that giant venue with a line of supporters stretching across the Gillett Bridge to the Gerald R. Ford Presidential Museum on the other side of the Grand River. To get in at 8:00 p.m., some people took their place in line at 9:30 that morning.

"If we win Michigan, we will win this historic election," Trump announced to wild applause.[5]

We had never seen anything like it in terms of energy, enthusiasm, and dedicated support (enough to sustain hours of line standing). Those intangibles count. They cannot be manufactured. They cannot be bought. And there was one more factor: there is an old saying in campaign politics that the candidate who's having the most fun wins.

Donald Trump was always having fun—especially at his rallies where he reveled in the excitement and adoration of his supporters and shared their enthusiasm. At his rallies, he was a rock star. The rally field staff would work the lines to sign up volunteers and register voters. In the past, the campaign would have to spend money to advertise a rally and drive people to attend. In Trump world, the cost was a mere tweet from the candidate.

⬛   ⬛   ⬛

On the morning of election day, I checked my phone and saw that Trump, at age seventy, was still an Energizer Bunny. He had campaigned into the late hours and was up again in the early morning.

At that point, the campaign had one remaining mission: to get on television and explain why we were going to win. Cable news outlets need to fill election day air time before the polls close, so it's another way to play get-out-the-vote. Confidence on election day is critical. The early misreporting about Bush's loss in Florida in 2000 almost sank him in the rest of the country as discouraged supporters avoided going to the polls. We couldn't let that happen again.

We were close to winning in ten states, not where we wanted to be, but well within the margin of error. We were convinced the polls under-reported Trump's strength among voters who were shy about announcing their support for a candidate excoriated by the media. The determining factors were whether our positive trend lines would continue in these final, critical hours and whether undecided but potentially pro-Trump voters turned out to vote.

■   ■   ■

I did a quick interview on MSNBC with Kate Snow, explaining some of what we saw in our internal polling data. While at the studio I tracked down Mika Brzezinski and Joe Scarborough in a small green room down the hall from their set. My assistant, Vanessa Morrone, and I walked them through our state-by-state polling data on an iPad that showed how we could hit the magic number of 270 electoral votes. They remained skeptical, but after the election, Joe Scarborough noted on the air multiple times that I had, in fact, shown him how Trump could win. That was notable not only because most of the media refused to believe our data but also because some outlets actually reported the opposite. *Politico*, for one, declared, "RNC Model Showed Trump Losing," which was absolutely not the case.

Next, I went to the Fox News studio where I did a short interview on Fox Business. When the interview was done, Bill Shine, then co-president of Fox News, entered the studio and asked if I had a couple of minutes.

We rode the elevator up to Bill's office on the executive floor.

Waiting for us in office chairs were Rupert Murdoch; Fox executive Suzanne Scott (now president of programming at Fox News); Jay Wallace, another Fox executive; Brian Jones, head of Fox Business; and several other executives. I had known Bill and some of the others, but this was my first conversation with Rupert Murdoch beyond an exchange of pleasantries at charity functions.

"So, Sean, can you give us the lay of the land?" Murdoch asked in his deep, gravelly, Australian accent.

I pulled out the iPad and explained what our internal data showed and how we were poised to exploit the trend. Murdoch leaned over the screen, asking informed questions about each swing state and why we thought we would win it. As I spoke about swing counties and key demographics, I could see the wheels spinning behind Rupert Murdoch's eyes. He was doing the math himself and arriving at the same number we did—and it would likely be one larger than 270.

I kept running the math through my head, playing with electoral maps, and by my guess, we could get to 270, 271, or 272, including Maine's second congressional district.

But not everyone in the media was interested in what the data said. Just about every news host, reporter, pundit, and political analyst thought we were going to lose.

At 7:30 p.m. on election day, a bunch of us—including Steve Bannon, Kellyanne Conway, Dan Scavino, Hope Hicks, Bill Stepien, Mike Pence, Reince Priebus, Jared Kushner, and Ivanka Trump—gathered on the fifth floor of Trump Tower. We were in a large utility room with a projector feeding us RNC and Associated Press election data on county-by-county vote counts. From the outset, Donald Trump had a laser focus on winning the electoral college, and we all knew that winning swing states was largely a matter of winning swing counties, which is why those county vote totals were so important—they were the best data we had on voter trends within a state.

The exit polls coming in were not good; but if exit polls selected presidents, Al Gore would have been in the White House. We didn't let the exit polls rattle us. More important were voter percentages within counties. If there was big turnout in Trump-leaning counties, that was an indication that the undecided voters we needed to win were breaking our way.

How was Trump faring in the Florida Panhandle compared to Romney and Bush? How were we doing in Broward County, Florida? How was the turnout for Hillary in Fairfax County, Virginia? Where were we outperforming? Where were we underperforming?

While we fielded one nervous question after another, Ivanka talked on the phone with her father. "You've got to come down to five," she said. "We're all here."

"No, have everyone come up to fourteen."

Bill Stepien, political director of the Trump campaign, packed up the projector and took it upstairs. Bill's computer was plugged into the projector, and the data was shown against a wall just off the stairway that connected the fifth floor to the fourteenth. Around 10:00 p.m., the outlines of a trend were starting to become clear. We did, indeed, have the wind at our backs. One by one, key states fell into the Republican-red column. Indiana, then Kentucky, West Virginia, South Carolina, Alabama, and a host of red states from Tennessee to Texas—that was all well and good but not enough. No surprises yet, but at least we had reason to be cautiously optimistic.

Just after 10:00 p.m., I sent Rebecca a text to tell her I was about to go live on ABC with George Stephanopoulos. She had just left an election return party at the *Washington Post* headquarters and walked across the street to have a drink with some colleagues. When she received my text, she immediately asked the bartender to change the TVs to ABC. She knew I would only be going on the air at that hour if we were seeing some encouraging returns.

Then, at 10:21 p.m., Ohio and its eighteen electoral votes were called for Trump. Better than expected returns in south Florida confirmed that we were in the running there, too. Then all of Florida came in, along with North Carolina, awarding us a combined total of forty-four electoral votes. Both states were must wins for us—and we had gotten them. We were also outperforming in states the media had predicted we would lose.

Our little crowd, which grew bigger by the minute, went nuts with cheers and high fives every time a state was called. Dana Bash on CNN said that fingers must be bleeding in Brooklyn "because there's no more nail to bite."[6] Our candidate, standing right behind me, was hardly biting his nails. Donald Trump was encouraged, but he was not about to tempt the gods by declaring a premature victory, just like when I called him "president-elect," and he replied, "not yet."

The Associated Press called Wisconsin in our favor but not Pennsylvania. Fox called Pennsylvania for us but not Wisconsin.

If we won any of the remaining battleground states, we would win the race. It felt like we had scratched off five winning numbers in the lottery—and were now starting to scratch off the sixth.

Just after 11:15 p.m., Trump went up to his residence to gather his thoughts. By 1:00 a.m., we led in the electoral college 244 to 215. Around 2:30 a.m., Trump headed over to the New York Midtown Hilton, just a few blocks away, as it looked likely that we would win Wisconsin and Pennsylvania, which would put us over the top. Julie Pace of the Associated Press texted Jason Miller that the AP was calling the race for Trump. Jason immediately shared the news with our candidate. Within seconds, Clinton aide Huma Abedin called Kellyanne.

The two aides connected their principals.[7] Hillary conceded.

The ballroom was electric. The crowd, warmed up by Vice President-elect Mike Pence, shouted, "USA. USA," with an enthusiasm I have never seen.

At 2:47 a.m., President-elect Donald Trump, his family, and top aides emerged from a balcony and descended to the stage.

At 2:49 a.m., he said, "Sorry to keep you waiting. Complicated business."

Melania stood behind him, beaming. Donald Trump made some kind remarks about Hillary Clinton and called on Republicans and Democrats to "heal the wounds that divide us."

The Trump I saw that night was elated but serious. He clearly appreciated the magnitude of what had just happened.

Shortly after 3:00 a.m., Wisconsin and Pennsylvania were called for Trump, their combined thirty electoral votes putting us over the 270 threshold. Michigan came in later that morning with another sixteen electoral votes, final confirmation that the Trump strategy of reaching out to blue-collar conservatives—people ignored by many Republicans, defined as deplorables by Hillary Clinton, and alienated by the elites— was the right one.

At 3:29 a.m., Trump's motorcade pulled up to the residence side of Trump Tower. As I stood there welcoming him back, I was somewhat surprised at the light police presence at the home and office of the president-elect of the United States. It wasn't until just after dawn that barricades started to go up.

Donald Trump won a historic victory that night. But the press immediately tried to deprive him of it by pointing out that he lost the popular vote and that his electoral college margin of victory was smaller than Obama's in 2012 and 2008. It was historic not only because the media had all but declared Hillary the victor before the event but also because virtually no one believed that Trump could win 306 electoral votes. When you win big after nearly being counted out, it is a victory like no other.

The media had invested their credibility in Hillary winning, and now they were proved utterly wrong. The *New York Times* had, after all, given Donald Trump at best a 15 percent chance of winning.

Many in the media rarely take any blame for their mistakes. Instead, they blame others. In this case, they blamed the polls, Nate Silver, Russian meddling, anything and everything but their own reporting and analysis. In their race to keep up with the twenty-four-hour news cycle, many reporters now spend less and less time trying to understand what's happening and more and more time pontificating—ill-informed pontificating at that. We had the data showing that we could win, and it had been dismissed.

■   ■   ■

In the morning, I stopped at a newsstand to buy a Powerball ticket.

"Let's see how long this lasts," I said to the perplexed man behind the counter.

It felt like luck, but our victory the night before had been anything but luck. A lot of work, strategy, and research was behind this election.

Later the next day, I took the train back to Washington and the RNC where we all pored over the results. In almost every state, we nailed our total vote goal—what we needed "to finish the house"—and Hillary underperformed.

In Ohio, RNC data had estimated Donald Trump needed 2.8 million votes to win the Buckeye state, and he got 2.84 million votes.

Our model showed Donald Trump winning Michigan by 0.2 percent. He won by 0.3 percent.

Our model also nailed the vote totals.

In Florida, our model projected that 9,409,777 people would vote. Actual voter turnout in that state was 9,420,039. In other words, the RNC had projected turnout to within 0.1 percent.

Ironically, the two battleground states that did not fully embrace RNC data and field operation were Nevada and New Hampshire, where both incumbent Republican U.S. senators lost, and we lost the presidential vote as well.

The RNC projected a national total vote of 135,824,656. The actual number was 136,401,627. We had predicted the total turnout to within four-tenths of 1 percent.

But more than anything else, we had won. We accomplished what we had set out to do—win the White House and maintain control of both the House and Senate.

The big questions now were what the new administration could achieve and what my role, if any, might be.

CHAPTER SEVEN

BAPTISM BY FIRE

Over Thanksgiving, our family gathered at my mom and dad's house in Barrington, Rhode Island. While we never openly talked about it (welcome to an Irish Catholic family), we were all thinking the same thing: these were my father's final days. The four young grandchildren weren't fully aware of what was happening, but they knew it was a special, somber time when my dad said goodbye to each one of them. It was the most difficult holiday of my life. My father was unable to eat solid food. While we sat as a family in the dining room eating takeout turkey, my dad was upstairs in his bed fading in and out, taking nourishment through a tube twice a day and wanting what he couldn't have—to sit down to Thanksgiving dinner with his family. It was painful to watch him fade. We had stayed close over the years, and I had often called him to share stories and debate the news. That was all coming to an end.

My father's immune system was highly vulnerable. And to make matters worse, the kids started getting sick, one after another. When my mother, the consummate caregiver, succumbed to the flu, we knew we had to get help.

We also needed to isolate the sick kids. Rebecca and I searched online to find a nearby hotel (let's just say that the choices on Route 6 in nearby

Seekonk, Massachusetts, are limited). My brother, Ryan, and my sister-in-law, Emma, decided that she would drive their sick child back to their home in Scarsdale, New York.

For my dad, we looked for home care, nurses, you name it, but none of these are easily found for a one-to-two-night, last-minute emergency. Thinking I was out of options, I remembered an old political buddy, Ben Marchi, who was now in the business of senior in-home care in Maryland. Ben called the Rhode Island franchise of the business and got us a night nurse—who turned out to be a godsend. We also called Father Barry Gamache, the pastor of St. Mary's church in Bristol, Rhode Island, to administer the last rites; we didn't know how long my father would live.

Rebecca drove our kids back to our home in Alexandria, Virginia, sensing that it would be a matter of days before she would be called to return to Rhode Island. My sister Shannon and brother Ryan were at the house with my parents, so I decided to return briefly to New York to work with the transition team.

The morning after I arrived in New York, I did a few television interviews and hoped to work through the day and take the 5:00 p.m. train back to Rhode Island. As I wrapped up a 9:00 a.m. interview, I got a text from my brother. He asked me if I could catch the next train.

Given how busy I was, my first instinct was to ask him why—but in my heart, of course, I knew.

I rushed to Penn Station and took the next train. The three hours between New York and Providence were long and tough, as I knew that life for my family, particularly my mom, was never going to be the same. Many memories of my father filled my mind. I recalled how, on election night, my dad had called to tell me how proud he was of me and our victory. I listened to the handful of voicemails I had saved that simply said, "Hi, it's your dad, just calling to say, 'Hi, I love you.'" In the coming months, often after tough days, I would put my headphones in my ears and play the voicemails to hear his voice.

When I arrived at the train station in Providence, my uncle Paul Grossman was waiting for me. I tried to read his face to gauge the situation, but Paul didn't know any new developments.

When we got to my parent's home in Barrington, it looked the same, but it was unusually quiet and had a somber air about it. I had a knot in my stomach, fearing that my father had already passed away and that I had missed my chance to say a final goodbye. But when I walked through the door, my mother greeted me with a long hug and sent me upstairs to see my father. He was barely conscious, but the doctors had told us that, appearances to the contrary, he could probably hear everything we said. So, I told him how much I would miss him and how I would try to keep making him proud. I made sure I told him how much I loved him, how proud I was of his fight against this disease, and how much I appreciated everything he did for me and our family. As he had previously requested, I assured him again that I would look after my mother.

Just after midnight, the nurse woke us. My mother, Shannon, Ryan, and I gathered around my father, held his hand, told him how much we loved him, and said goodbye as he went to heaven.

For nearly three years, he had fought through pain and fatigue so that he could work, sail, and travel with his wife. Even in declining health, he tried to spend every possible minute with his children and grandchildren. He absolutely cherished his grandchildren.

I tried to compartmentalize my grief, and I suppose, in a strange way, the hectic demands of the presidential transition helped me in that regard—though repressed grief takes its own eventual toll. I was back taking daily press calls—and, one morning, a call I didn't expect.

It was from Donald Trump. He wanted to express his condolences. The sincere compassion and empathy in his voice was something I will never forget. I wish more people saw that side of him. Trump had built up an image of toughness; however, in private, I have seen many instances of empathy and kindness from him.

My father's funeral was on December 5, 2016, at St. Mary's Parish in Bristol. Our longtime family friend, Father Gerald Hussey, presided over a beautiful Mass that celebrated my father's well-lived life. One of my father's only requests, which luckily we fulfilled, was that the music director at St. Mary's, Michael DiMucci—whose voice is truly a gift from up above—sing at the Mass. After the Mass, family and friends, including several who had flown up from D.C., gathered at Agave Restaurant & Lounge (now called The Beach House), which overlooks the calm water of the Bristol Harbor, for some clam chowder and a cocktail. There were a few tears but mainly laughter as we all raised a glass to honor my dad.

Dealing with the emotional impact of losing my father was not something I made time for. Within a day, I went back to New York to join the president-elect at a rally in North Carolina where he officially announced that Marine Corps General James Mattis was his pick for secretary of defense.

Donald Trump was personally involved in the transition communications team and messaging, and he gave me a steady accumulation of responsibilities, clearly evaluating my performance along the way. I never had anything like a formal job interview; I had an ongoing on-the-job interview.

During the transition, Jason Miller and I had been asked to draw up organization charts of the press and communications offices. So, it did not come as a shock when I was appointed press secretary on December 22 and Jason was appointed director of communications. I knew in my heart that I was better suited to take on the role of communications director, but the opportunity to stand at the podium was too tempting to turn down.

There were times I wished my dad had lived long enough to see me at the White House, and there were times, I must admit, when I was glad he did not.

■   ■   ■

Presidents, elected in November, originally had until March 4 to put their administrations together. Franklin Delano Roosevelt, impatient to get his New Deal policies in place, persuaded the nation to pass the Twentieth Amendment, moving inauguration day to January 20. For the candidate and his or her staff, there is no time to recover from the ordeal of the election. Given the difficulty every administration has in sorting itself out within that narrow window, I sometimes wonder if we would be better off moving the date back to March.

Fortunately, Washington has a process for every problem. The presidential transition is an established institutional arrangement that over time—especially since the terrorist attacks of September 11, 2001—has become much more formal (and government-funded) to ensure the world sees our continuity of government.

As early as May 2016, Donald Trump had asked New Jersey Governor Chris Christie to begin planning for a presidential transition. At the time, this was akin to being named mayor of the first colony on Mars. But Christie, who had been through a transition of his own as a two-term governor, took the task seriously and started building his transition team, including hiring veteran political consultants Ken and Keith Nahigian. The Nahigian brothers—with the help of Trump aides Andrew Bremberg and Bill Hagerty, the latter now ambassador to Japan—vetted top candidates for cabinet, department, and agency positions.

Before election day, the government provided office space for both Hillary Clinton's and Donald Trump's transition teams, just down from the White House on Pennsylvania Avenue. The winner on election night would take over the official transition office spaces at the corner of Eighteenth Street Northwest and E Street Northwest, inside the old Department of the Interior.

One of the Nahigians' deputies, Anna Stallmann, went to E Street to visit the transition offices. When she was there, an official from the government's General Services Administration (GSA) told her bluntly to make the most of her visit because she was not likely to see it again. Anna noted that the room set aside for the president's spouse might as well have had a framed picture of Hillary on its desk, so masculine was its decor, as if the GSA fully expected Bill Clinton to be taking up residence as First Gentleman. Needless to say, the GSA, like the rest of the Washington establishment, was in for a surprise.

But while Washington was seemingly paralyzed by shock in the aftermath of the election, the transition team prepared cabinet picks for Senate testimony and confirmation. Only one of Donald Trump's picks,

Elaine Chao, had been through the process before. We gave each nominee a "media Sherpa" to guide them through the process, and our team scoured social media, public statements, and family backgrounds to highlight areas where the media or Democrat senators might attack. We also matched potential surrogate speakers to rebut critics and highlight each candidate's strengths.

Inside our transition offices, a conference room was transformed into a mock Senate committee room—complete with similar lighting and staff members acting as senators. We even simulated disruptions by the likes of Code Pink. We grilled nominees in taped sessions that lasted up to two hours. We questioned them on their personal history and beliefs, and we quizzed them on the president-elect's policy platform. Afterwards, we'd play back the tapes, critiquing not just what nominees said, but their body language and facial expressions. We were confident that by the time we finished the preparation work, they would be ready to face a real Senate panel and the hot glare of TV lights.

In the end, all of Trump's nominees got through with one exception—Andrew Puzder, his nominee for secretary of labor. Given the controversy surrounding the new administration and the unalterable hostility of Democrats (and some Republicans), our near-perfect confirmation score was cause for celebration.

But Chris Christie would not be around to celebrate.

Just after the election, the president-elect announced that Vice President Mike Pence would take over as head of the transition team.

Christie was invited to remain as a member of the team, and Trump's campaign staffers became the transition team. Christie's removal had come at the worst possible time, leaving the transition team in limbo. Campaign staffers, still exhausted from the campaign, were now asked to help reorganize the transition. For better or worse the transition team had been focused on planning the key decisions we would need to make. The shake up would cost us valuable time as a new team was trying to get up to speed. While Trump was coming in with no government experience, the top staff had little if any senior executive branch experience. Neither Reince Preibus, Steve Bannon,

Jared Kushner, Kellyanne Conway, nor Katie Walsh had any real executive branch experience to speak of. Rick Dearborn, who had been Jeff
Sessions's chief of staff and had worked in the Energy Department
under President Bush, and I were the only two who had served in the
executive branch. But neither of us had served in roles that prepared us
for a transition of this magnitude.

Jason and I had to get down to work organizing a communications
shop. We couldn't wait for the leadership of the new transition to sort
itself out. We started working immediately with Hope Hicks to plan the
structure of the communications office of the transition as a first-draft
of the eventual White House staff. We consulted previous administrations and began to place people into jobs we weren't sure we had the
authority to place. The Nahigian brothers—like all transition officials,
unpaid volunteers—had set up a digital portal to receive and code
resumes in interested job seekers. They and their teams of volunteer
"experts" had created binders of potential candidates, as well as manu-
als for each office (the First Lady, legal, policy, press, vice president,
national security) on office structure, procedures, and outlines of priorities to review.

In our selections, we tried to choose people who had experience in
communications. We had plenty of candidates and resumes from people
who were long on loyalty, but short on experience. There was a list of
people who thought they deserved a West Wing job but few who had the
experience needed to get Trump's ambitious agenda implemented.

Ari Fleischer, George W. Bush's first press secretary, reached out to
Jason and myself and suggested that we start daily media briefings as
soon as possible to feed the media beast, lest it feed on us. Josh Earnest,
press secretary to President Obama, and Jen Psaki, the communications
director, also reached out to me. I visited them at the White House and
found them to be gracious and eager to share their time and counsel to
ensure a smooth transition.

While the transition office was technically in D.C., the real action
was in Trump Tower—cameras staked out in the lobby made watching
the elevators doors opening and closing must-watch television. The

media, meanwhile, was obsessed with the continuous stream of potential nominees being led past the cameras to the iconic Trump Tower by Madeline Westerhout. It was a media gauntlet where reporters snapped at the slightest bit of news. On this chaos, we tried to impose order, themes and facts.

When we weren't at Trump Tower, we were off at Trump's New Jersey golf club in Bedminister. Much like the elevator doors at Trump Tower, the golf club's wooden door with its brass fixtures became the new show. Through the door to meet with the president-elect came and went luminaries like General James Mattis, Rudy Giuliani, Safra Catz, Ben Carson, Michelle Rhee, Mitt Romney, Todd Ricketts, and Bob Woodson. While I was impressed with many of them, two stood out: Dr. Patrick Soon-Shiong and his wife Michele.

Patrick came to Bedminister at the invitation of his friend, the incoming Treasury Secretary Steven Mnuchin, to discuss his work to cure cancer and address many issues surrounding healthcare delivery and spiraling costs in the United States. Patrick is doing cutting-edge work in advancing a cure for cancer, and during our dinner conversation Michele offered to have him call my father's oncologist at Rhode Island's The Miriam Hospital, Dr. Howard Safran. As the dinner broke up, I left the second-floor room and called my mother, who was at her sister Joanne's house, to let her know about Patrick's work and offer. There are days when we can see God's hand at work clearly, and that night was one of them. Here I was, excited to be spending a weekend with the president-elect as he crafted his new cabinet and government but all the while knowing my father was struggling. This, I thought, was the answer—the reason this all makes sense. Meeting people like Patrick and Michele and seeing their kindness and concern.

During these long months of planning and anticipation, a pattern of leaks began to emerge from within the organization that would soon bedevil the White House. Announcements we were planning to make started appearing in the media before we were ready. In a foreshadowing of days to come, some people were up, some were down, was always unclear in the rumor cloud around the Trump operation. Everyone had a rumor, but only Donald Trump knew the truth.

※   ※   ※

The walk from the W Hotel in downtown Washington, D.C., to the northwest entrance of the White House grounds is just a few blocks. We had booked two rooms for ten Spicers on inauguration day. The hotel is known for its views of the White House, the Treasury Building, and the Washington Monument.

It was exciting to join the thousands of Americans gathering in the nation's capital to observe the swearing-in of the forty-fifth president of the United States. The morning of inauguration day, Rebecca and I attended services at St. John's Episcopal Church, at the corner of Sixteenth Street Northwest and H Street Northwest, across Lafayette Square from the White House. It's been called the "Church of the Presidents" because every president has attended the church at least once since it was built in 1816; most have attended services on inauguration day. Rebecca and I sat a few people away from the president-elect, Mrs. Trump, Rex Tillerson, Dr. Ben Carson, and other future cabinet members. We listened to inspiring Bible verses and an insightful sermon, reminding us about the awesome responsibility that each of us in that church was about to take on.

After the service, Rebecca headed back to the W Hotel to gather the family, and I boarded a bus headed for the Capitol. After making my way through the crowd and security, I sat on the upper part of the dais, watching the swearing-in ceremony and listening to the president's dramatic speech. After that, it was lunch in the Capitol with the senior staff before we were whisked away to the White House to see our new offices.

Every newcomer is surprised by how small and tight the West Wing is. The office of the press secretary is spacious by West Wing terms with a semicircle of a desk and a television set into a wall. The office also has the novelty of a working fireplace, something not found in most

Washington offices. I was told that if I wanted the fire lit, I should call a GSA team to do it. I thought that was a typical Washington bureaucracy. I was a former Boy Scout. I didn't need help lighting a fire. A few days into the job, I decided I should put the fireplace to use. Within minutes, the entire West Wing was filled with smoke, and the Secret Service was opening doors to ventilate the area. Apparently, the folks who light the fires also know about opening the flue!

In the Roosevelt Room, my assistant, Vanessa Morrone, and I were given our White House issued phones and laptops. Then I was off to monitor the inaugural parade and help prepare our first "pool spray"—a rotating group of twelve reporters, covering print, TV, radio, and wire services, and photographers—who cover an event on-site and file a report that their journalistic colleagues can use.

This first pool spray would be brought into the Oval Office to see the president signing his first executive actions and orders. The plan was for him to show and explain the executive actions and orders he was signing; it would be a great story to demonstrate how the administration was hitting the ground running.

Of course, it wouldn't be that easy.

The routine is the pool comes in, takes pictures, captures video and sound, annotates what the president says, and provides a summary of the event, which occasionally includes some background color about attendees and the surroundings.

Zeke Miller, then a reporter for *Time* and now for the Associated Press, was part of the pool and was ushered into the Oval Office. After the event, Zeke tweeted that a bust of Dr. Martin Luther King Jr. had been removed.

Every president puts his own stamp on the Oval Office—and Donald Trump famously gave prominence to a painting of Andrew Jackson—but Trump had not removed the bust, and he never intended to. Zeke Miller had just missed seeing it and leapt to an unwarranted conclusion. This seemingly small detail ignited a social media firestorm that insinuated the president was repudiating civil rights. Zeke didn't comment on the drapes or the rug but focused on this for a reason: he knew it would "make news." The tweet generated hurt feelings, even fear. This was not the start we were planning. It reaffirmed the way the media has been transformed: by believing that being first and sensational is better than being right. The problem is that, once tweeted or reported, a breaking story begins the narrative, and no correction ever has as much impact as the initial report, no matter how wrong it is.

When the story broke, Reince rushed to the Oval Office to snap a picture of the bust. He sent it to me to share with the media.

When I had pointed out to Zeke that the bust had been there all along, he tweeted that it had been "obscured by an agent and door."

It was the door's fault.

Aren't reporters supposed to be more careful?

When confronted with an obvious mistake, I found many White House correspondents are quick to excuse themselves with a quick, "Oops, let's all move along—next?"

Unfortunately, Zeke's post set the tone. The president had not even completed his first full day in office, and the media was playing gotcha. Never mind the executive orders—which were the serious, real, substantive news of the day.

I've known Zeke for a few years, and he's a good, decent person. The problem isn't him, it's the mindset of the press corps, the competition to get the first tweet or a viral clip, and an extreme ideological bias. It's not good for journalism, and it's not good for democracy.

After putting out that media fire, I raced back to the hotel to change into my tux and join my family—Rebecca, my mother, brother, sister, and sister-in-law—at the inaugural balls.

Saturday morning after inauguration day, just as Rebecca and I were getting the kids up, my new White House phone rang. It was the White House operator. The president was on the line.

"Sean, have you seen the news?"

I hadn't because our kids were watching TV, and six-year-old kids don't watch inauguration coverage.

The president had one particular story on his mind: a panel discussion comparing the Trump inauguration to that of President Obama's first inaugural. They were saying that the Trump crowd was noticeably sparse by comparison. The president was clear: this needed to be addressed—now.

I had planned Monday to be "day one" for me as White House press secretary, and I never expected our second major controversy, after the Martin Luther King Jr. non-story, to be about crowd size at the inauguration. I had two suits hanging in the hotel closet. They were okay for most occasions, but I wouldn't have called them camera-ready. Still, a suit, a blue shirt, and a tie—what more did I need? It wasn't like I was going to be on camera.

I planned to be a press secretary in the model of my predecessors—Ari Fleischer, Tony Snow, Dana Perino, Marlin Fitzwater, Mike McCurry, Robert Gibbs, Josh Earnest. I would get the facts out, articulate the president's priorities and agenda, be forceful with reporters when necessary, and above all remember that I was serving the country that I love, all the while trying not to "commit news" myself.

What could go wrong?

Inauguration weekend is traditionally a time when political disputes are momentarily set aside. As RNC communications director in January 2013, when President Obama was sworn in for the second time, that was the approach I took. "This is President Obama's day." We stood down and made it about the country—inaugural weekend was when we celebrated the peaceful transition, or continuation, of presidential power after an election. Our role at the RNC in 2013 was to be the loyal opposition, to hold the president accountable at every opportunity. But on inauguration weekend, that could wait.

It was a short walk to the White House from the W Hotel, but my mind was racing—this was a new administration, and I was a key part of that administration, and not all of us were sworn-in yet. And most staff hadn't even been granted access to the buildings. That meant the press office was comprised of just Vanessa and me until more staff received their badges.

While I knew the president wanted me to address the question of the crowds at his inauguration, when I reached my desk, I thought my real priority should be to highlight his executive orders that were focused on jump-starting the economy. I also had hoped for a dry run at the White House press podium, but there wasn't time for that now. The press would be in the James S. Brady Press Briefing Room in a few hours, and I had work to do—first off, figuring out how to get accurate attendance figures for the inauguration.

While I wanted to talk about the president's policy agenda—thinking that's how we should set the tone—I focused on the president's point, that the media was making an issue of the inaugural crowd to belittle and disparage the incoming administration from the get-go. If we were to have any chance of fair coverage, if we were to stop the press from making a habit of being endlessly negative about the administration, it made sense to confront them now. I called Tom Barrack, a successful businessman and close friend of the president who had served as the chairman of the Inaugural Committee. His staff at the Inaugural Committee gave me some numbers, quoting the Metropolitan Police Department of the District of Columbia's estimates of Metrorail ridership that day. But I didn't have hard and fast stats on attendance, and as far as I could find out on a Saturday morning, no one else did either.

I continued to dig, of course, calling the National Park Service, the Department of the Interior public affairs staff, the Metropolitan Police Department, the Secret Service. Almost everyone I talked to had the attitude of "It's over, who cares?" They had all worked incredibly hard for months to make inaugural day a success. Now they were relieved it was behind them. The National Park Service told me that they had once collected inauguration numbers but had stopped because there was too much second-guessing. I knew many people hadn't made it onto the National Mall at all because of the crowds. My own family barely made it through the long lines and delays at the security checkpoints. It had taken them more than two hours to get from the hotel to the Capitol grounds. There had been reports of extensive lines at each of the security-perimeter checkpoints that inaugural attendees had to clear before getting on the National Mall. That certainly could have diminished the crowds.

I examined images on social media. There were aerial photographs of the National Mall, but they excluded people along the parade route and the checkpoints.

Some calculations could be made. An estimated 250,000 people could fit in the area between where the president was sworn-in and Fourth Street. The area between Fourth Street and the media tent could accommodate another 220,000 people. Another 250,000 people could occupy the area from the media tent to the Washington Monument. Inaugural staff told me that an estimated 420,000 people had used the D.C. Metro system (compared to the 317,000 who had used the Metro for Obama's second inauguration). Based on these numbers, it seemed possible that President Trump had, in fact, a larger inaugural audience than Obama.

While I researched, Reince called for updates, and I developed a plan for how to present the administration's case. I knew the president appreciated a forceful press conference I had managed at Trump Tower on January 11. During that briefing, I had knocked down false reports from BuzzFeed and CNN and challenged the media directly, pushing back on their assumptions.

I assumed that was the approach the president would want to see again: strong, aggressive, no questions.

I was wrong.

At 4:51 a.m., the president had tweeted, "Wow, television ratings just out: 31 million people watched the Inauguration, 11 million more than the very good ratings from 4 years ago!"

From his vantage point when he was sworn-in and from the vantage point of everyone who was on that dais, the National Mall looked packed. But a rebuttal cannot be based on impressions. As I drafted my statement for the press, I still needed facts and figures to support the president's assertion. As I thought about it, one thing was clear: technology had improved so much in even just the last four years, let alone the last eight, that it was far easier to watch the inauguration from almost any device, from anywhere around the world. Watching live events on Twitter, Facebook, or Periscope wasn't possible eight years ago, and live viewing on a tablet or a phone was much more popular now. Twitter had announced that a record breaking 6.82 million unique viewers had watched the inauguration on its live feed.[1] Fox News Channel's ratings for the inauguration were off the charts. News websites reported record traffic, and CNN itself claimed almost 17 million live streams that day.[2]

Regardless of the final numbers, it did seem clear that the press—CNN and NBC in particular—were creating a story where there was no story. So, I crafted a simple, straightforward statement: "This was the largest audience to ever witness an inauguration—period—both in person and around the globe." (I'm not sure why I have to always send these dramatic moments with, "period," but I'm going to work on this.)

I felt I had done the best I could. Still, I asked Tom Barrack to talk with the president and try to refocus him on the *success* of the inauguration rather than the *numbers*, especially when there was so little definitive information. The president respected Tom, and Tom made a compelling argument, but my orders from the president remained the same.

I got the word that the press had assembled, the cameras were ready, and the lights were on. I gathered my thoughts before I stepped through the small door to the briefing room. At least, I thought to myself, a Saturday afternoon briefing on inaugural crowd size from a White House press secretary few people had ever heard of was not going to be big news. When this was over, I thought, I could get back to the important stuff.

It was now about 4:30 in the afternoon. I was keyed up from my calls with Reince and the president. As I stood in my office, I felt like a boxer who gets the pep talk of his life in the ring corner and then rushes forward seeking a knockout punch. The first punch I threw connected, a solid blow. I denounced the media's pettiness and reminded them of the non-story about the Martin Luther King Jr. bust being removed. I accused them of "deliberately false reporting," trotted out some of the statistics I had acquired, and said photos that centered on the National Mall where white tarps on the grass highlighted large gaps between groups of people were "intentionally framed...to minimize the enormous support that had gathered on the national mall." I thought I had worded my statement in such a way to make my case, but I was even more certain that the media was trying to make an issue out of nothing. It was appalling that no elder statesmen in the media called on their colleagues to focus on more serious issues. Still, in retrospect, I should have lowered the temperature and not so broadly questioned the media's motives. I left the room without taking questions because I was in no position that Saturday afternoon to talk about the president's appointments or policies.

The rest, you could say, is history. Fact checkers said my pants were on fire, fashion critics mocked my light gray pinstriped suit for the way it rode up my neck, and my first appearance before the media in the Press Briefing Room set an unfortunate precedent of a belligerent press confronted with an equally belligerent press secretary.

I went back to my office, expecting an "attaboy" from the president; instead Reince was waiting for me and said the president wasn't happy at all with how I had performed. He didn't like my not taking questions. He thought I was hung up on the wrong issues. He wanted to know why I hadn't run my statement by him. Minutes later, the president himself called, and he was not pleased. And I started to wonder if my first day would be my last. In fact, as I drove past the White House gates that night, I wasn't sure I'd be driving back in. In the end, I didn't get fired, but that day did cost me a few thousand dollars. I immediately went out and bought four new—dark, well-fitted—suits ASAP. For weeks afterward, I would get emails and letters from tailors and personal stylists all looking to "help." What a first day.

But my not-ready-for-prime-time suit was the least of my mistakes. I had wrongly assumed I knew what Donald Trump wanted. Instead of bringing the White House press corps to heel, he had wanted a polished, nuanced argument defending his position. Every time the president had checked in with me, I had said like a good soldier, "We're on it, Mr. President." Instead, I should have talked with him more and understood exactly what he wanted me to do.

I had made a bad first impression, and looking back, that was the beginning of the end.

■   ■   ■

As I travel and speak around the country, people will walk up to me, wince sympathetically, and say, "Can I ask you something?"

I nod, knowing what's coming.

"What did it feel like to see Melissa McCarthy play you on *Saturday Night Live*?"

On the first Sunday in February, Rebecca and I were getting ready for Mass. She had gone to bed before me and awakened before I had.

"Did you stay up to see SNL?" she asked.

"No, I was right behind you. Why?" I wondered.

"You are going to want to see the skit they did on you."

As usual we were running late, so I said I would watch it when we got back. We got in the car and headed to church.

Throughout the hour, while I sat in church, I heard the buzzing of my phone. Glancing down, I saw the screen fill with text messages. As soon as church let out, I looked down with horror to find Twitter ablaze with my name.

What was it now?

At first, I feared something truly terrible had happened. I soon sorted out that I had been referenced the night before on SNL. Like most of my generation, I love SNL and grew up on the antics of Dan Aykroyd, Eddie Murphy, Tina Fey, Dennis Miller, Chris Farley, and Bill Murray. With tough jobs and kids to put to bed, Rebecca and I rarely watched it live, but it was set to record on our DVR each week.

Taking a deep breath, I went to the DVR and saw Melissa McCarthy wearing my suit, downing gum by the bucket (guilty as charged, but never at the lectern), and yelling at the media. I had no choice but to laugh. Like many SNL sketches, I think they milked it too long, but there was no denying it was funny. In the sketch, McCarthy-as-Spicer sprayed a reporter with a Super Soaker. And sure enough, thanks to a friend, my office soon had a Super Soaker of its own.

The sketches kept coming, but they didn't bother me. When you play in the NFL, you can't complain about getting tackled.

Did the sketches bother the president?

I wondered about that. But then, we were all in for SNL punishment—Kellyanne Conway, Steve Bannon, and most of all, the president himself.

■   ■   ■

After my poor debut on Saturday, I had stewed for the rest of the weekend, determined to set this right.

My maiden conference was scheduled for Monday.

By this time, my staff was coming on board, providing me with needed reinforcement. On Monday morning, I gathered with my deputy and assistant press secretaries, received their updates on each of their specific focus areas, and reviewed my script, written for me by the very capable Natalie Strom.

Then I went through a pre-brief practice session with the staff, volleying questions and answers with my deputies. It felt like I was a freshman cramming for a final exam in a class I had barely attended.

I walked out to the briefing room to face the harsh television lights. This time I was dressed for the part—dark blue suit, white shirt, and red tie. I think half the staff came in for that first one—both to support me and to see what would happen.

I started with a humble joke about my predecessor, Josh Earnest, not having to worry about losing his title as "most popular press secretary." I had a lot of news to present and take questions about. At the top of the agenda was the president's decision to withdraw the United States from the Trans-Pacific Partnership (TPP), a trade agreement with almost a dozen other Pacific Rim countries, minus China. As an assistant U.S. trade representative for President Bush, I had helped promote the TPP as a good deal for working Americans. Now I was announcing our withdrawal from the TPP because President Trump believed it was hurting working Americans.

It felt strange, but I reminded myself that I was a spokesman whose job it was to explain the president's policies, not express my own opinions.

I had a brisk set of announcements to make about the president's meeting with leading CEOs in the morning and with labor leaders in the afternoon to discuss ways to create good American jobs. I described the president's executive action of freezing hiring on non-military federal personnel. Beyond that were many high-profile personnel announcements—including the upcoming swearing-in of General James Mattis as secretary of defense and General John Kelly as secretary of homeland security.

I hoped to convey the urgency with which Donald Trump was approaching the task of fulfilling his campaign promises. By any measure, that message got through.

"If other new occupants of the White House wanted to be judged by their first 100 days in office, President Trump seems intent to be judged by his first 100 hours," the *New York Times* reported. "No president in modern times, if ever, has started with such a flurry of initiatives on so many fronts in such short order."[3]

On my first day, I wanted to make a statement and take back some control of the briefing room that had been ceded by previous administrations to an admiring press.

Tradition had it that after a press secretary made a short statement, the first question would always come from the AP White House beat reporter, then Julie Pace. The press secretary would usually turn deferentially to the mainstream media giants of the first row—ABC, NBC, CBS, the *Washington Post*, the *New York Times*, Reuters, and the AP, which were, in short, the major networks, papers, and wire services— and then work back to where reporters from the smaller or niche media outlets dwelled. In some ways, the AP reporter was in charge because by tradition it was up to that reporter to decide when to end the press briefing by saying, "Thank you very much."

I threw this protocol out the window in four ways.

First, I gave the first question to Daniel Halper of the *New York Post*. We wanted to send a signal that this was a Trump presidency, and giving the first question to a New York paper clearly conveyed that. It also made it clear that the days of the establishment media dominating the briefing were over.

Second, I looked beyond the media giants to regional papers, business media, ethnic media, and other outlets. I did so not out of spite but out of the recognition that even the largest media outlets were being marginalized by social media and media fragmentation. Other reporters also had a right to question the White House press secretary.

Third, when Julie Pace, the AP reporter on duty that first Monday, said, "Thank you very much" about forty-five minutes into the briefing, which traditionally should have signaled the end, I looked down and said, "Thank you. I'm going to keep going." This wasn't an attempt to slight Julie but rather another small gesture to signal that the press was not in charge of the briefing, we were.

Fourth, I announced that we would have four "Skype seats" reserved for journalists who worked outside the Washington beltway. In a digital age, it made sense to use technology to widen access to the White House. There was also a deeper point to this move—the White House Correspondents' Association and its members had become a comfortable guild separated from the media pack by nineteenth-century standards of proximity and access. There were too many print publications, online news sites, and radio and TV affiliates that were being left out.

The mainstream media hyperventilated about censorship and dangers to the First Amendment, which was ludicrous, as we were *expanding* access to the White House press briefing. What the major media outlets were really upset about was our recognition of reality—that the American media landscape extended far beyond three TV networks, a wire service, and a couple of major newspapers. Mainstream media is outraged by attacks on itself but never seems to find issue with launching attacks on conservative media. I guess it's only an attack on the First

Amendment when mainstream media is questioned. During the Obama administration, Fox News was ostracized by the president and his staff, and the ring leaders of the mainstream media didn't seem to express the same concerns about the First Amendment.

I ultimately took question about everything from the high cost of prescription drugs to the coming order to permit the building of the Keystone pipeline. Then ABC News correspondent Jonathan Karl, a journalist I had known for almost twenty years, asked a question that went to the heart of my credibility.

> Karl: Before I get to a policy question, just a question about the nature of your job.
>
> Spicer: Yeah.
>
> Karl: Is it your intention to always tell the truth from that podium, and will you pledge never to knowingly say something that is not factual?
>
> Spicer: It is. It's an honor to do this, and, yes, I believe that we have to be honest with the American people. I think sometimes we can disagree with the facts. There are certain things that we may miss—we may not fully understand when we come out. But our intention's never to lie to you, Jonathan. Our job is to make sure that sometimes—and you're in the same boat—I mean, there are times when you guys tweet something out or write a story, and you publish a correction. That doesn't mean that you were intentionally trying to deceive readers and the American people, does it? And I think we should be afforded the same opportunity. There are times when we believe something to be true, or we get something from an agency, or we act in haste because the information available wasn't complete, but our desire [is] to communicate with the American people and make sure that you have the most complete story at the time. And so we do it.

This led to a discussion of the police-reported Washington Metro numbers I had issued in haste on Saturday. Those were the numbers I used because those were the numbers I had, and I defended my statement that Trump's inauguration had been the "largest watched inaugural ever" with social media live streaming and television. This time, I was prepared to walk through the numbers in a more careful way.

In doing so, I wanted to rebut the press's double standard. Almost all veteran reporters have filed stories that, in retrospect, they wished they had made clearer and provided more context for, or that they later realized were flat-out wrong. Yet rarely do reporters have their integrity questioned the way Jonathan questioned mine. In the previous administration, he had asked the press secretary if the administration would pledge to tell the truth, but now he was making it very personal.

And, of course, he was not alone. The January 11 press conference was the start of a new era for CNN's Jim Acosta. That day, he took on the role of carnival barker, yelling at the president-elect and grandstanding for the camera. He was joining with Jonathan to try to portray me as a liar.

Standing at the podium can be a game of gotcha—having to remember every detail of policy proposals ranging from trade deals to healthcare reform, to immigration, to national security, to tax reform and beyond (not to mention the specifics from various meetings, the names of every domestic and foreign leader, and the proper pronunciation of those names). Some reporters ask questions at the briefings to get information to write strong stories; other reporters try to throw curveball questions at the press secretary, in hopes of knocking him or her off balance and creating a moment that can go viral.

With so much to convey, it was inevitable that mistakes would happen. But I did promise that if we ever issued an inaccurate statement, we would correct the record.

I again called out Zeke Miller for his "racially charged" tweet that the president had removed the bust of Martin Luther King Jr. from the Oval Office. I noted that Miller had tweeted out an apology to "my colleagues." Where was his apology to the president? Or to the White House staff who had to respond to his false report? Or to the American people who had been misled by it? I thought the fact that he had only apologized to his colleagues showed just how clubby and insular the White House press had become and how so much of what they did was to impress each other rather than to accurately inform the American people.

I stood my ground and answered questions for almost two hours.

When I left the podium, I was mentally exhausted but thinking I had righted the ship. I wanted to sit down, but there was one more thing I needed to do. I almost sprinted to the Oval Office and the president's back dining room. This was it—was I back or not? The television at the end of the room was on, and President Trump was leaning back in his chair at the end of the table, remote in hand, and beaming. To my eternal surprise, he rose up and gave me a bear hug.

"That's my Sean. Good job," he said. "Right way to do it."

■   ■   ■

I had found my footing   many friends told me approvingly after the press briefing, "That's the Sean Spicer I know"—but I still faced a media that reported rumor as fact and put stories about alleged, White House palace intrigue ahead of substantive reporting about policy.

I got a taste of this before I had even left the RNC. Just before Christmas 2016, the RNC put out a statement: "Over two millennia ago, a new hope was born into the world, a Savior who would offer the promise of salvation to all mankind. Just as the three wise men did on that night, this Christmas heralds a time to celebrate the good news of a new King. We hope Americans celebrating Christmas today will enjoy a day of festivities and a renewed closeness with family and friends."

The big tent of the RNC includes people from just about every religion. We routinely issued religious tidings, extending our best wishes to Jewish Americans at Passover, to Muslim Americans at Ramadan, and so on.

And yet, this time heads exploded on social media and cable news.

Jonathan Chait, a writer for *New York* magazine, tweeted: "The distinction between a president and a king is not trivial."

MSNBC producer Kyle Griffin said, "No joke—This line is actually in the RNC's Christmas message."[4]

"I hope you are kidding," I replied when asked by BuzzFeed about whether Donald Trump was the "King" in question. "Christ is the King in the Christian faith," I replied. "To ask this on Christmas is frankly offensive." Ben Smith, BuzzFeed editor in chief and a veteran of *Politico*, took to Twitter to stand by BuzzFeed's "reporting."

Over the years, I have experienced many spats with reporters and media outlets, but this disagreement at Christmastime was a new low.

This was just the beginning of a landslide of negative media coverage. Over a three-month period in the following year, the conservative Media Research Center found that coverage of President Trump was 91 percent negative.[5] In an analysis of the media coverage of Trump's first one hundred days as president, a paper from the Shorenstein Center at the Harvard Kennedy School noted, "Trump has received unsparing coverage for most weeks of his presidency, without a single major topic where Trump's coverage, on balance, was more positive than negative, setting a new standard for unfavorable press coverage of a president." It went on:

> Trump's coverage during his first 100 days set a new standard for negativity. Of news reports with a clear tone, negative reports outpaced positive ones by 80 percent to 20 percent. Trump's coverage was unsparing. In no week did the coverage drop below 70 percent negative and it reached 90 percent negative at its peak....The best period for Trump was week 12 of his presidency, when he ordered a cruise missile strike on a Syrian airbase in retaliation for the Assad regime's use of nerve gas on civilians. That week, his coverage divided 70 percent negative to 30 percent positive. Trump's worst periods were weeks 3 and 4 (a combined 87 percent negative) when

federal judges struck down his first executive order banning Muslim immigrants, and weeks 9 and 10 (a combined 88 percent negative) when the House of Representatives was struggling without success to muster the votes to pass a "repeal and replace" health care bill....

CNN and NBC's coverage was the most unrelenting— negative stories about Trump outpaced positive ones by 13-to-1 on the two networks.[6]

There are reportedly three big Trump rules: 1) when you are right, you fight, 2) never apologize, and 3) controversy elevates the message. When Donald Trump lashes out on Twitter, it is to express his message without distortion, told in his own words, not left up to interpretation or spin. He believes that if you get hit, you hit back twice as hard. I don't always agree with that strategy, but Trump usually makes it work. I think the president sometimes calls attention to attacks from marginal people that would be better left alone, but I understand his frustration. Americans may not always agree with what he says, or how he says it, but many people understand why he's frustrated.

■   ■   ■

Donald Trump came to office determined to disrupt the status quo at all levels. From the get-go, I tried to channel that spirit into the way we interacted with the White House press corps.

The leaders of the White House Correspondents' Association had already briefed me on the traditional protocols of White House press briefings, and I had questioned whether these old practices were best practices. The more I probed, the more defensive their body language became.

They could see changes coming, and they didn't like it.

I wanted to expand access to the briefing without taking up prime real estate in the West Wing. I considered moving our briefings to a recently renovated space on the ground floor of the Eisenhower Executive Office Building, right across West Executive Avenue Northwest from the West

Wing and "Pebble Beach" where television reporters do their live reports from the North Lawn of the White House. The space we identified was significantly larger than the James S. Brady Press Briefing Room—it could accommodate many more journalists and bloggers. Of course, I realized this move would have created the mother of all media backlashes, not because it was a bad idea but because the major news outlets would scream that they had been banished from the White House. They would also fret about their prestige taking a hit as more reporters got to attend. But more reporters meant more sources of information for the American people. Jeff Mason of Reuters, then the president of the White House Correspondents' Association, had told me there would be initial interest in the briefings and they would be carried on camera for a few weeks, maybe a month or two, but then interest would subside. As the calendar flipped from February to March, and the briefings became "must-see TV," attracting millions of daily viewers, I would gently remind him of that prediction.

With so much going on during the transition and in the early days of the administration, my idea to move the daily briefing wasn't a top priority for Reince Priebus, Kellyanne Conway, or Steve Bannon. And without their full backing, I figured I wouldn't and couldn't do it.

The current briefing room has forty-nine seats and standing room for others. My proposal would have opened that capacity up to about 250 reporters. I think most people would consider that a good thing, but the establishment media likes the current situation because it protects them. There are seats for all the big, mainstream outlets, and they control the White House Correspondents' Association, the organization that has assigned the seats for decades, deciding which network, newspaper, or other outlet gets which of the forty-nine seats. Most of the regular reporters who cover the White House have access to small, work-space areas, located in the back of the Press Briefing Room. But for years, that area has been cramped and uncomfortable—plus it hasn't been made available to newer news organizations. So, while a larger room and more work-space might have been good for journalism in general, the mainstream media folks already had what they needed and weren't concerned with "up-and-coming" media outlets.

The changes I did make were enough to send the White House Correspondents' guild into orbit.

Ben Schreckinger of *Politico* warned the republic about the dangers of Skype: "[T]he Trump team has gotten to work quickly, stacking its briefings in its favor. In its first week in the White House, Trump's communications team installed screens in the briefing room to allow journalists outside Washington—including conservative talk radio hosts—to participate [in them]." Perhaps those screens hadn't been used in eight years, but I remember when those screens were inserted a decade ago by the George W. Bush administration. Beyond Ben lacking the facts about the screens, he also didn't accurately note that the majority of journalists who attended the briefings via Skype were reporters for local affiliates of major networks. When *USA Today* did a story on my use of Skype to give access to more reporters, it noted that the issues raised by these outside reporters differed drastically from the questions asked by the White House press corps. That was the point. The D.C. press corps has a pack mentality, asking the same questions about the same subjects over and over—especially if they needed their own "cutaway shot" to include in their coverage—whereas the reporters on Skype generally asked about issues important to their communities. *USA Today* tabulated that the top five issues raised by the Washington press corps were, in order, intelligence and wiretapping, the continuing Russia controversy, health care, communications issues and the president's tweets, and immigration. The top five issues for reporters who participated via Skype were, in order, immigration, taxes, coal and energy production, local issues, and infrastructure. In short, reporters who attended through Skype were more interested in real news and policy than the D.C.-based reporters who were more interested in controversy. Trump had been elected by disenfranchised voters in the so-called "flyover states," and it was important to include their questions and address issues important to them.

Bringing in remote reporters via Skype helped restore competition to the marketplace of ideas and journalism. I didn't set out to settle scores or to clip wings. I set out to change the ossified rules of the White House press office and to bring in more diversity, including Spanish-language outlets and minority-owned American Urban Radio.

With Skype I was also able to bring in geographically and ideologically diverse voices. Consider Lars Larson, a radio personality in Oregon. In one interview, Lars asked me, "The federal government is the biggest landlord in America. It owns two-thirds of a billion acres of America. I don't think the founders ever envisioned it that way. Does President Trump want to start returning the people's land to the people? And in the meantime, for a second question—since that's in fashion these days—can he tell the Forest Service to start logging our forests aggressively again to provide jobs for Americans, wealth for the Treasury, and not spend $3.5 billion a year fighting forest fires?"

Now, if you're a White House correspondent, that's a "wasted" question, time wasted in the briefing that could have been better spent on palace intrigue or any number of issues that have been covered ad nauseam. If you happen to live in the rural American West where about one-half of the land is owned and managed by Washington, D.C., it is a very important question.

In that same briefing, Kim Kalunian from WPRI in Rhode Island wanted to know if the president would retaliate against the city of Providence, Rhode Island, by withdrawing grant money because it had declared itself a "sanctuary city" in defiance of federal law.[7]

Again, a silly question if you're a Capital Beltway journalist. I was soon fielding questions from Skype reporters who actually asked about things that millions of overlooked Americans cared about. I thought this was a good thing, but many in the mainstream press did not.

According to *Politico*'s Ben Schreckinger, one of the sins committed by this larger group of journalists occurred when President Trump and Canadian Prime Minister Justin Trudeau were asked a question about national security, instead of about General Michael Flynn's resignation (over his misleading Vice President Mike Pence about the nature of his conversations with Russian Ambassador Sergey Kislyak). "Trump and Trudeau were *instead* asked questions about trade and border security," Schreckinger opined.

Why the "instead"?

While questions about the resignation of the NSC director, Michael Flynn, are appropriate, why is a truly substantive and relevant question, in the context of a joint press conference between the U.S. president and the Canadian prime minister, allegedly out of line?[8] The reporter who asked the question—Kaitlan Collins, then of the *Daily Caller*—was eviscerated by her colleagues. After that, I noticed her reporting became more aggressive and more in step with the "mainstream reporters" in the Press Briefing Room. She now works for CNN.

Back in April 1999, Jeff Zeleny—then of the *New York Times* and now of CNN—asked President Barack Obama the following question during a presidential press conference: "During these first one hundred days, what has surprised you the most about this office? Enchanted you the most from serving in this office? Humbled you the most? And troubled you the most?"

CBS News reported Zeleny's question as a "light moment" in the press conference while his colleagues met the question with "laughter."[9] The differences between how the media covers Republicans and Democrats are pretty clear.

At one joint press conference, the media accused the president of not having a headset on to listen for translation—the problem was that he was wearing a single earpiece with a single cord rather than the headphone headset the media had been issued. So, rather than ask for or check the facts, a quick tweet got sent from a reporter's phone, establishing a narrative.

At the end of January 2017, the *New York Times* reported that President Trump had signed the executive order demanding a temporary halt, and eventual enhanced screening, for foreign visitors from seven countries where terror networks are prevalent—the so-called "Muslim travel ban"—before then-Homeland Security Secretary John Kelly could be fully briefed.

Josh Rogin of the *Washington Post*—an opinion writer—wrote that Steve Bannon had dictated policy, going over the head of the Department of Homeland Security, and then set up a damage-control, 2:00

a.m. phone call with then Secretary of State Rex Tillerson. Rogin never contacted me or anyone in the press shop about the story or to check his facts.

Neither the *New York Times* story nor the *Washington Post* story had any basis in truth. In the case of the *Washington Post*, I spent a good part of a day talking with its editors, and in the end, its story was "updated" twice, noting the newspaper should have called the White House prior to publication. The "update" was a way to get around saying they were wrong or admitting fault. I demanded a full correction which never came, but the paper kept Rogin out of commission for a week.

As for the *New York Times* report, Secretary Kelly had in fact been briefed multiple times on the "travel ban" and had directed his staff to amend the order as necessary. And the Department of Justice's Office of Legal Counsel had vetted it and found it compliant with the law. As was so often the case, whoever leaked this story didn't know what he or she was talking about. Secretary Kelly himself contradicted the *New York Times*'s reports on television interviews, but it was frustrating that we had to spend so much time knocking down false media reports that went viral.

This was par for the course. False reports in one part of the media spread through all the others like wildfire, and reporters never seemed abashed when they were corrected. The editors usually wanted the corrections kept quiet, the reporters adopted the attitude that "Oh well, these things happen," and both groups focused on their game of gotcha in which any small error on our part was a headline and the countless errors on their part were barely acknowledged. In one briefing, I finally had had enough and said, "Oh, okay, so I apologize if NBC News's reporting is based on the *New York Times*'s false reporting."

I also wondered if the presence of cameras was an unhealthy influence on some journalists.

I wondered about this in early January, even before the inauguration.

That was the period when then FBI Director James Comey told President-elect Trump about the "Steele" dossier, a compendium of negative information about Trump and his associates compiled by a former British intelligence official, Michael Steele, for Fusion GPS—a private, opposition research outfit that was paid by a law firm employed by the Clinton campaign.

The dossier included an allegation that Donald Trump, as a private citizen, had visited Moscow, was filmed consorting with prostitutes, and was entertained when one of them urinated on a bed on which Barack and Michelle Obama had slept. If true, the tape would have supported the Left's narrative that Donald Trump was being blackmailed and controlled by Russian intelligence.

At 2:00 p.m. on January 10, 2017, I received a voicemail from Jake Tapper of CNN. He wanted me to give him a call about a story. I called him back about an hour later, and he texted me, saying he was on-air and would touch base soon. Then around 5:00 p.m., Tapper said he was about to air a story on the Steele dossier. He gave me less than an hour to give a response. Considering the magnitude of the charges being leveled, that was not enough time to prepare a response. CNN reported that on January 5, during a meeting at Trump Tower in New York City, the heads of the intelligence agencies had briefed Trump about the dossier, and he had been presented with a two-page summary of the document. That did not happen. The summary was not ready when they briefed the president-elect. As the meeting with the four intelligence chiefs—Director of National Intelligence James Clapper, National Security Agency Director Admiral Mike Rogers, CIA Director John Brennan, and FBI Director James Comey—was concluding, Comey asked to speak with Trump privately in the back corner of the room. By his own admission, he verbally briefed Trump on the allegation of the prostitutes in the hotel, and Trump cut him off quickly, denying it. CNN's story, which highlighted the president-elect being handed a two-page document, was wrong.

I began a mad dash to actually get a hold of the dossier, which, was classified and not easily obtained, though it had already been leaked to the media. Before we could really do anything, CNN ran its story, and we had to play catch up. Ironically, CNN would go on to win an award for its reporting despite Comey telling Fox News's Bret Baier in an interview that he never showed the two-page summary to Trump.

James Clapper, former director of national intelligence, later confirmed that the president was *not* shown the dossier but had been given a vague warning about it by former FBI Director James Comey. Not having seen the dossier, we could not respond to it. But then BuzzFeed published the whole lurid account.

Not only did we not have a copy of the two-page report, we had not even seen it. So, we called Mike Pompeo, then a congressman from Kansas who had been nominated to be the CIA director, asking him about how we could get a copy and requesting that he call us on a secure line to brief us on its contents.

One of the allegations in the dossier is that Michael Cohen, who worked in the Trump Organization and was one of Trump's personal attorneys, had been in Prague to meet with Russian agents. I called Michael. He told me he had never been to the Czech Republic and on the day in question had visited his son at college in California. I asked him if he had his passport.

"It's in my pocket," he said. "I always carry it with me."

"Where are you?"

"I'm on my way home, a half-hour away."

"Can you come back to Trump Tower right now?"

"Are you serious?"

Michael Cohen came back. I asked to see his passport and personally verified that his passport had no stamps exiting this country or entering another around the time alleged in the Steele dossier.

But at this point, the media was ready to run with anything. With CNN and BuzzFeed, no matter how many facts we debunked in this manner, the burden of proof remained on us to continue to disprove the next allegation. In short, a newly elected president was getting sandbagged by reporting on baseless gossip on the eve of his inauguration.

We held a press conference on January 11 in Trump Tower. The president-elect asked me to deliver a statement calling out CNN and BuzzFeed for their erroneous reporting before introducing him to reporters. The president-elect called BuzzFeed "a failing pile of garbage" and denounced CNN for "going out of their way" to promote the dossier allegations without investigating their veracity.[10]

Here is where the cameras came into my thinking. In that press conference, Jim Acosta went into a rage, red-faced and shouting at Donald Trump. President-elect Trump refused to call on him, calling him "fake news."

Acosta—who had covered Hillary Clinton's campaign in relative obscurity—had quickly improved his visibility by becoming dramatic and hyperbolic on the air. At the end of that press conference, I told Acosta he was rude and disrespectful to the president-elect. He said that he thought the president-elect had been rude and disrespectful. He went on-air immediately after that, saying that I had threatened to kick him out of the press conference, which simply was not the case. And the president's anger at the media's endless stream of baseless, partisan rumor-mongering was just beginning.

■   ■   ■

While their facts were wrong, the media had a point about the rollout of the so-called "travel ban." One problem with disruption is that it can disrupt itself. The executive order on travel had been coordinated by Stephen Miller, an engaging fellow who would not bridle at the description that, at age thirty-two, he is an old man trapped in a young man's body. He had been Senator Jeff Sessions's communications director and came into the Trump campaign through an early alliance between the senator and the candidate. In short order, Miller demonstrated an uncanny ability to capture Trump's voice—and thus, win his ear. So, when Stephen Miller led the effort on the executive order, he captured the president's intentions to a T. A poll from Rasmussen Reports found that 57 percent of likely voters favored a temporary ban on refugees from Syria, Iraq, Iran, Libya, Somalia, Sudan, and Yemen until the U.S. government could do a better job of vetting them.

While we ran the executive order through the proper channels to have it reviewed, we did not anticipate all the legal traps liberal, activist judges invoked to stymie it, in part because we were not yet fully staffed and did not have time to do that sort of analysis or the experienced hands that might have helped guide us to the smooth implementation of complex policies like this.

I knew Steve Bannon as the force behind the Breitbart News Network. Using money from Rebekah Mercer and other big donors, Steve had frequently unleashed Breitbart to attack the RNC as a den of out-of-touch, political elitism. After enduring a few broadsides, I had asked Steve for a meeting to see if I could get him to cool it down a bit. When we met, Steve and I found we shared some experiences in common, including our working-class backgrounds and service in the Navy. Next up was furthering an understanding between Reince and Steve, who shared more goals than they might have initially realized. As they got to know each other better, Breitbart eased up its criticisms, at least a bit.

The core principle of Bannonism—as expressed through Breitbart, which remained his mouthpiece even when he was in the White House— is to tear down establishment Republicans. That is his number one priority. In the White House, I learned something else about Steve Bannon. He is adept at playing the populist angle while also maintaining deep back channels to the very mainstream journalists he publicly denounces. Despite all of his talk about draining the swamp, Steve Bannon was an expert navigator of every cove and eddy.

His most consummate skill, though, was as an inside, political knife fighter. Steve somehow won the acquiescence of incoming National Security Advisor General Michael Flynn to give him a voting seat on the National Security Council (NSC). Many senior staff attended NSC meetings, but to have a vote was something else. And to give a vote to a politically oriented staff member was unprecedented.

Donald Trump was blindsided by the decision and the firestorm of criticism that ensued. The president was furious and called both men into the Oval Office. At that moment, Steve deftly turned to General

Flynn in front of Donald Trump and said, "I thought you had run this by the president?"

The mainstream media narrative that the new administration was in chaos gained considerable traction from the embarrassingly short tenure of General Flynn as national security advisor. I had come to know General Flynn during the campaign. He was always well-dressed, buttoned-up, and never had a hair out of place, the quintessential, former three-star Army general. Moreover, he had grown up in Middleton, Rhode Island. We developed a quick and easy relationship, but the one sticking point was that, during the transition and the early days of the administration, I found it nearly impossible to get information out of Flynn's office. The short-lived tenure of Fox News contributor Monica Crowley as his communications director didn't help.

During the transition, the media claimed General Flynn had met with Russian Ambassador Sergey Kislyak on more than one occasion—contrary to what Flynn had told me, Reince, and Vice President Pence.

I questioned Flynn about it again, and he quickly pulled out his phone to show me a text message to Kislyak, wishing him a happy new year and offering his condolences for members of the Russian Red Army Choir who had died in a plane crash. Flynn convinced me that the media was chasing a non-story. Vice President Pence and I gave flat-out denials that General Flynn had any important contacts with Russian officials.

But then in a high-profile interview with Adam Entous of the *Washington Post*, Flynn implied that he had conducted more extensive conversations with the Russian ambassador.

General Flynn's evolving account of his Russian contacts—and the fact that he had misled us—sank his credibility as national security advisor. The president promptly fired him. It was a painful decision for the president because he liked and admired General Flynn and valued his counsel. Flynn was later indicted for lying to FBI agents about whether he and Russian officials had discussed the prospect of lifting economic sanctions. From what I understand, having conversations with future foreign counterparts was well within the bounds of his responsibilities. But there is no question that he was wrong to mislead the FBI and others, particularly considering the level of trust our government places in his position.

There is also no question that some in the media got this story wrong.

In December 2017, after I had left the White House, ABC suspended its "investigative correspondent" Brian Ross for reporting that General Flynn was ready to testify to Special Counsel Robert Mueller that *presidential candidate* Donald Trump had directed him to contact the Russians. In fact, it was *President-elect* Donald Trump who had instructed General Flynn to initiate communication with the Russians. That is what incoming presidents do. Moreover, such contact occurring *after* the election had nothing to do with "collusion" and everything to do with a president-elect preparing to stake out his foreign policy.[11]

In the quick-draw culture of the media, Ross's story spread like the proverbial wildfire. Even when the story was reported correctly, the breathless tone of the media overlooked the fact that it was entirely appropriate, indeed expected, that someone named to be the national security advisor should be in contact with foreign governments.

After General Flynn's departure from the White House, MSNBC's Chris Hayes reported that Vice Admiral Robert Harward had turned down an offer to become the new national security advisor. Harward did so, according to MSNBC, after he saw the president's performance in a press conference.[12] I had to clean up that impression in a briefing in which I relayed what I knew to be true—that Vice Admiral Harward was deeply enthusiastic about working in the administration, that he had financial and family concerns that precluded him from accepting, and that he wanted to be kept in consideration for future opportunities in the White House.[13]

The same sort of issue occurred around the nomination of Phil Bilden to be secretary of the Navy. Major Garrett of CBS News reported that Bilden would be revoking his name from consideration. After talking with Phil, who said the report was not true, Major Garrett challenged my credibility when Phil ultimately withdrew his name over a week later. On February 28, Phil sent me a note that read, "I want you to know that you were factually correct when you reported 'those people would be wrong' in response to the CBS rumor. I was 100 percent committed and fighting the OGE [Office of Government Ethics] hard then. It was not until Friday 24 Feb that I decided to withdraw, realizing then the fight would waste valuable time and money and delay President Trump having a SECNAV in office."

This was just another example of the relentless negativity—and selective use of facts—with which White House stories were being reported. When I asked a *Washington Post* veteran about reporters calling out other reporters in stories, she said the "higher-ups" get very skittish. Think about that. They treat that kind of news—news about their peers—very differently than all other kinds of news.

■   ■   ■

President Trump wanted to get a lot done right away. We had an aggressive agenda. Perhaps inevitably, given our inexperience and the shrill opposition of the Democrats, the media, and even some Republicans, we had our fair share of stumbles, mistakes, and embarrassments. We could produce incredible results one day and fall flat on our face the next. In February 2017, for example, Mexican President Enrique Peña Nieto cancelled a tentatively planned trip to Washington after a testy phone call with President Trump. Peña Nieto wanted President Trump to publicly renounce his promise to "build a wall and make Mexico pay for it." Trump refused. That was the issue—a matter of policy—not, as some in the media reported, that Trump had insulted the Mexican president.[14]

While the administration has caught a lot of flak for its turnover of personnel, that's largely because it took a while for the president to realize what sort of people he needed in which positions. Remember, he wasn't hanging curtains in the Oval Office before election day, and he wasn't lining up a White House roster during the campaign months either. But once we started building a roster, the discipline and thoroughness with which we prepared cabinet nominees and senior agency appointments was unprecedented. Unfortunately, we were unprepared for the Democrats' obstruction of nominees, slowing the process of Senate confirmations as much as they possibly could. Sixteen of President Trump's nominees to head major departments or agencies were still waiting to be confirmed at the end of January 2017—that was nine more than President Obama had at the end of January 2009 and fourteen more than President Bush had at the end of January 2001.[15]

The leaks, which were an annoyance during the transition, took a more serious turn within the White House. Rough drafts of domestic policies were handed to the media. Worse, the details of the president's private phone calls with the prime minister of Australia and the president of Mexico were leaked. This release of the call transcripts was far worse than an embarrassment; it was a major hindrance to the president's ability to conduct foreign policy. It signaled to foreign leaders that the United States could not be trusted to keep leader-to-leader conversations private. It undermined the president's ability to have candid conversations with top alliance leaders and adversaries. It threatened to shut down candor on both sides. The person who leaked transcripts of the president's calls committed a serious crime—embarrassing the administration is bad enough, but undermining this country is dangerous.

Trump's opinions on controversial issues were pretty transparent. Anyone who wanted to know what he was thinking only had to read his tweets. Keeping an eye out for his early morning, late-night, and weekend tweets was part of my new world order. I soon learned that there were two kinds of Trump tweets. There were the early morning and late-night tweets that were pure and unfiltered Trump when he had no staff around him. Then there were the business-hour tweets that were filtered through or drafted by the social media director, Dan Scavino. The former often caused me trouble because the press would latch onto any statements they saw as potentially embarrassing or controversial. The latter, on the other hand, were typically incisive and confrontational, but constructive. Dan Scavino was an invaluable editor for Trump, but he couldn't be on call twenty-four hours a day. One example of a late-night tweet that got a lot of media, but was really rather harmless and amusing, was this famous fragment, issued at 12:06 a.m. from the president: "Despite the constant negative press covfefe."

I assumed he meant "coverage," and his thumbs simply hit the wrong button. But the minute I saw it, I said to myself, "Oh brother, here we go." I would later see how even the most trivial events could go viral in the media. I later assured reporters in the most serious tone, "Only the president and other select people know what that means."

But then there were many things that went right, at least from a media standpoint, where Donald Trump spoke with the most convincing language of all—action.

At the end of January, acting Attorney General Sally Yates—a holdover from the Obama administration—refused to enforce the administration's call to enhance the vetting of visa applicants from seven countries that were either known sponsors of terrorism or that had unstable governments endangered by terrorists. It is understandable why Yates, one of the luminaries of the liberal legal establishment, would find executing a Trump order distasteful. But the Constitution doesn't give law enforcement officers leeway to veto legally binding instructions they do not like.

Sally Yates was setting herself up to be a liberal martyr. She got what she wanted. She was fired. In my press briefing on January 31, I broke through the media hysteria by calmly and rationally explaining why firing Sally Yates was a constitutional necessity, not a choice. That same day, I also announced, speaking of the constitution, that the president had nominated Neil Gorsuch to the open seat on the Supreme Court.

Former Democratic Senate Majority Leader Harry Reid had established the precedent that the Senate could not filibuster a Supreme Court nominee. When Supreme Court Justice Antonin Scalia died in February 2016, Republicans, holding a majority in the Senate, decided to hold the seat open until the November presidential election. President Obama disagreed with that decision and nominated D.C. Circuit Court Chief Judge Merrick Garland for the seat.

Neil Gorsuch ticked all the boxes—Columbia, Harvard, Oxford, a Supreme Court clerkship, U.S. circuit court judge—and was well respected.

And yet, with a thin Republican majority in the Senate and Democrats feeling that Judge Garland had been wronged, Neil Gorsuch was not a shoo-in.

Jason Miller, originally slated to be our communications director, had resigned for personal reasons, and for a while I doubled as White House communications director and press secretary. That was a challenge, but in the Gorsuch nomination, my team and I managed to get everything just about right.

Our White House communications team worked hand in glove with Judge Gorsuch, the Office of White House Counsel, and key staff on Capitol Hill. We developed a thorough media plan. We armed surrogate speakers with talking points and deployed them on cable shows. We briefed legal organizations. We blanketed the Hill with information about why Gorsuch was an excellent pick for the Supreme Court. We worked with all our usual conservative allies—including The Heritage Foundation and Leonard Leo of the Federalist Society—to energize conservatives in support of Gorsuch.

The media stumbled in its reporting, and this only added to the drama of our initial announcement of Gorsuch. The media was keeping tabs on the short list of potential nominees. One strong potential nominee, Judge Thomas Hardiman of Pennsylvania, had been seen jumping into his car to go to a meeting. The rumor circuit assured Washington that Judge Hardiman was heading to D.C. to meet the president. Even though Hardiman never left Pennsylvania, there were rumors that he had been seen around the White House. The media's obsession with this rumor provided us with the perfect foil to keep Neil Gorsuch under wraps, a secret that did not begin to leak until after 6:00 p.m. on the East Coast, less than three hours before our announcement.

The president entered the East Room at precisely 9:02 p.m. at the request of the broadcast networks. We had invited senators from both parties to the East Room, but only Republicans accepted. And we arranged for the media to interview them in the East Room immediately following the announcement, allowing us not to miss a single beat. That way many Americans could and did see their home state senator praising the nomination of Judge Gorsuch. Our rollout and execution of Gorsuch's confirmation was pure teamwork, and it showed.

In the end, Neil Gorsuch was confirmed as an associate justice of the U.S. Supreme Court. For millions of Trump voters, this was easily the president's most important accomplishment of his first year in office.

■   ■   ■

On January 29, 2017, I donned a tux to attend the Alfalfa Club's annual, black-tie banquet, an evening in which establishment Washington lets its hair down and presents mild roasts of senators, the president, and media figures. Once I got there, I was called away by Reince Priebus.

"We've just conducted a special forces operation against a terrorist base in central Yemen," the chief of staff told me. "A U.S. Navy SEAL was killed during the operation."

This was the first military operation of the new administration. The president had ordered men into harm's way, and we had lost one of our best. I knew the media would treat this as a test case of our competence, and I knew that the president would want to speak to the brave Navy SEAL's widow.

Days later, I listened as Donald Trump called Carryn Owens, the widow of Senior Chief Petty Officer William Ryan Owens. I had known Donald Trump as a billionaire, a reality TV show host, a Republican donor, a celebrity, a Republican candidate for president, and now I saw him truly as the commander in chief, a man who cares deeply about our troops, a man who knows how tragic it is to see loved ones lost, and a man who has—as I learned when my own father passed away—a deep vein of compassion and sympathy. The president joined the family at Dover Air Force Base for the return of Chief Owens.

The media inevitably questioned the success of the mission of which Owens had been a part. I walked them through the history that led up to the raid on the terrorist compound. On November 7, 2016, the United States Central Command (CENTCOM) submitted a plan for the raid to the Department of Defense. The raid was subjected to immediate legal analysis. On December 19, the Department of Defense recommended that the plan be moved ahead. It was sent then to the National Security Council staff.

On January 6, 2017, an interagency deputies meeting was held. The deputies approved the military action for the next "moonless night," which wouldn't occur until after Donald Trump was sworn in as president. On January 24, President Trump's secretary of defense, Jim Mattis, read the memo authorizing the raid and submitted it to the White House, saying he supported the action. The next day, the president was briefed by General Flynn on the potential operation.

The president wanted to discuss the matter further with his top advisers, so he held a dinner meeting whose attendees included Vice President Pence, Secretary Mattis, Chairman of the Joint Chiefs of Staff General Joseph Dunford Jr., Reince Priebus, CIA Director Mike Pompeo, and others. The planned operation was laid out and analyzed in great detail.

In the morning, the interagency deputies reaffirmed their support of the mission. On January 26, President Trump signed the memo authorizing the action.

I thought the process behind the mission was important, but the press didn't care about that. They only wanted to know whether the White House considered the mission a "success" and were clearly trying to maneuver me into implying that Chief Owen's life was expendable. I explained in the briefings and in private, as patiently as I could, that 1) the mission was strategically a success; 2) it would not have been allowed to proceed if we had known in advance we would lose a sailor; 3) in the fog of war, you never know how even the best planned operation will play out.

Barbara Starr, CNN's Pentagon correspondent, saw our point.

She reported that, during the raid, Special Forces had seized laptops and cell phones that allowed U.S. intelligence to identify hundreds of al-Qaeda contacts, including potential terrorists in the West.[16]

■   ■   ■

Holding two, high-profile jobs in the White House meant a lot of pressure, but it had its rewards. I was in the Oval Office when Vice President Pence told President Trump that he planned to attend the Super Bowl and watch the New England Patriots take on the Atlanta Falcons.

Growing up in Rhode Island, I had been a Patriots fan my entire life—even during the team's lean years.

"Sean's a big Patriots fan," the president said. "He should fly down with you."

After scrupulously making sure that I complied with government ethics rules, I splurged and spent $2,000 of my own money to purchase two Super Bowl tickets (one for a friend) and flew down to Houston, Texas, on Air Force Two. After we landed, the vice president made an impromptu stop at a barbecue spot. It is always fun to watch people's eyes light up when they see the president or vice president walk in unannounced on a spontaneous visit.

Even with the money I had invested in game tickets, I had the last seat in the last row of the stadium, section 400, above the end zone. My head almost touched the fencing at the top of the stadium. In the third quarter, when defeat looked inevitable for the Patriots, the vice president, out of respect for the fans, decided to leave the stadium early, lest fans get snarled up in his security detail. The entire ride back to Air Force Two, we listened on AM radio as the game tightened up and the Patriots staged one of the greatest comebacks of all time. The Patriots won 34–28.

When the motorcade pulled up to the plane on the tarmac, the vice president jumped out of his limo, looked around, and shouted, "Where's Sean?"

I walked up and gave Mike Pence my hardest high five.

CHAPTER EIGHT

TURBULENCE, INSIDE AND OUT

B y February, I had settled into the routine of my new job.
Most mornings, I rose just after 5:00 a.m., checked Twitter (I had notifications set up from @realDonaldTrump so that I knew in real time when tweets happened), drove the seven miles from Alexandria, Virginia, to the White House, drove through two sets of gates and Secret Service checkpoints, and parked my car on West Executive Avenue (just a few spaces from the vice president's limo). My first stop each morning was the gym on the first floor of the Eisenhower Executive Office Building for a fifty-minute workout on the elliptical while taking in the morning news. In between commercial breaks, I would multitask on my iPhones, looking at emails, Twitter feeds, and transcripts of overnight news. To say that I "worked out" in the morning was truly an insult to working out, but it got me moving and was better than nothing.

Just before 7:00 a.m., after shaving, showering, and getting dressed, I would drop off my gym bag in my car as I crossed back over to the West Wing to meet Deputy Press Secretary Raj Shah, a former research director at the RNC. Raj would be ready to brief me on the stories and issues he thought were popping that morning. I would read his digests until about 7:20 a.m. The top members of our press team would join us, and we would create an informal first draft of the day's briefing. We wanted to get a handle on the day's big stories and issues and decide whether we could play offense or, more likely, if we had to play defense. After a while, we had a pretty good sense of which stories would pick up steam and dominate our day and which stories would dissipate.

The press staff had specific issue areas they focused on, and they kept me briefed on news involving their respective departments and agencies so that I could avoid being blindsided.

At 8:00 a.m., I went to the senior staff meeting where I briefed Reince and the other senior staffers—Steve Bannon, Jared, and Kellyanne, in addition to people in institutional positions such as the national security advisor, the chair of the Council of Economic Advisers, the White House counsel, the director of legislative affairs, the head of scheduling, the political director, and the head of presidential personnel—about what they could expect over the course of the day. They, in turn, informed me about things we might have missed, especially changes to the president's schedule or late-night developments in Congress or with foreign governments.

At 9:30 a.m., I met with my staff for more in-depth briefings, often with experts from, say, the Afghan desk of the National Security Council or the Office Legislative Affairs who would discuss legislation pending on the Hill. Sometimes, these briefings included a member of the Office of White House Counsel who would advise us on what we could or could not comment on.

At some time between 10:00 a.m. and noon, Sarah Huckabee Sanders and I would poke our heads into the Oval Office and get the president's take on the issues of the day.

He was always full of questions, wanting background on where a story came from and, of course, curious to know what we were going to say about it. And he was never shy about giving us directions. I'd be peppered throughout the day with calls from the president as stories evolved. He was extremely engaged, very particular, and insistent about how he wanted his points delivered. The more time I spent with him, the more I came to understand that President Trump wanted me to repeat his answers to the press *verbatim*.

Sometimes I referred these responses to a lawyer in the Office of White House Counsel. If that attorney told us, "Hey, you can't say that," we'd meet with President Trump in the Oval Office to hash out what we could say.

At 12:30 p.m., I'd have lunch. Most days, I ate at my desk. I would call the White House Mess, a small dining facility operated by the Navy and located on the lower level of the West Wing across the hall from the Situation Room, and order blackened salmon and salad with oil and vinegar. (If I was feeling a bit wild, I'd order chicken tenders.) While I ate, I read reports and long articles. After lunch, I would take meetings with staff members, conduct interviews, and prepare for the afternoon briefing. I would then review all that I had heard and read, finalize any last-minute changes in my opening statement with Assistant Press Secretary Natalie Strom, leave my office, and walk down the hall about fifty feet to face the harsh lights of the briefing. Before I walked out, I would try and have a moment of reflection and read a daily passage from the book *Jesus Calling* for inspiration. I mentioned a version of the book during a *Fox and Friends* segment with Abby Huntsman, and a viewer of the segment sent a shipment of the book so that everyone in our office could have a copy. Behind my desk was a wooden table with two drawers. On top of the table sat a box with a picture of St. Gabriel on it that Rebecca had given me as a gift when I took the job. In the box, I had two medals that I would slip into my pocket: one of St. Michael in honor of my dad and another of Mother Teresa—now Saint Teresa of Calcutta— that was blessed by the Holy Father and given to me early in my tenure by John Gizzi of *Newsmax*. In his note to me, John wrote, "it will guide you through times." Man, was he right.

After the briefing, I typically felt drained, but there was no time to relax. There were always loose ends to tie up—answers I had promised reporters, official statements that needed elaboration or clarification, and phone calls that needed to be returned.

Between 6:00 p.m. and 7:00 p.m., I would order a takeout dinner (very similar to my lunch choices) from the White House Mess and call the whole press team into my office for a wrap-up meeting to analyze our day and preview what we would likely have to do tomorrow. On a normal night, I'd leave the White House between 8:30 p.m. and 9:30 p.m., too late to see my kindergarten-aged children before they went to sleep. If I missed my kids for three or four days in a row, I'd pick a day when the president was traveling and no briefing was scheduled (often on days when a foreign leader was visiting) to break away and get home early. But there were times when I'd go an entire week without seeing them, even though I was in town.

Not surprisingly, I often had more "face time" with the president than with my family. Of the countless everyday exchanges I had with him, one stands out—the evening before the White House St. Patrick's Day Reception in March 2017. The tradition of a White House St. Patrick's Day celebration began under President Ronald Reagan and has been continued by every president since. In recent years, Ireland's prime minister, the Taoiseach, has made a point of making an official visit to the White House to join the event.

As I got ready to leave that night, I called the president at the residence.

"Sir, just a reminder about the St. Patrick's Day event tomorrow—do you have a green tie?"

"Yeah! Of course I have a green tie," President Trump said.

"For tomorrow?"

A long pause.

"Well, I have one in New York, but I don't have one here."

"I've got an extra green tie. Would you like me to bring it in?"

"Thanks, sure, but let me see what I can do. It'd be great to have a backup in case I can't find one. Let's touch base in the morning."

I'm thinking to myself, *It's 8:00 p.m., and you are the president. Unless you're going to dispatch the military to get your green tie, it is not going to get to the White House by tomorrow.*

The next morning, I put on a green tie with my suit and packed a second green tie in my bag to take to work with me. First thing that day, I delivered the green tie to the Oval Office and set it on the Resolute desk. The eighth-grade boy in me had to pause for a moment and marvel at the fact that a kid from Rhode Island, who as a student had never seen the inside of the White House, was now making sure that the leader of the free world had the right tie to wear. The billionaire president wore my green tie that entire day, including to the events with the Taoiseach. He must have liked it because I've never seen that tie again.

■   ■   ■

One of the central pledges of the administration was to control the nation's borders. As with all his campaign pledges, Donald Trump worked hard to see it fulfilled, beginning with more aggressive enforcement of immigration law. The 2015 killing of Kathryn Steinle on a San Francisco pier at the hands of an illegal alien who had already been deported five times was still fresh in the president's mind. Angered by this and other preventable crimes, the president became especially aggressive in deporting illegals with criminal records. In the first months of his administration, illegal immigration declined, and the nation saw a 53 percent drop in arrests along the Southwest border, a direct result of the deterrent effect of enforcing laws already on the books.[1] The immigration issue turned in the president's favor, though, I think the media and the Democrats were—and are—slow to sense it.

The administration's redrafted order, which halted visitors from terror-ridden countries in order to give the United States time to develop better vetting procedures before issuing visas, continued to enjoy strong support from the American people. It became increasingly clear that while liberals and the media crowed at federal judges who had struck down previous versions, most Americans considered it a just and fair effort to protect our country.

As Donald Trump acted, the Democrats dug themselves into increasingly extreme positions on certain issues. One was the "sanctuary cities" debate in which municipalities alleged the right to nullify federal law and refused to deport illegal immigrants, including those with criminal histories. When Steinle's killer, Garcia Zarate, was found not guilty of murder after claiming he had just picked up a Sig Sauer handgun that had been left on Pier 14 and accidently fired it, liberals in San Francisco erupted in a Twitter storm of celebration.

The more the Democrats, especially in California, embraced open borders and nullification, the more popular the president's approach to immigration became. Today, in fact, some conservative local governments in California are rebelling against the state's sanctuary policies, calling them dangerous, if not illegal. We all want America to be that shining city on a hill. But most Americans understand that when we fail to enforce our immigration laws and lose control of our borders, and thereby our national security, we endanger one of Franklin Delano Roosevelt's Four Freedoms—the freedom from fear.

The Trump agenda continued to unfold in other ways. The announcement that the United States would withdraw from the Paris Agreement on climate change was universally panned by liberals but praised by the Trump base, especially in coal country in West Virginia and Ohio. Whether one agrees or disagrees with that action, it demonstrated an unprecedented resolve by a newly elected president to implement his campaign promises.

The president's decision to reverse the Obama administration's executive veto of the Keystone and Dakota Access pipelines—and the decision to build them with American-made steel—deepened Trump's connection to blue-collar voters. I couldn't help but think that if any other administration, especially a Democratic one, had lived up to its promises and solidified its hold on its base so soon, it would have sent the bards of the media into rhapsodies of praise.

Of all the high points I witnessed during my White House tenure, the highest was President Trump's address to the nation before a joint session of Congress. Stephen Miller was the chief architect of that speech, but it was very much a team effort. Everyone reviewed Stephen's draft, including staff from the Office of Legislative Affairs, the National Security Council, and other key parts of the administration. And we had a brainstorming session about who should sit as guests in the First Lady's box, to be acknowledged by the president and incorporated into his speech.

I felt particularly proud to have suggested an early line in the speech that set the bipartisan tone of the evening. But the real game changer was the president himself who took his pen to Stephen's first draft, rewrote sentences, revised word choices, and inserted new lines and paragraphs.

Reince, Steve Bannon, Jared, Dina Powell, Hope Hicks, Kellyanne, and I sat with the president in the Map Room on the first floor of the residence and further refined the speech. As the president practiced reading the speech on a teleprompter, he made further edits, and I went to work confirming that we had every fact in the speech nailed down, that we were ready to support each theme the president touched on, and that we had an army of surrogates ready to hit the air the minute the president finished.

After the speech, as Trump strode off the floor of the House of Representatives, I walked behind him and followed the president into a hold room that was just off the House floor, accompanied by the vice president and other senior staff. Our mood after the address was even more jubilant than what we felt at the inauguration. It felt like hitting a home run on your birthday and winning the lottery at the same time. I had not seen that many happy faces and high fives since election night. President Trump had done well—and so had our entire team. We shared in the glory.

Everyone—from the mainstream media, to Democrats, and even to Never-Trump Republicans—agreed that the president had done a fantastic job, his delivery and tone were perfect, and his remarks on policy were well thought-out and well stated.

We motorcaded back to the White House, and a small group of us went into the living room in the residence with the president and First Lady to absorb America's reaction while pilfering cookies and Diet Coke. Looking back, I think it was the best night we had—and the praise continued for days.

"Trump delivered a grand slam…" the *New York Post* enthused. "[T]he best speech of his life and the most remarkable speech in decades by a chief executive to a joint session of Congress."

"Trump's best day in the White House," declared the *Arizona Republic*. "This man looked presidential."

"[S]truck an inspiring, even bipartisan tone," said the *Minneapolis Star Tribune*.

The president's "style is direct and not eloquent," observed the *Toledo Blade*. "But it is sincere and powerful."

"If I am the Trump team, I am very happy with this speech," said Obama's top strategist, David Axelrod.

"That moment (with Carryn Owens) was one of the most extraordinary moments we have ever seen in American politics," exclaimed former Obama official Van Jones.

■   ■   ■

Media around the country was ready to give Trump his due. But not the White House press corps. This had been true from the beginning—not just of his presidency but of his campaign.

Maggie Haberman of the *New York Times* had been offered an exclusive on Donald Trump's announcement that he would run for president, but she took a pass because she didn't think he was credible.

When Katy Tur, a correspondent for NBC News, was asked by her editors to leave London and return to the United States to cover Trump, she reported in her book that she was told it would only be for awhile—the Trump candidacy was not serious.

Whether you support him or not, it's important to understand the persistent barriers Trump has faced time and again—and surmounted, time and again.

First, he was told by reporters, pundits, and many establishment political types that he would never really run for president—he was just looking for publicity. Then he announced he was running—seriously, more seriously than the press ever understood. Then the narrative was that he would never file a financial disclosure form, which is a presidential candidate requirement. And then he did. Then he was told he would be crushed by the strong Republican field in the early primaries and caucuses. Instead, he kept winning. Then his doubters insisted that, despite these surprising victories, he would never be the Republican nominee. When they were proved wrong on that point, they remained absolutely certain that the Clinton political machine and Hillary's massive campaign apparatus would destroy him. All the way to election night, the media and so-called experts said Donald Trump had no path to victory; there was no way he could win enough states to reach the required 270 electoral votes. Yet he managed to win 306 electoral votes.

Trump repeatedly proved his critics embarrassingly wrong, but they never gave him credit for it and never stopped criticizing him. Such an endless negative headwind would take its toll on anyone.

Still, at every point, Donald Trump overcame the relentless negativity. I understand that many people, and most reporters and commentators, don't like him or his policies, but objectively Trump has never received anywhere near the appropriate credit from the mainstream media for his successes. This refusal to report good news about the president is bad for the media's credibility and certainly bad for their relationship with Donald Trump. He knows—and we certainly experienced this—that many in the media will find a negative angle to every story involving him no matter how positive it might otherwise be. And maybe worse, the media are happy to act as an unofficial adjunct to the Democratic National Committee. That's not just me saying that—the *New York Post* made essentially the same point while dissecting the reporting of the *New York Times*.

Get this from the "Gray Lady" (for younger readers, that is the *New York Times*): "Despite [President Trump's] lament that he was handed 'a mess'…Trump inherited a low unemployment rate" and "a lack of international crises requiring immediate attention."

As the *New York Post* pointed out, this is a stunningly brash whitewash of the Obama administration, during which the share of the U.S. population that had given up even looking for work (and so doesn't count in the unemployment rate) reached historic highs during the most lackluster "recovery" in history.

But beyond that, when it came to a "lack of international crises": "The Times' reporters (and editors and fact-checkers) somehow forgot Syria, where nearly a half-million have been killed and whose refugees are overwhelming nations across the region. And also ISIS [later to be evicted from their 'caliphate' by Donald Trump], North Korea, Iran, China—and Russia, which the Times now deems quite the threat."[2]

The negativity began to influence the coverage of Mika Brzezinski and Joe Scarborough of MSNBC, who were former friends of Donald Trump. They were critical of many things then candidate Trump had proposed and said—but they had given him a lot of coverage and airtime, leading some to imagine they were almost Trump boosters in his early phase. Once Trump was in office, however, Mika accused the president of "lying every day and destroying the country."[3] When they criticized the president's tweets and orders on travel, Trump, who as a candidate had gone out of his way to accommodate their media requests and who regarded them as genuine friends, was hurt and angry by what he regarded as a betrayal.

As Mika and Joe displayed tidbits of inside information, they seemed to the president to be sanctimonious in their conviction that they had full situational awareness of what was happening inside the White House, who was doing what, and what the best solutions were. It sounded to the president as if Mika and Joe kept implying, "If you listened to us, you would be perfect."

Too many media outlets have adopted, consciously or not, the click-based media attitude that it is more important to be first than to be right. *Politico*, in my opinion, was the anchor that dragged down media standards and too often read like a tabloid. One of the worst examples was when *Politico* reporter Julia Ioffe tweeted, "Either Trump is f[***]ing his daughter or he's shirking nepotism laws. Which is worse?"

Ioffe was fired for that post. But given that it was her last day at *Politico*, the move wasn't exactly a managerial profile in courage. She was moving on to an even better job at *The Atlantic*. When I spoke with ex-*Politico* staffers, they told me that sensationalism and crudity were encouraged as a valued part of that newsroom's culture. I was on a train heading back to D.C. when I heard about Ioffe's tweet. I called her soon-to-be new boss at *The Atlantic*, Jeffrey Goldberg. We didn't know each other, but I said we could probably agree that that tweet was entirely unacceptable. To my surprise, Goldberg dismissed it as a mistake that had since been deleted. A mistake, I told him, is getting a fact wrong, misspelling a word, or mixing up two names. What she said, in the crudest terms, about the president and his daughter was, regardless of your politics, disgusting and despicable, and it raised serious questions about Ioffe's judgment. Jeffrey responded by saying, "Look, why don't we just move on; we can put this behind us." I told him, "There's no moving on. You don't get to make these kinds of comments, defend them, and then say, 'Hey, by the way, let's be buds.'" Unreal—*a mistake*. Her tweet was based on "reporting" that Mrs. Trump was not going to have a First Lady's office and, instead, Ivanka was taking over the East Wing and creating a First Family's office, all of which was incorrect information— and still no excuse.

Ioffe now frequently appears on CNN.

By contrast, months later, Goldberg hired a right-leaning (but Trump-hating) writer from *National Review*. Leftists immediately mounted a campaign to get the new writer fired and found a controversial, anti-abortion tweet in his past. Goldberg promptly fired him.

While I was often at odds with many reporters in the White House press corps, there were many straight-shooting, solid reporters. I did not always agree with their reporting, but generally, I thought, they tried to be objective. Jennifer Jacobs of Bloomberg, Jon Decker of Fox News Radio, Eamon Javers and Kayla Tausche of CNBC, David Brody of CBN, Steve Holland of Reuters, Margaret Brennan of CBS, John Gizzi of *Newsmax*, John Roberts of Fox News, Jonathan Swan of *Axios*, and Sarah Westwood and Gabby Morrongiello of the *Washington Examiner* were some I thought could be tough but fair. And here is one more: Maggie Haberman of the *New York Times*. It's no secret that I have had my issues with Maggie's reporting, and in many cases I believe rightly so. Over time, though, I have realized that while I might not always agree with her reporting—and for very valid reasons—she is a smart and tenacious reporter with good sources. I've also realized the importance of listening to each other. Over time—a therapist could have made a fortune from the amount—Maggie and I have learned how to hear *and* listen to each other, and we have built a more respect-ful relationship.

That list of reporters is hardly exhaustive, and it is important to note that many reporters are still committed to solid, old-school, shoe-leather journalism that focuses on facts and not conjecture. Interestingly, while a few of those reporters are from television, many that I mentioned aren't. I've noticed over time that there are two types of journalists—those who are curious, ask tough questions, take time to get the facts right, and love the thrill of writing a complete and interesting story and those who want to make a name for themselves and become famous (usually by appear-ing on TV).

One group that I find interesting is the self-appointed "fact checkers" of the *Washington Post* and other media outlets, who could learn a thing or two from their more careful brethren.

For example, when Vice President Pence said there are more Amer-icans at work today than ever before, the *Washington Post* "fact checker" Nicole Lewis took him to task for failing to note that the United States population has risen, swelling the numbers of those at work. The vice president was awarded three "Pinocchios" out of four for "significant factual error and/or obvious contradictions" when, in fact, what he had said was the plain truth, though Lewis made a fair point about context. When someone tells the truth and the *Washington Post* deems that person a three-Pinocchio liar, is that "fact checking" or partisan nitpicking?

After substantial criticism, a *Washington Post* editor added, "[T]he fact that Pence's remark elicited applause was a strong indication that it was misleading."[4] Really? Did the fact checkers rate President Obama's applause lines the same way? Actually, surprise, they didn't. David Har-sanyi at *The Federalist* noted this:

> Obama was constantly offering simplistic claims about the
> state of the economy. Without offering any context, the for-
> mer president would take credit for authoring the greatest
> economic recovery in history. While this statement was

technically true—certainly undeserving of three Pinocchios—
Obama also happened to have prevailed over the worst economic recovery in history, despite the fact that, historically
speaking, the worse the recession the stronger the recovery.
Not once that I can tell did the former president mention that
weak labor force participation rates helped bolster his impressive unemployment numbers.[5]

Or consider how AP fact checkers treated this statement from President Trump: "There has never been a presidency that's done so much in
such a short period of time." You could fairly criticize that statement as
political hyperbole (especially if you didn't like what the president was
doing). You could also defend it (given not just the president's flurry of
executive orders and the bills he had signed into law, but his ambitious
initiatives that were getting underway in various departments). But AP
fact checkers Jim Drinkard and Calvin Woodward made the following
response: "THE FACTS: Trump's first month has been consumed by a
series of missteps and firestorms and produced less legislation of sig-
nificance than Obama enacted during his first month."[6]

Is that a fact? Or is that an opinion? It is the latter if you regard the
signature acts of the administration's first month as irrelevant, which is
what these "fact checkers" did. In reality, most mainstream media fact
checkers are opinion checkers.

Early on, I realized there were no less than four things that distorted
the White House press corps' coverage of the Trump administration.
They are the following:

1. An unshakable focus on palace intrigue (who's up and
   who's down) over substantive stories—something I first
   encountered when Kaitlan Collins got attacked for asking
   a question about national security at a press conference
   with the president and the Canadian prime minister rather
   than asking a question about General Flynn. Because she
   failed to follow the media herd, she was attacked—and

since then has turned into one of the president's fiercest critics....and moved to CNN.

2. A desire to break a story rather than doing real reporting and journalism to get a story right.

3. The desire to use cameras to become a cable star by generating fake controversy and outrage. In this category, I put not only Jim Acosta but also April Ryan and Brian Karem. Both April and Brian (who is the freelance reporter for *Playboy*) are veterans of the briefing room. April and I had a very public back and forth about her shaking her head in response to an answer I was giving, and Brian had his moment in a similar circumstance when Sarah Huckabee Sanders was at the podium. After both instances, these veteran reporters were offered cable contracts on CNN. Let's be clear—they were offered TV contracts not because they broke a story or won an award based on great sources. They got these contracts for making a scene, for making themselves the story. Think about that for a second—is that what being a reporter is all about? I saw how reporters, who had been attending these briefings for years, were suddenly thrilled to be recognized on the street. But they weren't being recognized for their reporting; they were being noticed for their place in the briefing room.

4. And finally, a partisan, pack mentality. One that decides it is necessary to litigate everything Republicans say and do to the nth degree but has limited curiosity about the shortcomings and outright scandals of the Obama administration, Democrats, or the Left.

If you doubt this, imagine the media reaction if the Obama administration's IRS scandal—using the power of the audit to punish political enemies with willful lying to Congress and destruction of subpoenaed evidence—had occurred under the Trump administration. The media would have howled and demanded a special prosecutor. But during the

Obama administration, the importance of the investigation—and scandal—was downplayed by most members of the media.

If I was as wrong in my understanding of the electorate as the media has been, at some point I would ask myself whether I needed to find better sources. Instead, when confronted with political realities they don't like, many journalists seek the comfort and reassurance of the herd. And when they get it wrong, the herd closes ranks.

Pity the press secretary who broaches, ever so gently, such criticisms of the media. Those who do will immediately be told that they are a threat to the First Amendment. The media criticizes freely (as it should) and also freely questions motives (as it is allowed to under the First Amendment). But the media regards any questioning or examination of its own motives to be beyond question. In the minds of many in the press, the First Amendment is solely about them and their rights. In reality, it's about all of us and our ability to express ourselves. I believe that a free press is crucial to a robust democracy. But the same First Amendment that allows the media freedom to print or broadcast a story also affords me freedom to critique it, to state denials when they report something wrong, and to offer corrections when they make mistakes. We all know that freedoms come with limits and responsibilities and can have consequences and repercussions, which is why we have professional standards and why journalists should strive to be correct and open, like everyone else, to criticism.

In an attempt to get the media to focus on issues of substance rather than palace intrigue, our communications staff often tried to establish legislative themes. Every Monday morning, we dispatched talking points to House and Senate leaders and key staff members to coordinate the week's message. We had Energy Week, Workforce Week, and the like, but as Congressman Thomas Massie told *The Hill*, "It might as well be Easter Bunny Week" as far as the media is concerned.

Kellyanne once told ABC's *Good Morning America*, "Even when you look at the network coverage: in a five-week period between May and June, 353 minutes spent covering Russia, FBI, Comey—a totally fantastical, hypothetical charade. Less than a minute spent on tax reform, five minutes spent on jobs. I mean, this is the culture we live in now."[7]

Then there were random acts of sheer media meanness in the style of Julia Ioffe.

About Jared Kushner, Chris Matthews remarked, "So the son-in-law—you know, one good thing Mussolini did was execute his son-in-law."[8]

Reza Aslan, CNN's "religious scholar," tweeted, "Like a piece of s[**]t father, like a piece of s[**]t son."

No one went over the line, however, like Kathy Griffin, who posted the infamous photo of herself holding a realistic-looking bloodied head of Donald Trump, ISIS-style. Both Aslan and Griffin were let go by CNN and tried to position themselves as media martyrs. In each of these incidents of media meanness, the culprit usually, but not always, apologizes and moves on.

■   ▦   ■

The annual White House Correspondents' Association dinner used to be one of the prime events on Washington's spring social calendar. Every year, a comedian is chosen to rake over the incumbent president and other newsmakers, and reporters bring guests that include Hollywood stars, big money advertisers, and even fellow reporters.

Given the media's unprecedented hostility toward the president, there had been intense discussion among the senior staff about how we should handle the dinner. However, no one but the president could make the decision. When I asked him about it, President Trump said, "I really don't see any reason to go."

President Trump saw it the same way I did. To attend that dinner would be to submit to an evening-long public immolation, not really Trump's style. The president realized—correctly—that the evening was a chance for the liberal, elite media and their Hollywood friends to bash Republicans. So, I informed Jeff Mason—a reporter for Reuters and then the president of the White House Correspondents' Association—that the president would not be attending.

I told him I knew he wasn't going to like our decision. Then I explained that in recent years the event often went beyond ribbing to become downright mean, and we didn't see any reason to attend.

"Can you think it over?" Jeff asked. "Talk to the president?"

I promised I would give it a second attempt, but I knew the president was firm on this point. He saw no benefit in spending a night pretending everything was okay with a press that was at war with him. When I checked back with the president, he reaffirmed he was not going to attend and added that he didn't see any reason for the vice president or senior staff to go. I asked them, and they agreed—they stood with the president.

This was further bad news for Jeff Mason and the White House Correspondents' Association Board. I must admit that on a personal level, I was a little disappointed. I knew the president's decision was the right one, but this was my chance to sit at the head table. Small and petty, yes, but as a press secretary in Washington I had always looked at that table with fondness and admiration. However, I and all the other White House staffers knew that if we laughed at a harsh joke, the press would assume we were making fun of our boss; if we sat silent, they would accuse us of being humorless and unable to take a joke. I also felt bad for Jeff. He had waited a long time to become the group's president and had put a lot of time and effort into organizing the dinner where he would get to serve as master of ceremonies with the president of the United States at the head table. While not attending was the right call, I knew it was a major let down for him professionally.

So, we skipped the dinner, a culmination of a five-day Woodstock of the elites (with brunches, lunches, and cocktail parties) that raises some money for journalism scholarships. True to form, some in the media started to buy into the notion that by not going to a dinner, we were somehow assaulting the First Amendment. But attending a dinner of celebrities and advertisers is hardly the bellwether test of support for the First Amendment. There was no reason to validate the White House Correspondents' Association dinner when it had degenerated into an excuse for big media and Hollywood elites to bash Republicans.

With opposition from the media and much of the bureaucracy, Republicans fight against the odds in Washington. To succeed, it is essential to have a coherent message and strategy. Too often, we didn't.

This lack of strategic thinking became apparent at an early meeting to discuss the Republican answer to the Affordable Care Act, or Obamacare. I turned to Tom Price, then the secretary of Health and Human Services, and asked, "Who's with us on this? What outside groups?"

Secretary Price looked at me, a little surprised.

The secretary couldn't name a single ally.

I was so stunned that I asked the question again. No one? Secretary Price confessed that we had no alliance of political action groups, K Street allies, corporate groups, doctors, or trade associations to back our efforts.

"How are we ever going to be successful without having a comprehensive plan and allies?" I reminded him that Obama had lined up the big healthcare trade associations to support Obamacare. "That's how Washington works."

And in this instance, Washington didn't work. The failure of the administration and Republicans in Congress to replace Obamacare almost doomed the party, causing bitterness that would not fade until the success of tax reform later in the year and the clear revival of the economy.

Then there was the challenge of managing the message whenever the president himself set a new and often unexpected agenda for the day's news with a morning Twitter feed.

While Twitter, or some future platform like it, will certainly continue to be used by future presidents, I don't think you're going to see another politician rely upon it the way President Trump does. The president sees Twitter as a way for him to speak directly to the American people. The media has no choice but to report his tweets verbatim.

But there is often a cost attached to the president's early morning and late evening tweets.

In the warm afterglow of the president's address to a joint session of Congress, I left the White House thinking, "We're back. This is what a successful White House feels like."

But as Philip Rucker and Ashley Parker of the *Washington Post* pointed out, our plan to capitalize on the tailwinds of the president's speech by promoting new policy initiatives was sidelined by presidential tweets. The president was furious at harsh criticisms he was receiving from Joe Scarborough and Mika Brzezinski, who he thought were trying to curry favor with their MSNBC bosses and liberal media peers. He was dismayed by the fact that in person they had one persona and on-air quite another. He attacked "low I.Q. Crazy Mika" and "Psycho Joe" and criticized Mika Brzezinski's purported plastic surgery.[9]

In the face of these outbursts, the media often expected me to be an ombudsman if not an outright apologist for Donald Trump's tweets. I never did that. And I consider my stance on this to have been a matter of principle. The job of the press secretary is to communicate the thoughts and views of the president when he or she is unable to do so. It is not to interpret the president's thoughts and words. It is not to massage or tweak them. Sure, I made suggestions and gave my advice and counsel all the time, but in the end my job—and that of any spokesperson—was to accurately reflect the person I represented.

Unfortunately, that tweet gave every critic who had reluctantly praised the president's speech permission to return to form. Double-edged sword is an apt cliché for Donald Trump and Twitter. Sometimes he's cutting up the opposition and sometimes he's cutting up his own best messages.

■   ■   ■

The media insisted that the White House press and communications shop was more than a messenger for the president—we were a story. It was hard to find talented people who could, or wanted to, endure that spotlight. In my search for a communications director, I reached out to several people, including Brian Jones, who had worked on the Romney campaign. Brian's business was going well. He knew a White House job meant precious time away from his family, and he declined. He recommended one of his partners, Mike Dubke. I didn't know Mike well, but I was aware that he was regarded as a talented strategist and experienced campaign adviser.

I brought Mike into the West Wing to meet some of the senior staff and then to the Oval Office to meet the president. By chance, the president had just decided to hold a press conference within a few hours. Mike's interview soon turned into a press conference preparation session. But the two seemed to hit it off, and we offered Mike the job of communications director.

No sooner had we announced Mike's new role than he got caught in the Washington spin cycle. He had ownership in a media-buying company, Crossroads Media, which served American Crossroads, a super PAC affiliated with Karl Rove. Within days, the media had conflated these facts and were characterizing Mike as an acolyte of Karl Rove, the mastermind of the George W. Bush administration, whom many Trump supporters had issues with.

In fact, Mike only recalled briefly meeting Karl in passing at a baseball game.

Mike was a consummate professional, not a showboat. He was exactly what we needed—someone who checked his ego at the door, managed staff well, and could provide effective, long-range planning and coordination. And yet he became a story, especially in the alt-right blogosphere where it was reported that Trump had turned to Karl Rove's right-hand man for help. I found myself facing backlash from Reince and others about whether we had made the right decision. The attacks were especially intense from Breitbart, though Steve Bannon denied any involvement.

Within a few months, Mike Dubke resigned because the Office of Government Ethics required him to get rid off all the small business interests he had spent twenty-five years building up, making me, again, the acting communications director as well as press secretary.

As press secretary and (often) communications director, I had to work within a White House that was not exactly organized for message discipline. It was hard to keep everyone from freelancing because the senior staff was structured to operate as a warren of fiefdoms rather than one cohesive unit.

Within the White House, Steve Bannon had his own PR machine, which was run by Alexandra Preate and backed by Bannon's Brietbart News empire outside the White House. Jared had his own press person, and Kellyanne, of course, was an official surrogate but not technically a part of the communications operation. And finally, we had the ultimate press secretary—the president himself—who was often on the phone with journalists. His openness and candor was frequently rewarded with even more negative stories.

I was ultimately held accountable for messages coming out of the White House. I knew we couldn't have everyone devising their own media strategies, but, to an unfortunate degree, we did. I had run the communications of many organizations and could predict the results of having everyone talking from a different page—not exactly a recipe for an effective press operation, or an effective White House.

And yet, here we were.

In the spirit of St. Francis's famous serenity prayer, I had come to terms with the things I could not change in order to focus on the things I could. And if the efforts of others went wrong, it became easier for me to be at peace and say, "Well, I had nothing to do with *that*."

One more point about my former colleagues—there's an old saying that I use to describe relationships: "Friends vs. Roommates." You can work with colleagues, hang out with them, and regard them as friends while never wanting them as roommates. But working in the White House is different. Due to the nature of our jobs, we often spent eighteen hours a day together, six days a week. We were all roommates whether we liked it or not.

■　　　■　　　■

Meanwhile, the president remained concerned—that's a mild word for it—about the continuing information leaks, not just about his calls with foreign leaders, but also lower-level invasions of his privacy, like verbatim accounts of things he had said at dinners with friends.

Some senior staffers naively assumed that if there were press leaks, they must be coming from one of the forty people working in the press office. I'd occasionally ask reporters who was leaking to them, and they'd reply, "It's not your team." Meanwhile, pressure kept coming from above to plug the leaks. And there were a few times when I wondered about internal sources when I saw something embargoed or held by my office leak out, especially after leaks from a planning meeting with some of my staffers.

My communications staff was made of two distinct groups. One group was comprised of people I had worked with at the RNC, sometimes for years. The other group included Trump "loyalists" who had come from the campaign, though some of them had only worked there for a short while. There was some friction between the two groups. And where there is friction, there is the potential for someone to get even by leaking against a colleague.

As I tried to track leaks within my own staff, I came to learn something about the art of it. The smart leakers cover their tracks with burner phones. The less smart ones simply download data-driven voice apps that allow them to make calls from their smartphone, text, and then delete all evidence. The latter did not realize that when they did this, their whole email contact list received a notice about the downloaded app, including me.

After an early morning meeting with my team, I discovered that someone had leaked something. So, I worked with the Office of White House Counsel to plan an approach. I gathered twenty of the men and women who worked for me and gave them an impromptu pep talk about teamwork and trust.

"We've got to be able to work together," I said. "We've got to be able to trust each other."

So, I asked them to allow me or one of my deputies to look at their phones, whatever they were carrying on them, from personal phones to the iPhones issued by the White House. We looked for Confide,

WhatsApp, Signal, and other messaging apps that could potentially violate the Presidential Records Act.[10]

I should have known what would happen next. My effort to contain the leaks got leaked to the press. Within days, stories about me confiscating phones and snooping on employees were reported by *Politico* and became talk-fodder for cable news. I realized with a sinking feeling what would happen next.

Sure enough, the president called me in to explain why I had done this.

"Sean," he said, "what were you thinking?"

I tried to explain, but the president's stern expression of disapproval showed me he didn't buy it. He reprimanded me, not raising his voice but speaking like a disappointed parent.

I can only say in my defense that I was under relentless pressure to find leakers. I am not given to self-pity, but my team and I worked tirelessly to support the president's message. So, it was especially upsetting to read the numerous, anonymous leaks attacking our performance and undermining our efforts. I sometimes felt like a scuba diver, abandoned in the middle of the ocean, treading water. Of all my experiences with the president, that one was the worst.

※   ※   ※

As I struggled to keep my equilibrium, accusations of Russian meddling in the presidential election began to spill into discussions of domestic and foreign policy, especially into what the White House press corps loved to focus on—supposed scandal.

On February 14, 2017, the *New York Times* ran a front-page story:

> WASHINGTON — Phone records and intercepted calls show that members of Donald J. Trump's 2016 presidential campaign and other Trump associates had repeated contacts with senior Russian intelligence officials in the year before the election, according to four current and former American officials.[11]

I could, of course, name three of these current/former officials in my sleep. The implication was twofold: the Trump campaign was a Russian front organization and was working hand in glove with Russian intelligence to hack the Democratic National Committee and demoralize Clinton supporters with fake news. This ignited media speculation that the president was somehow indebted to Russia.

I knew that Donald Trump—the *real* Donald Trump—believed America's current state of affairs with Russia was an aberration, that we have many of the same foreign policy concerns, and that our countries should be natural allies against terrorism and the ISIS caliphate.

But when Vladimir Putin has acted against the world order, Trump has proven to be as tough as he needs to be. He was visibly proud of his ambassador to the United Nations, Nikki Haley, who faced the UN Security Council and strongly denounced the Russian occupation of Crimea. President Trump has twice ordered air strikes against Russia's ally Syria when the Syrians used chemical weapons against their own people. And he expelled sixty, Russian diplomat-spies after a Russian-linked nerve-gas attack on a former Russian agent and his daughter in England.

The deputy director of the FBI, Andrew McCabe, informed Reince that the *New York Times* story was "a bunch of bull." To knock down this story, which cited four unnamed current and former intelligence officials, I needed more than McCabe's assurance. So, I asked CIA Director Mike Pompeo and Senate Select Committee on Intelligence Chair Richard Burr to talk with reporters from the *Washington Post* and the *Wall Street Journal*.

I was asked about this in my February 27 press conference.

> Q: Sean, there's a report this morning that you reached out directly to CIA Director Pompeo. Did you directly contact Director Pompeo and ask him to knock down the *New York Times* story on the Russia connection?
> SPICER: …The FBI deputy director was at a meeting here at the White House that morning. After the meeting

concluded, he asked the chief of staff to stand back a second; he wanted to tell him that the report in the *New York Times* was "BS." For viewers at home, I think you can pretty much figure what that means, but I'll leave it at that....

Q: You don't think there's something strange about—something odd about the White House press secretary getting the CIA director on the phone to knock down a story about an investigation?

SPICER: ...Now, remember, this all started with the FBI coming to us, bringing to our attention, saying that the story in the *Times* was not accurate—in fact, it was BS—and all we did was simply say, that's great, could you tell other reporters the same thing you're telling us? And I would think that other reporters, yourself included, would think that that would be a helpful thing to get the story straight.

You would think.

But many in the media acted as if bringing the most authoritative people into the discussion was an imposition, not a benefit; they did not appreciate it when high-ranking, well-informed officials defended the administration rather than leak against it.

The never-ending, always-changing Russia narrative began to reshape the administration. General H. R. McMaster was widely praised as a strong candidate to replace General Flynn as national security advisor. Unlike Flynn—a retired, three-star general—McMaster was an active-duty, three-star general who wore his uniform on alternating days. I found McMaster to be affable, kind, and personable but also—I say this as a Navy man—very Army.

That meant General McMaster described every decision-making process the Army way—with bulleted and sub-bulleted courses of action, each point lined up with its pros and cons. Many previous commanders in chief would have eaten that up. However, the linear McMaster style, accentuated with a PhD vocabulary, was not Donald Trump's style. He considers it a waste of time and doesn't want to discuss five different options and their corresponding pros and cons. He wants his advisers to come to him with their best assessments of what should be done and to defend, or modify if necessary, their advice after he questions them.

I knew from the outset that General McMaster, great man that he is, was likely not going to last long in that post.

Meanwhile, Attorney General Jeff Sessions was almost pulled into the same quicksand that had engulfed General Flynn. As a senator, Sessions had been a member of the Armed Services Committee. In his confirmation testimony before his then fellow senators, Sessions had answered a question from then Senator Al Franken affirming that he had not, as an adviser and supporter of the Trump campaign, had conversations with Russian officials about the 2016 election. Sessions had not mentioned that he had, as a United States senator, been visited by the Russian ambassador in his office with his staff present. The Democrats and the media were on a mad chase to convict Sessions of perjury, but as Sessions's spokeswoman pointed out:

> There was absolutely nothing misleading about his answer. He was asked during the hearing about communications between Russia and the Trump campaign—not about meetings he took as a senator and a member of the Armed Services Committee. Last year, the Senator had over 25 conversations with foreign ambassadors as a senior member of the Armed Services Committee, including the British, Korean, Japanese, Polish, Indian, Chinese, Canadian, Australian, German and Russian ambassadors.

On March 2, 2017, I took questions from the press about Sessions while aboard Air Force One.

> MR. SPICER: I know the Attorney General is going to speak very shortly, so let's just—I'll leave it at that. But I think

the president made his views clear with you guys just a short time ago.

Q: He doesn't have any concerns about whether he should have given a more clear response at the time?

MR. SPICER: Well, obviously—I mean, I'll let the Attorney General speak for himself. But I think that clearly if you listen to what he was responding to, he's clearly referring to his role as a campaign surrogate. That's what the question was about. And I think there's no—

Q: So, in that role as a campaign surrogate, does that mean, like, if he was asked at a campaign rally, he's a campaign surrogate? If he's at his office, he's a senator? Like, where does one role begin and the other one stop?

MR. SPICER: We're moments away from him addressing this. And it was really silly for me to try to talk about what he may or may not think. But I think most people—almost a clear—I don't think there's very few other ways to read it when you look at the transcript and see the back and forth that he was clearly referring to himself. He was very—he was clear in referring to himself as a campaign surrogate and believed that that's what the question was about. But I will let—I mean, we're literally moments away from him addressing this, and I think the president made his view clear.

Q: Sean, I had a big question of what he told the Senate. Is the White House annoyed that he wasn't completely forthcoming with you guys?

MR. SPICER: Forthcoming about what? I mean, he's a United States—

Q: (Inaudible) with the Russian ambassador.

MR. SPICER: Wait, hold on, he's a United States senator who speaks to countless—I mean, that's—I mean, he was a campaign surrogate and gave the candidate at that time some ideas and advice in very important—he had the value— the president values his opinion tremendously, as you can tell by the fact that he wanted him in his cabinet…I'm going to let the Attorney General speak for himself, but the bottom line is, is that for six months now we've heard the same thing over and over again, unnamed sources talking about nebulous, unnamed things, and keep having to say the same thing. At some point, you have to ask yourself where the "there" is.

In the end, Sessions stared down the effort by Democrats to portray him as a perjurer. In fact, it was Senator Claire McCaskill of Missouri who inadvertently came to the attorney general's rescue with a perfect illustration of the frailty of human memory. She tweeted, "I've been on the Armed Service Com[mittee] for 10 years. No call or meeting w/ Russian ambassador. Ever. Ambassadors call members of Foreign Rel[ations] Com[mittee]."

Unfortunately for her and the Democrats' attempt to smear Sessions, this accusatory tweet had been written without reference to the senator's own Twitter feed. In 2013, she had tweeted, "Off to meeting w/Russian Ambassador. Upset about the arbitrary/cruel decision to end all US adoptions, even those in process." In 2015, she had tweeted, "Today calls with British, Russian, and German Ambassadors re: Iran deal."

The truth is that Washington officials, with their perjury traps and gotcha questions, take far too little stock of the deficiencies of human memory. It's easy to question motives, assume someone is lying, or try hiding something nefarious, especially when you don't like a politician or his policies, even when the reality is much more innocent and straightforward.

To pacify his critics, the attorney general recused himself from any investigations into Russian interference in the 2016 election. In May, in the face of a rising chorus of Democratic accusations of alleged "collusion" between the Trump campaign and the Russians, Deputy Attorney General Rod Rosenstein appointed former FBI Director Robert Mueller as the special counsel in charge of investigating possible ties between the Russian government and the Trump campaign.

President Trump was quick to realize the magnitude of this threat, the origin of which he blamed on Jeff Sessions.

"Jeff Sessions takes the job, gets into the job, recuses himself," President Trump told the *New York Times*, "which frankly I think is very unfair to the president. How do you take a job and then recuse yourself? If he would have recused himself before the job, I would have said, 'Thanks, Jeff, but I'm not going to take you.'"[12]

The die was cast. The Trump administration was condemned to invest a lot of energy and attention into the investigation, distracting it from policymaking. Given the legal complexities and murky nature of the subject, I began to refer Russia questions to outside attorneys.

*   *   *

Among the press's many observations about the president is the criticism of his evangelical supporters for backing a man the press believes is lacking in Christian virtues. I think the press is wrong about that.

Once, during the transition, I attended a dinner in Bedminster, New Jersey, with the president-elect, the vice president-elect, and Reince Priebus.

"Let's all go to church tomorrow," Donald Trump declared around 10:00 p.m. It would be an OTR (an unscheduled, off-the-record movement) to a small Presbyterian church a mile or two away.

Donald Trump looked to Mike Pence, an evangelical, and Reince, who both nodded in the affirmative.

All eyes were on me.

"Thank you for the kind offer, Mr. President-elect, but I am going to Mass tomorrow."

"It's all church, so let's go together," the president-elect said.

Mike Pence, who had been raised Catholic, intervened to explain that Catholics go to Mass, not church. I didn't mind going to a Protestant service, but I didn't want to miss Sunday Mass—something I tried not to miss any week during the campaign or while I was at the White House.

Then I realized something—the president-elect was a little crestfallen. He had seen our whole excursion as a brotherly moment, a sharing of the church experience. It made me feel bad to say no to him.

Donald Trump may not quote scripture like an evangelical, but I know he is a man of Christian instincts and feeling. I saw this in his desire to share communion with me. I saw it in the way he interacted with the children of the late Navy SEAL William Ryan Owens. You see it in his compassion for the victims of opioid addiction. You see it in his support of victims of crime. It influences his economic policy, his concern for blue-collar workers, and his foreign policy—like when he responded forcibly to Syrian, chemical-weapons attacks on civilians.

Many people don't see—or want to see—that side of him, but I still see it from time to time when I visit the White House or see the president on television interacting with people from around the country.

That's the Donald Trump I know.

CHAPTER NINE

MEMORABLE MOMENTS, MEMES, AND MISTAKES

Since leaving the White House, I am often asked what I remember most about the experience. I put my memories into three categories: moments, memes, and mistakes.

There are moments I will cherish forever: events where I saw history being made and encounters with luminaries and officials I was honored to meet. Then there are the memes and mistakes—those times when I became a story, sometimes as a result of my own actions and sometimes as a result of the media creating a meme.

On April 6, 2017, President Trump flew to his Florida resort, Mar-a-Lago, to hold his first high-stakes summit meeting with a foreign counterpart, Xi Jinping, the most powerful leader of the People's Republic of China since Mao Zedong.

While the two leaders began to get to know one another that afternoon, I strolled through the Spanish-Moorish archways and sumptuous rooms of the great estate, which was built by Marjorie Merriweather Post in the 1920s. I walked out to the pool through an underground walkway that goes under the road seperating the estate from the beachfront. I stopped and stared at the Atlantic Ocean, wishing for an instant that I could jump in and relax. But there was no time to for that. I turned around, went inside, and got back to work.

Earlier that day in the White House and on Air Force One's television screens, President Trump had seen, and been deeply affected by, the heart-wrenching images of dying children, victims of a poison-gas attack launched by the Syrian regime of Bashar al-Assad against the city of Khan Sheikhoun. In terms of foreign policy, the attack was interpreted as a gesture of defiance against the United States and a test of the new administration. The president acknowledged that, but he viewed it even more as an outrage against human rights and innocent children.

On the flight down to Florida, reporters were inquiring about rumored retaliatory strikes. As the day wore on in Florida, I grew convinced that something was about to happen. That evening, at Mar-a-Lago, I was summoned to a Sensitive Compartmented Information Facility (SCIF)—an enclosed area where classified information can be freely discussed without fear of eavesdropping, electronic or otherwise. Surrounding the president were Reince, Lieutenant General McMaster, Deputy National Security Advisor Dina Powell, Secretary of State Rex Tillerson, Chief Economic Advisor Gary Cohn, Treasury Secretary Steve Mnuchin, Commerce Secretary Wilbur Ross, Deputy Chief of Staff for Operations Joe Hagin, National Security Council spokesman Michael Anton, Stephen Miller, Steve Bannon, Jared Kushner, and military aide Major Wes Spurlock.

Defense Secretary Mattis joined us by video.

The president had ordered a secret air strike earlier in the day—fifty-nine Tomahawk cruise missiles against Syria's Shayrat Airbase—and now we were gathered to review footage of the strike. Secretary Mattis provided a preliminary assessment of the mission and a timeline for when we would know more.

The president led the discussion with Secretary Mattis. Early indications were that the raid had been a tremendous success, destroying perhaps twenty Syrian aircraft, inflicting severe damage to hangars and smashing military support facilities—everything from supply depots to air defenses.

We were focused on Syria, but there was other big news developing. That same day, we received word that the U.S. Senate had confirmed Neil Gorsuch, President Trump's nominee for the vacancy on the U.S. Supreme Court. The president beamed at the news of the confirmation. He had promised to appoint a conservative to fill the "Scalia seat" on the court, and he had succeeded.

That evening, the president dined with President Xi. At the end of dinner, over chocolate cake, the president informed the Chinese president of the strikes.

■   ■   ■

I've had many roles as a communication director or press secretary in my career, and I have helped countless candidates, party officials, and elected officials undergo media training.

Media training isn't as formal as it sounds. It's basically teaching people how to prepare for an interview, especially on camera. The trainee sits in a chair in front of a camera while a staffer asks practice questions. And there are some basic rules. If you're preparing for an in-studio interview, you look at the interviewer, not the camera; if your interview is in a remote studio, you look directly at the camera. Don't move your hands too much. Don't repeat a question. Don't validate a premise with which you disagree. And the number one rule I gave every Republican was don't ever, ever talk about rape or compare anything or anyone to Hitler or the Holocaust.

Ever.

I can't tell you how many times I've repeated these rules to everyone from candidates to state party chairmen. But on April 11, 2017, I violated my own number one rule, setting off another controversy from the White House podium.

Earlier, I had been part of a small, impromptu briefing in the dining room off the Oval Office where Secretary Mattis had explained to the president the degree of the current atrocities committed by Syria's leader, Bashar al-Assad. He noted that not even Adolf Hitler had dared to use chemical weapons on the battlefield (note the word "battlefield"). I left the meeting wanting to make sure that the horror of Assad's actions was fully communicated. I wanted everyone to understand just how evil Assad is and why the president had acted so swiftly.

When I went into the briefing room to begin the daily briefing, echoes of Mattis's words were still with me.

The briefing started with a reflection on a tragic shooting in San Bernardino, California, and a readout of a meeting the president had had with private sector CEOs on modernizing the government. Then I opened up the briefing for questions. Eleven of the first fifteen questions focused on Syria. The video showing the pain and suffering of the Syrian people that had gone viral was clearly on the minds of the reporters. I was doing well, talking about the president's reaction and concern. But then came the sixteenth question.

"The alliance between Russia and Syria is a strong one; it goes back decades. President Putin has supplied personnel. He's supplied military equipment to the Assad government. What makes you think that at this point he's going to pull back in his support for President Assad and for the Syrian government right now?"

I thought to myself, "I got this." I had been in a groove expressing the president's concern and Assad's horrific actions. But instead of staying on the messages that had been working just fine, I tried to turn it up a notch:

> I think a couple things. You look—we didn't use chemical weapons in World War II. You had someone as despicable as Hitler who didn't even sink to using chemical weapons. So, you have to, if you're Russia, ask yourself is this a country that you and a regime that you want to align yourself with? You have previously signed on to international agreements rightfully acknowledging that the use of chemical weapons should be out of bounds by every country. To not stand up to not only Assad, but your own word, should be troubling.

Russia put their name on the line. So, it's not a question of how long that alliance has lasted, but at what point do they recognize that they are now getting on the wrong side of history in a really bad way really quickly.

And again, look at the countries that are standing with them: Iran, Syria, North Korea. This is not a team you want to be on. And I think that Russia has to recognize that while they may have had an alliance with them, that the lines that have been crossed are one that no country should ever want to see another country cross.

That was it—like the previous eleven questions on the subject, I thought I had sufficiently described the outrage we had toward both Assad and Russia. The questions in the briefing room are asked at the speed of light. I would answer one question while anticipating the next one. In my mind, I thought I had answered the question, but clearly what had come out of my mouth was not the full explanation that I had envisioned saying. I kept going, oblivious to the damage I had done.

The next question was about the president's tax returns. Then came a question about the Easter Egg Roll. My corny response about it being "egg-cellent" evoked laughter from the briefing room. That was followed by a question on the White House visitor logs. After that, more questions focused on Syria and North Korea, and a question was asked about taxes and infrastructure. At this point, I thought I was doing great. Nothing seemed out of the ordinary because of the pace and intensity of the briefings.

Then I called on ABC News's Cecilia Vega.

"Sean, thanks. I just want to give you an opportunity to clarify something you said that seems to be gaining some traction right now."

What now?

Then she started reading from her phone.

"'Hitler didn't even sink to the level of using chemical weapons.' What did you mean by that?"

What? Frantically, I'm thinking, "What did I do?"

I responded, "I think when you come to sarin gas, there was no—he was not using the gas on his own people the same way that Assad is doing, I mean, there was clearly—I understand your point, thank you."

Cecilia then tried to throw me lifeline number two, which I failed to grab.

She said, "I'm just getting—" but I cut her off and stepped in it deeper and deeper.

"Thank you, I appreciate that," I said. "There was not—he brought them into the Holocaust center, I understand that. But I'm saying in the way that Assad used them, where he went into towns, dropped them down to innocent—into the middle of towns. It was brought—so the use of it—I appreciate the clarification there. That was not the intent."

What had I done. Holocaust centers?

And I didn't realize until later that I had inadvertently omitted General Mattis's important phrase "on the battlefield."

Hitler, of course, *had* used chemical weapons to murder Jews and other victims during the Holocaust.

I read the body language of not only the reporters but also my own staffers along the side of the room. I was beginning to realize I had misspoken badly.

The instincts that kick in behind that podium are similar, I imagine, to those of a quarterback facing a blitz—just get rid of the ball and don't get knocked down. But after a bad play, a quarterback can call a time out and get his thoughts together and confer with his team. A press secretary behind the podium doesn't have any time outs to call.

In the heat of the moment, I still hadn't realized what I had said wrong. I was so fully focused on condemning Assad that I failed to see how badly I had stumbled by omitting that phrase, "on the battlefield."

By this point, I was feeling flustered, still not fully understanding what had just happened. My remarks were not quite right, and I had the alarming sense that I was digging myself into a deeper hole with each word.

This may have been the lowest moment I had in the White House. I alone had fumbled; no one else had made me do it.

The irony is that this was a question that I had been waiting for, that I had been prepared to answer. And I had been given two chances to clarify the record.

After the briefing, I went to my staff. I knew it was bad, but I still asked, how deep am I? Sarah Huckabee Sanders, Natalie Strom, and Raj Shah gave me a look that said, "Deeper than the Titanic." Then I noticed the calendar on my computer. It read, "First day of Passover."

Reince came into my office.

"Remember the first thing you taught me in media training?" he asked.

"Yes," I said sheepishly. *Never compare anyone to Hitler.*

I made a mistake, a big one, and I needed to say so.

I went to the Oval Office to see the president.

"Mr. President, I need you to know that I just stepped in it really badly, and I screwed up."

"I saw it. But I know what you meant, Sean. It's going to be okay."

"Thank you, sir, but I think I've embarrassed you and the administration and insulted the Jewish people. I need to make it right."

"Look, Sean, you screwed up, but I know what you meant. You clearly didn't mean…" He trailed off. When he spoke again, his tone was gentle. At a moment when I felt my worst, he tried to reassure me and was gracious, caring, and forgiving. Finally, he said, "Do what you think is right."

I felt like I had a fever that was going to get worse before it broke. And despite the president's support, I was again wondering if this was my last day at the White House.

I asked Natalie, who is Jewish, how the story was playing. Natalie is as loyal as they come, but she had to confess it was getting much worse. Many people echoed the president, telling me they "knew what I meant," but millions of other people did not and were deeply offended.

In this moment, I knew I had three choices: one, do nothing and hope it blew over; two, look for a friendly interviewer or reporter and try to put my spin on the story; or three, find the most challenging interviewer I could, own the mistake, and ask for forgiveness. I chose number three.

I asked my team to check which news shows I could get on ASAP. They came back with several options, including appearing on CNN with Wolf Blitzer at 5:00 p.m. I knew from the outset that it wouldn't be an easy interview. Wolf always asks tough questions. And he is the son of two Holocaust survivors.

"I was obviously trying to make a point about the heinous acts that Assad had made against his own people last week, using chemical weapons and gas," I told Wolf. "Frankly, I mistakenly used an inappropriate and insensitive reference to the Holocaust, for which, frankly, there is no comparison. And for that I apologize."

Many public apologies aren't really apologies at all. To say, "I am sorry to those who took offense at my comments," isn't an apology. Either you are sorry or you aren't. I wanted to make it clear that I was sorry—that I had said something I hadn't meant to say and truly regretted it.

Wolf kept boring down on me. Wasn't I aware that in addition to the Jews, others had been victims of Hitler's poison-gas chambers?

Of course, I told him.

"Have you spoken to President Trump about your blunder today?" Wolf asked.

"Obviously, it was my blunder," I said.[1]

To think that I had offended people—especially those whose families had been victims of the Holocaust—twisted my stomach in a way I had never felt before and hope to never feel again. I had created this mess. I had embarrassed myself, my team, and the president.

House Minority Leader Nancy Pelosi, other Democrats, and even a Republican congressman from Colorado were soon calling for my resignation.

That evening, I was as down as I ever was. Some people can shrug off bad moments, but I have a hard time forgiving myself when I make a mistake, especially when I hurt others. It grates on me. Fortunately, Rebecca and the kids were waiting for me at home, and that made all the difference.

Marlin Fitzwater, who had served in both the Reagan and the George H. W. Bush communications shops, wrote me early in my days at the

White House with a bit of sage advice: "You don't have to explain what you don't say." His words would have served me well on that day.

■   ■   ■

A few days later, the job became a little more cheerful. I was in the middle of a briefing when the New England Patriots came to the White House to meet the president in celebration of that big, surprising Super Bowl win in Houston, Texas.

Andrew Giuliani, who worked in the Office of Public Liaison, was coordinating the team's visit and let them know the briefing was happening. We were well into the briefing when all of a sudden, Rob Gronkowski, the team's tight end and one of its biggest stars, opened a door leading into the briefing room and popped in.

"Need any help here?" he asked.

The briefing room erupted in laughter. I chuckled, paused to process what had just happened, and responded, "I got it. Thanks, man."

It was a much-needed laugh by everyone in that briefing room.

Later that day, some of the most popular Patriots came to my office to talk with my kids and meet my mother, brother, and sister. As a young boy, I had attended one game with my dad in the old Foxboro Stadium and sat on metal benches. They were most likely up in the "nosebleed" section. Now, here I was with the team in my office.

My kids had brought a "few" of their favorite Patriots items in hopes of getting them signed, including their team helmets and kid-sized Gronkowski jerseys. My daughter brought the pink Gronk jersey a friend had given her for her sixth birthday. The kids spread the items perfectly across my desk with black Sharpies strategically positioned close by. When the players arrived at my office, I asked Gronk if he would sign a few things for my kids, and he graciously responded by pulling up a chair and reaching for a Sharpie. As he sat down at my desk, he eyed a box of leftover chicken tenders my kids had left on a nearby table. He asked the kids, "Anyone know where I could get a chicken tender around here?" Right on cue, my son grabbed a chicken tender and handed it to Gronkowski. He devoured it and went on to sign every item sitting on my desk.

Later that day, my family had the privilege of attending a ceremony on the South Lawn that honored the Patriots' Super Bowl win. After the event, the president invited the entire team into the residence. I got a message that I had been called to the residence, too. Robert and Jonathan Kraft, the owners of the Patriots franchise, and head coach Bill Belichick wanted to see me before they departed from the White House. After finishing their visit in the presidential family's private quarters, they walked down the Grand Staircase to the State Floor with the team in tow. My family and I were standing in the Grand Foyer, at the base of the staircase, when we saw the president, Bob Kraft, and coach Belichick arrive. The coach had a Patriots helmet in his hand. He walked up to me and said, "We brought this for you. For what you deal with every day, you've earned this."

As my family departed the residence and headed back to the West Wing, my mother leaned over to me and said, "You know who would have loved this day?" Yes, we were thinking the same thing: my dad would have loved it. His family, the Patriots, the White House—what a combination. As he was getting ready to leave this earth, my dad asked me to take care of my mom. I remembered that—the last conversation I ever had with my father. Somehow, I knew he had been with us, sharing in the excitement of that special day.

■   ■   ■

April 27 was the annual Take Our Daughters and Sons to Work Day. We had identified that date as an opportunity to invite the children of the press corps to join their parents at work and go behind the scenes at the White House. We thought it would be a way to strengthen relationships with members of the media. Deputy Press Secretary Lindsay Walters spearheaded a fantastic event complete with commemorative media credentials for the children, a tour of the White House and the Eisenhower Executive Office Building, meetings with members of the administration, and a mock press briefing in which the kids could ask their own probing questions. Many of the children came well-prepared with substantive policy questions. They sat in the briefing room's blue chairs, and I stood at the podium providing answers. We had a lighthearted, fun exchange.

In the early afternoon, we took the children into the Rose Garden where the president and vice president greeted them. President Trump and Vice President Pence posed for pictures with the children and signed their media credentials.

Unfortunately, no good deed goes unpunished. In the middle of this children's event, the ABC News team whipped out a camera and took advantage of the situation, asking the president a series of questions.

When word got out that ABC had used the children's event to interview the president, I was suddenly on the wrong side of every other reporter. Why had I allowed ABC to have access that no other media outlet had? How could ABC get something they didn't have? Other outlets whose correspondents did not have children attending the event said it wasn't fair to them. Meanwhile, the president asked how this could have happened. I tried to explain to both the president and members of the press corps that it wasn't supposed to have happened; ABC's action had violated the spirit of what was supposed to be a friendly, off-the-record event, focused on the kids.

After the fact, ABC News tracked down Lindsay to ask for permission retroactively, but the damage had been done. Later, I called Jonathan Greenberger, ABC's Washington bureau chief, for an explanation. He offered no apologies and expressed no regret.

What had been meant as an olive branch to the press corps had been trampled on by ABC—and yet not a single person in the press corps or the White House Correspondents' Association criticized the network for its action.

■   ■   ■

Memes.

They can make us laugh, and we all share them. However, the longer I was behind the podium, the more convinced I became that there is something deeply dysfunctional in the way our culture uses memes to elevate tiny details into national moments of outrage or ridicule that push aside any deeper consideration about policy and simple fairness.

One internet meme featured spinach caught between my teeth while facing the press.

Another showed my flag pin upside down on my suit lapel—after it had slipped—during a briefing.

One (falsely) displayed me wearing different colored shoes. (I was wearing one brown shoe and one black medical boot.)

A story in *Politico* falsely claimed that I was "butt tweeting" from the @PressSec Twitter handle, however, *Politico* failed to realize that the "butt tweet" in question was actually from an unverified, fake account, @Press5sec.

Another story dug up a tweet about Dippin' Dots I had posted years earlier.

Mike Bender of the *Wall Street Journal* falsely accused me of taking a mini fridge from junior staffers.

And, of course, there were the constant stories about my habit of chewing Orbit cinnamon gum. (Admittedly, I chewed a lot of gum, but not quite to the level the memes suggested.)

Some memes were sweet. One, for example, captured a colorful, beaded bracelet that spelled out the word "DAD," which my son had made for me and which I often wore behind my watch. (Melissa McCarthy even wore one on SNL.)

Any person who stands in front of cameras day after day is going to have some detail, quirk, or imperfection that gets noticed and turned into a social media meme. It just comes with the territory. What bothered me, however, was how the memes made the briefings about me, not about the president and the administration's policies. Some memes overshadowed the news. And in meme-world, truth and fiction can get blurry.

Take @sean_spicier, a truly funny Twitter feed in which someone parodies not just me, but the Left, the Right, and everyone in between. For example, "Sean Spicier" tweeted, "Nothing at all to worry about, everyone! The people who said you can keep your doctor also say you can keep your guns."

Kurt Eichenwald, a *New York Times* writer turned author, took the bait, tweeting, "...and @seanspicer returns to hollow-headed, inflammatory fear mongering in his desperate attempt to seem enough of a propagandist to land a job at @FoxNews. Or anyplace where lies are cherished." Eichenwald got my handle right in his attack of me, but he didn't notice the difference. I may be Spicer, but I am not Spicier.

My alleged quote got a lot of online attention, thanks to Eichenwald's marketing, eliciting anger in the blogosphere and commentariat before a sheepish Eichenwald corrected it. But, like all good memes, the truth or correction will never get the attention that the original meme did.

And I was about to become the subject of the mother of all memes.

■   ■   ■

Around 4:00 p.m. on Tuesday, May 9, 2017, I was called into the Oval Office. Nothing unusual there—it happened about five times a day. Sarah Huckabee Sanders and I arrived to find Reince, Stephen Miller, and several attorneys from the Office of White House Counsel standing near the two couches and chairs in front of the fireplace.

"Hand Sean the copies," the president ordered.

One of the lawyers thrust copies of two letters at me. One was from Deputy Attorney General Rod Rosenstein to the president; the other was a terse missive from Attorney General Jeff Sessions to the president. Both laid out the case of why FBI Director James Comey should be relieved of his duties.

"We need to get this out," the president said.

The president's advisers wanted to slow this process, and I agreed. Before we went public with this news, congressional leaders needed to be briefed. Our communications needed to prepare statements and talking points. We needed to line up allies to support us, and they needed to know our rationale.

And, of course, James Comey needed to be notified privately that he was out of a job.

The president acknowledged each point but kept coming back to "We need to get this out."

I suggested that the president should at least call the Republican and Democratic leaders of the House and the Senate because I knew that one of the first questions I would get was whether the president had given a heads-up to Congress. I knew that, in addition to the decision itself, the story would also be about how we handled it. The president agreed to start making calls to the congressional leadership. Keith Schiller, the director of Oval Office Operations, was tasked with getting in a car and driving to FBI headquarters, a few blocks from the White House, to hand-deliver the letter that would fire Comey, who—as it turned out—was in California to give a speech for a diversity recruitment event.

The conversation turned entirely toward process and away from why this was being done. The "why" was in the letters from Rosenstein and Sessions I held in my hands. The Rosenstein letter took Comey to task for his handling of the Hillary Clinton email scandal:

> The director was wrong to usurp the Attorney General's authority on July 5, 2016, and announce his conclusion that the case should be closed without prosecution. It is not the function of the Director to make such an announcement. At most, the Director should have said the FBI had completed its investigation and presented its findings to federal prosecutors. The Director now defends his decision by asserting that he believed Attorney General Loretta Lynch had a conflict. But the FBI Director is never empowered to supplant federal prosecutors and assume command of the Justice Department.... On July 5, however, the Director announced his own conclusions about the nation's most sensitive criminal investigation, without the authorization of duly appointed Justice Department leaders.

Compounding the error, the Director ignored another longstanding principle: we do not hold press conferences to release derogatory information about the subject of a declined criminal investigation. Derogatory information sometimes is disclosed in the course of criminal investigations and prosecutions, but we never release it gratuitously. The Director laid out his version of the facts for the news media as if it were a closing argument, but without a trial. It is a textbook example of what federal prosecutors and agents are taught not to do.

"Let's go, let's go—let's get this done," the president said.

As Donald Trump spoke, Reince turned to me as if to intensify the command "Get it done now."

The decision was made; there was no second-guessing, no slowing this down.

I took the two letters to the lower press office, a very small workspace adjacent to the Press Briefing Room where the deputy press secretaries, the assistant press secretaries, and the press assistants work under several television screens turned to various news channels. (It's the room right behind the door where the press secretary enters the briefing room.)

Turning the two letters into attachable, digital documents would be relatively easy to do from a home computer. But it was not so easy to do in the federal government, especially in the White House.

One of the press assistants had to feed the two letters into a scanner and then send them to the government system, GovDelivery. The system had a maximum of one gigabyte of information that could be fed out as an attachment. When converted into PDFs, the DOJ letters were 1.01 gigabytes, one one-hundredth of a percent over the maximum allowed.

We tried feeding the documents through the system in hopes of getting the files under that limit, but the system continued to say they were too large. Meanwhile, my phone kept ringing. Reince was now telling me sternly, "Get it out now."

The letters finally went through GovDelivery.

The attorneys from the Office of White House Counsel had given me clear guidance on what to tell the press: this was a Department of Justice decision because the FBI director reports to the deputy attorney general, so the DOJ would take the lead on this—100 percent.

I composed a short blurb announcing the firing, attached the two documents, and hit the "send" button, igniting an instant wildfire that spread throughout the press, the networks, and the cable news stations. Within minutes, as the president flipped through the media coverage on television, he realized that the Comey firing was almost universally getting panned.

Democrats, Republicans, reporters, and pundits were all questioning why this decision was made. Even Comey's detractors wondered, why now?

I got a call from Reince.

"Where are our surrogates?"

I wanted to say, "Oh, you mean all the surrogates I lined up during the few minutes of heads-up time you all gave me? You mean those surrogates?" But I knew he was just reacting to all the negative coverage—the reaction was just rolling downhill, and I was the guy squarely at the bottom of the hill.

My team joined the Office of Legislative Affairs to call every Senate Republican to find out who was willing to go on a show that evening or the following morning.

As I could have predicted would happen after people have been taken by surprise, we got a universal, 100-percent "no" from Republican senators.

"Where are our people?" the president asked me over the phone. "What are we doing to get anyone out there?"

We were now calling friendly members of the House and all our top surrogates outside of Congress.

No one wanted to go on the record until he or she had time to evaluate the decision, and the few who were willing to appear on morning shows were turned down by show producers. Even the public affairs shop at the Department of Justice—which, according to the Office of White House Counsel, was responsible for talking to the press—was keeping the firing at arm's length. They said they had no plans to make anyone available to the press. What? They claimed it was a tradition that the deputy attorney general never does television. Tradition? Really? Didn't they get the memo that tradition was over and a fresh administration was creating new traditions?

One thing was clear to me: had the president fired Comey in January, he would have been universally applauded. The FBI director's bizarre handling of the Clinton email investigation was still a news story then, and the new administration would have been praised by some for cleaning house. But now everyone wanted to know about the timing and questioned what had happened to move Comey's firing to the forefront.

Our inability to answer those questions kept any potential ally from going on-air to offer support or an explanation for the firing.

The president wanted us to counter the media's criticism, so Kellyanne, Sarah, and I sat down and divvied up the networks. I took Fox Business, Kellyanne took CNN, and Sarah went to Fox News. Despite the Office of White House Counsel's advice about the Department of Justice taking the lead, we recognized that the president was right—the White House had to say something. We could not continue to be silent on such an important matter. The critics were on every show, and we had no one—zero, nada—representing the president's point of view.

Every night at 9:00 p.m., the Secret Service closed the door between the briefing room and the press staff offices. Reporters, now unable to access our offices, had gone outside to "Pebble Beach" on the northwest corner of the White House driveway. Pebble Beach is now a paved area that is shaded by green awnings, but years ago it was covered in pebbles. It is still a prime work area for reporters doing live reports and interviews for networks and cable news; most television news reporting from the White House takes place there.

I walked outside, stepped up to the lights, and did my part with Fox Business, doing an interview with Lou Dobbs. As I finished my interview, one of our press assistants, Janet Montesi, pointed to a huge gathering of reporters. I knew I had to say something to them.

"Tell them I'll be right there," I said.

I walked down a slate walkway to where the press corps had collected on the White House driveway, and I took a deep breath. For over ten minutes, I answered every question, hewing as closely to Rosenstein's memo as I possibly could.

Prior to beginning, I said to the reporters and their cameramen, "If you guys turn off your cameras, we can go into the Roosevelt Room, and I'll give an interview to anyone who wants one." I thought I was being "media friendly." They had waited patiently and were doing their jobs. It was my job to make sure the president's position was known. Since it was pitch dark, and we were standing in the middle of a driveway, I figured offering to bring all the camera crews into the Roosevelt Room, which had television lights, would make for a much better shot for their morning show reports.

We wanted to make sure that everyone got an equal chance to have his or her questions answered. And true to our word, every network got its time. I thought we had done our job the best we could, considering the circumstances.

I called the president to update him.

Some of the interviews I had done would be held for the morning news shows. As luck would have it, I was due to report to the Navy for my reserve duty the following day at the Pentagon. I called the president to remind him. "I just want to make sure that's okay, sir."

"Sarah will be here, right? She can handle it."

"Of course. She's ready to go."

"No problem. Fine."

The next morning, I dressed in my uniform and scanned the *Washington Post,* in which reporter Jenna Johnson wrote that I had been hiding in the bushes before briefing the reporters who had assembled by Pebble Beach.

There is a row of tall bushes on the perimeter between the slate path that leads to Pebble Beach and the driveway that goes to the West Wing of the White House. I was on the path the entire time, a very short path, maybe ten yards to the driveway. Not only had I never hidden from the press, I had gone out of my way to make myself available with a camera-friendly opportunity. A retrospective story about the Trump White House later included coverage of that night, showing very clearly where I was and where I wasn't.

The irony of Johnson's report is that I could have completed that first round of interviews, walked back into the White House, and called it a night. But I knew the press was frustrated and wanted more, and I was intent on answering the questions of reporters who had stayed late. My reward for trying to be helpful to the press was Jenna Johnson inventing a whole-cloth untruth of me hiding in the bushes.

It wasn't until the afternoon that I found time to get away from my desk at the Pentagon to deal with Scott Wilson, the *Washington Post* editor who had overseen Johnson's story. I told Scott it was not possible for me to have been in the bushes, and I sent him pictures of the event and area to prove it.

So, the *Washington Post* ultimately relented and issued an "update": "Spicer huddled with his staff among bushes near television sets on the White House grounds, not 'in the bushes,' as the story originally stated."

So, I was now "among bushes." I guess you take what you can get.

Does a guy looking to hide from the press go out on the White House driveway where the media gathers all the time? Several journalists, who were there, told me that what Johnson had done was wrong, but the meme had already been launched.

I asked Lynn Sweet, the bureau chief of the *Chicago Sun-Times*, what she saw that night and she responded, "I saw a press guy looking to deal with a press scrum. I'm not sure how this got turned into hiding. From what I saw, you weren't hiding from anybody. Even before this (the driveway), you were accommodating to the print press."

Of all the things to hit me on, the press picked the time I went out my way to be helpful, and it is now part of an indelible image of me. I could have given the scoop of the firing to a friendly outlet or let the letter stand or just let my comments on Lou Dobbs's show stand, but I didn't. I played it straight while Jenna Johnson clearly did not.

I tried as best I could to put in my Navy drill day. Unlike the old recruiting commercials, it's not always about a weekend a month and two weeks in the summer. In the modern-day reserves, many of us IMAs (Individual Mobilization Augmentees) are attached to an active-duty unit and come in on weekdays to fill in for someone on leave or to work on a special project; in essence, we are support staff for an active unit or command.

While I was sitting at my desk in the Pentagon, I heard that reporters were checking to confirm that I was really in the building and not off hiding somewhere.

By midday, Facebook and Twitter were full of images of my head popping out from behind bushes. Then came the late-night hosts with their jokes and skits. Once again, I had become a story.

It was easy for those pushing this meme to say that it was all in good fun. But most memes—and certainly this one—don't emerge from a spirit of fun. They emerge from a spirit of malice and a desire to wound.

While I was on duty at the Pentagon, Sarah had taken the podium with poise and confidence. By all accounts, she had done a strong job of fielding questions about the firing. The president was impressed. And, watching with one corner of my eye from my desk at the Pentagon, so was I.

Some in the media appeared to fault me for reporting for Navy duty during those three days. Rebecca, who had received her first paycheck from CNN years ago, was watching CNN in her office that day. The lower-third "Breaking News" banner on the screen wasn't about Comey. It was about me. "SPICER TO MISS PRESS BRIEFING DAY AFTER COMEY WAS FIRED," the banner read. And the commentary from the pundits matched the banner. "[Y]ou're a former White House correspondent, and so am I," Wolf Blitzer said to David Gregory on-air. "I think it's pretty extraordinary, though, for Sean Spicer to decide that he's going to go forward with his routine Naval Reserve duty over at the Pentagon, at a time like this, instead of stepping up and doing this major briefing." David Gregory responded to Blitzer, "But they don't have a real concern about being accountable and giving the press corps answers."

Two things stood out about that exchange. The first was Wolf saying that it was odd for me to fulfill my Navy duty and suggesting that I had not "stepped up." The second was David Gregory insinuating that the White House wasn't being "accountable" even though the rest of the press team had been accessible that day and Sarah had conducted a full, on-camera briefing from the podium.

In the span of twenty-four hours, I had gone from presenting the White House response to media questions and criticism about the FBI director's firing, to being pilloried by a false meme about hiding in bushes, to having reporters question my service to the Navy. That last part really got me angry.

Joining the Navy remains one of the greatest decisions of my life. I have had the honor of serving alongside some of the most talented, patriotic, and brave individuals I could ever hope to meet. Each of us decides how to serve and fulfill our duties as a citizen in our own way.

■   ■   ■

On May 11, while I was still on duty at the Pentagon, the president sat down for an interview with NBC's Lester Holt. It was recorded in the Cabinet Room and replayed on several NBC shows as well as other news outlets.

"I was going to fire Comey—my decision . . . I was going to fire regardless of [the] recommendations" of Deputy Attorney General Rod Rosenstein, Trump said.[2] The president also stated that Comey had to be fired because he was a "showboat" and a "grandstander"— observations that were well borne out by the behavior described in Rosenstein's letter.

I knew what Donald Trump was thinking: *Here I am, a president who has begun to dismantle the regulatory state, reshape the appellate bench to conservative principles, establish policies that favor economic growth, and reset international relationships to better serve the needs of this country—yet day in and day out, I have to deal with this other narrative on Russia.* I interpreted the interview as saying that Rod

Rosenstein's memo reaffirmed what the president had already been thinking—that America needed a new director of the FBI. But the media didn't see it that way.

The president was clear in the interview that he wanted any investigation into Russian interference in the election to be "absolutely done properly." He also understood that firing Comey would not end any investigation and might lengthen it. That wasn't the point. The president had decided to fire Comey, who, as director of the FBI, served at the pleasure of the president (as Comey conceded), and Rosenstein had valid reasons for recommending Comey's dismissal.

"Trump is putting a lot on the backs of his spokespeople, while simultaneously cutting their legs out from underneath them," Alex Conant, a former Marco Rubio adviser told Glenn Thrush and Maggie Haberman at the *New York Times*. Newt Gingrich added that the president "resembles a quarterback who doesn't call a huddle and gets ahead of his offensive line so nobody can block [for] him and defend him because nobody knows what the play is."[3]

Another curveball came our way when the president tweeted, "James Comey better hope that there are no 'tapes' of our conversations before he starts leaking to the press!"

For older Americans, talk of "tapes" brought back memories of Nixon and Watergate. The president later admitted that there had been no recordings made of his conversations with James Comey. So why this particular shot across the bow?

A sense of injustice over double standards has been a sore point for Republicans for years. For anyone who has dealt with classified information, the rules are clear. You may not reproduce or distribute classified information, period. To do so is to commit a serious crime. Hillary Clinton and her long-time aide, Huma Abedin, had copied classified information and stored it on unsecure servers. Abedin sent her classified information to her husband, Anthony Weiner—now imprisoned for illicit sexual communications with a minor—for him to store on his computer and print out for her.

Consider this exchange between Comey and Republican Senator John Kennedy of the Senate Committee on the Judiciary when the former was still director of the FBI:

> SEN. JOHN KENNEDY, R-LA: Morning, Mr. Director, I guess afternoon, now. I'll assume for second that I'm not a United States senator and that I don't have a security clearance to look at classified information. If someone sends me classified information, and I know or should know which classified information, and I read it, have I committed a crime?
>
> COMEY: Potentially.
>
> KENNEDY: Has the person who sent me the information committed a crime?
>
> COMEY: Potentially, if they knew you didn't have appropriate clearance and a need to know.
>
> KENNEDY: OK. Was there classified information on —on former Congressman Weiner's computer?
>
> COMEY: Yes.
>
> KENNEDY: Who sent it to him?
>
> COMEY: His then spouse, Huma Abedin, appears to have had a regular practice of forwarding e-mails to him, for him I think to print out for her so she could then deliver them to the Secretary of State.
>
> KENNEDY: Did Congress—former Congressman Weiner read the classified materials?
>
> COMEY: I don't—I don't think so. I think it is descriptive— I don't think we've been able to interview him because he has pending criminal problems of other sorts. But my understanding is that his role would be to print them out as a matter of convenience.
>
> KENNEDY: If he did read them, would he have committed a crime?

COMEY: Potentially.

KENNEDY: Would his spouse have committed a crime?

COMEY: Again, potentially, it would depend upon a number of things.

KENNEDY: Is there an investigation with respect to the two of them?

COMEY: There was, it is—we completed it.

KENNEDY: Why did you conclude neither of them committed a crime?

COMEY: Because with respect to Ms. Abedin in particular, we—we didn't have any indication that she had a sense that what she was doing was in violation of the law. Couldn't prove any sort of criminal intent. Really, the central problem we have with the whole e-mail investigation was proving that people knew—the secretary and others knew that they were doing—that they were communicating about classified information in a way that they shouldn't be and proving that they had some sense of their doing something unlawful. That was our burden and we weren't able to meet it.

So, James Comey investigated the importation of classified information onto Anthony Weiner's computer without interviewing either of the subjects. He then exonerated Huma Abedin (and, by association, Hillary Clinton) because "we didn't have any indication that she had a sense that what she was doing was in violation of the law."

Huma Abedin had been the deputy chief of staff at the State Department. She would have had clear instructions about the handling of classified material.

Now put the shoe on the other foot. Imagine if any one of us had illegally copied classified information and placed it on the computer of a sex offender. How many special prosecutors would that entail?

It is this kind of double standard that stokes Donald Trump's ire and erupts in his tweets and statements.

■   ■   ■

I also saw the media straining to read hidden meanings in even the most mundane observations. *Business Insider* ran a piece on Gary Cohn's salary that correctly reported the salary of the then director of the National Economic Council was $30,000 a year. In the White House pecking order, salaries—which are publicly reported—are usually clear markers, along with job titles, that signal where one stands in that order.

The story also noted that Steve Bannon and Kellyanne Conway each made $179,700 per year.

"It's unclear why Cohn's salary is lower than nearly every other employee on the White House payroll," the story noted.

The implication was that, judging by his salary, Gary Cohn's place in the White House pecking order was lower than most junior staff. The reason why this was unclear is that the reporter never bothered to ask me. Cohn, who had a salary and bonus at Goldman Sachs worth more than $7 million, asked for this reduced salary. It was understood by his peers that Cohn was acting out of sheer patriotism by asking to be paid $30,000. That was the lowest amount he could receive and still get benefits.

RawStory also published a piece about intrigue surrounding White House salaries. The premise of the story was the following: "Why does Steve Bannon make less per year than Omarosa?" The piece included a link to *Politico*'s list of White House staff salaries, which showed Steve Bannon's salary *was exactly the same* as Omarosa's salary.[4] The accurate list refuted the very premise of the story.

Rachel Maddow jumped into the money game when she promised to reveal on-air an illegally leaked copy of Donald Trump's 2005 tax return, which MSNBC had been hyping into a big "reveal" event. Like Geraldo Rivera when he opened Al Capone's vault on live television in 1986, Maddow attracted a huge audience. And like Rivera, she found nothing…except that in 2005 Donald Trump had paid $38 million in federal income taxes on about $150 million in income, a rate of about 25 percent.[5]

Or consider how the media spun the story when Democrat Jon Ossoff came close to beating Republican Karen Handel in a special election for a House seat in Georgia. The media treated the Democrats' loss as a win that discredited the administration. Hallie Jackson of NBC asked if the president was spending "too much political capital on a race Republicans should be winning easily."

"The Democrats went all in on this race," I told her. "They spent over 8.3 million dollars. They said on the record that their goal was to win this race. They lost, and the reaction has somewhat been that they *almost won*. No, they lost."[6]

■   ■   ■

As the relationship between the administration and the media grew more heated, the briefings began to feel less like press conferences and more like the British Parliament's Question Time where opposing members of Parliament make faces, bang desks, grumble, and loudly protest statements with which they disagree. Many in the media were creating an environment that felt like an opposition party, less interested in reporting the facts than in contesting our positions and trying to undermine and embarrass the administration at every turn.

This confrontational attitude began to infect almost all my interactions with the media, including with April Ryan of American Urban Radio Networks (AURN). April and I had initially gotten along well. AURN was one of the outlets I called on more often in my effort to broaden media access beyond the normal Beltway reporters. Things fell apart, however, in the March 28 briefing. My repeated "no's" are in response to her vigorously shaking her head in dissent.

> Q: ...[W]ith all of these investigations, questions of what is
> is, how does this administration try to revamp its image?
> Two and a half months in, you've got this Yates story

today; you've got other things going on. You've got Russia. You've got, you've got wiretapping. You've got—

MR. SPICER: No, we don't have that.

Q: There are investigations on Capitol Hill—

MR. SPICER: No, no—I get it. But you keep—I've said it from the day that I got here until whatever that there is no connection. You've got Russia. If the president puts Russian salad dressing on his salad tonight, somehow that's a Russian connection. But every single person—

Q: It's beyond that. You're making it—

MR. SPICER: Well, no—I appreciate your agenda here, but the reality is—

Q: It's not my agenda.

MR. SPICER: No, hold on. No. At some point, report the facts. The facts are that every single person who has been briefed on this subject has come away with the same conclusion. Republican, Democrat. So, I'm sorry that that disgusts you. You're shaking your head. I appreciate it, but—

Q: I'm shaking my head, and I'm listening. And I'm trying to get—

MR. SPICER: Okay, but understand this—that at some point, the facts are what they are. And every single person who has been briefed on this situation with respect to the situation with Russia—Republican, Democrat, Obama-appointee, career—have all come to the same conclusion. At some point, April, you're gonna have to take "no" for an answer with respect to whether or not there was collusion.

Q: How do you change the perception of—

MR. SPICER: We're going to keep doing everything we're doing to make sure that the president's—that what the president told the American people he was going to do—to fulfill those pledges and promises that he made, to bring back jobs, to grow the economy, to keep our nation safe—that's what he's been focused on since day one. We're going to keep focusing on that every single day.

Q: But when Condi Rice comes Friday. Condi Rice did not support this president. She did not go to the convention. She comes—what is on the agenda? And, and how is their relationship? Has it healed since 2006 when he used a very negative word to describe her?

MR. SPICER: So, here's what I'll you—it's interesting that you ask those two questions back-to-back. On the one hand, you're saying what are we doing to improve our image. And then here he is, once again, meeting somebody that hasn't been a big supporter of his. Hold on—

Q: But he called her that negative name in 2006.

MR. SPICER: No, no, but you—but, April, hold on. It seems like you're hell-bent on trying to make sure that whatever image you want to tell about this White House stays because at the end of the day—

Q: I am just reporting what—

MR. SPICER: Okay, but you know what? You're asking me a question, and I'm going to answer it, which is the president—I'm sorry, please stop shaking your head again. But at some point, the reality is that this president continues to reach out to individuals who've supported him, who didn't support him—Republicans, Democrats—to try to bring the country together and move forward on an agenda that's going to help every American. That's it, plain and simple.

Sarah Huckabee Sanders had her own moment when she took the lead for a briefing in June. She made an eloquent statement that a relentless focus on negativity caused the media to overlook stories that the American people want to hear.

Sarah said:

> I think that there are a lot of things happening in this world that,
> frankly, a lot of people would like to hear about—whether it's
> job growth, whether it's deregulation, whether it's tax reform,
> healthcare....All we are saying is, you know, I think that we
> should take a really good look at what we are focused on, what
> we are covering and making sure that it's actually accurate and
> it's honest. If we make the slightest mistake, the slightest word
> is off, it is just an absolute tirade from a lot of people in this room.

Exactly. While upholding the First Amendment right of journalists to question the administration, Sarah was upholding her own
First Amendment right to question the way journalists report the
news today.

Enter Brian Karem, the White House correspondent for *Playboy*—
apparently, it does have articles, and political ones at that. Sarah's opinion
left Karem so indignant that he shouted:

> You're inflaming everybody right here and right now with those
> words! This administration has done that as well. Why in the
> name of heavens—any one of us, right, are replaceable, and any
> one of us, if we don't get it right, the audience has the opportu-
> nity to turn the channel or not read us. You have been elected
> to serve for four years at least. There's no option other than that.
> We're here to ask you questions; you're here to provide the
> answers. And what you just did is inflammatory to people all
> over the country who look at it and say, see, once again, the
> president is right and everybody else out here is fake media. And
> everybody in this room is only trying to do their job.

Sarah responded, "Well, I just—I disagree completely. First of all,
I think if anything has been inflamed, it's the dishonesty that often
takes place by the news media. And I think it is outrageous for you to

accuse me of inflaming a story when I was simply trying to respond to his question."

Sarah and I were frustrated the briefings had turned into rituals in which reporters asked the same questions about Russia-related issues— over and over—knowing that they would get no different answers but upping the volume and emotion with each pass, realizing full well that their self-serving eruptions on camera ensured them eternal YouTube fame if not CNN contracts. Realizing the cameras were too much of a temptation for some reporters, I began expanding our off-camera briefings during the summer. I told the president I wanted to create a space for more thoughtful interaction between reporters and, often, the president himself. The media continued to rebel, sometimes in funny ways. (Acosta tweeted an image of his socks, and CNN engaged in a stunt by sending in a sketch artist to draw an image of me at the podium.) But the president supported me in doing what I had to do to try to improve our relationship with the press. Even after I relented to allow audio recordings of our off-camera briefings, the reaction among some in the media was fierce and predictable—that somehow the administration was trampling the First Amendment. But I received welcome support from former White House Press Secretaries Ari Fleischer (George W. Bush) and Mike McCurry (Bill Clinton), who both tweeted an interesting proposal: "We support no live TV coverage of WH briefing. Embargo it & let it be used, but not as live TV. Better for the public, the WH & the press."[7]

In a joint piece for the *Columbia Journalism Review*, the two former press secretaries elaborated on their proposal: "If the briefing is 'embargoed' until its conclusion, it will become just one of several raw ingredients that journalists can use to prepare their reports on the work of the president and the White House. It would instantly become a toned-down briefing, and reporters would use the information from the briefing and test it against other sources as they prepare coverage."

And here's the kicker: "It would not be a 'news event' in and of itself."[8]

Ari and Mike hit on exactly what was eating away at me—the briefing should convey news, and it shouldn't ever *be* the news.

The media, however, *wanted* the briefings to be news and sought out any possible misstep as a "gotcha" moment.

I knew my relationship with the press was radioactive, and I told the president and Reince that I would happily support the appointment of a new press secretary so that I could focus on being the director of communications, a post better suited to my disposition and talents. We approached a handful of people, but none of them were quite right.

■   ■   ■

The anger that was displayed in the media against the administration sometimes spilled over into personal attacks on me.

One spring day, I was browsing around an Apple Store when a woman started berating me: "How does it feel to work for a fascist? How does it feel?...Have you helped with the Russia stuff? Are you a criminal as well? Have you committed treason too just like the president?"[9]

In this case, I was a victim of an "activist" who had previously inflicted herself on Secretary of Education Betsy DeVos and who likes to broadcast her bizarre interactions on Twitter and Periscope. As *National Review* noted about this encounter, "It takes a true social-justice warrior to accuse Spicer [of] destroying the country, working for a fascist, and being involved in *treason*, and still have the nerve to call him a racist for smiling and affirming her right to harass him. But when you are sufficiently self-possessed, any encounter can make you a hero."[10]

That encounter happened on a Saturday that I'd spent mostly in the office. (My work-at-home day was Sunday.) Rebecca's birthday was coming up, and I wanted to swing by the Apple Store in Georgetown on my way to a 5:00 p.m. vigil Mass to buy her an Apple Watch. She had been almost single-handedly raising our children and running our household while balancing her own career; this would be one small gesture of appreciation for all she had done.

But when it all went viral, I had both the president and my wife asking me what I was doing in an Apple Store. For the president, it was one more example of his press secretary becoming a story. And regarding Rebecca, I had to hem and haw as I worked to keep her birthday gift a surprise.

People asked me all the time if I felt safe with my newfound notoriety. For the most part, I did because I arrived early and worked late in one of the most secure places on Earth, and I rarely ventured out during working hours.

What did concern me was the security of my family. We installed security cameras, got rid of all the shrubs around our house, had countless pieces of anonymous mail and packages screened, and got to know the amazing officers of the Alexandria Police Department on their frequent patrols.

One Sunday, our good friend John Sankovich had gone to our house to help set up some furniture (since I wasn't ever around to help with home projects). While he was there, a package arrived at our front door. As she was prone to do, Rebecca put on plastic gloves and a surgical mask, took the box outside, and then cut it open. "You just never know, and I'd rather be safe than sorry," she would say. John had to admit that she was being a bit too cautious. However, it turned out that there was a mysterious item in the box, and she notified the authorities. And that was just one example.

One afternoon, a neighbor contacted Rebecca to see if we were moving. When she inquired why, we found out that our house had been posted on the real estate websites Zillow and Trulia. That might sound funny at first, but the listing made defaming alterations to the picture of our house and to its written description. We learned that the real estate community takes such fraudulent posts very seriously, and a realtor— whom we did not know—filed a fraud report with the companies, which promptly took the postings down.

The day I resigned, quite a few TV trucks showed up on our quiet, narrow street. One news outlet—Reuters—put a camera in my front yard to live stream coverage of my house. I don't know what the news agency expected to see, as I was still at the White House that day, but it did get a riveting video of our neighbor's kid taking our aging, black Labrador, Bailey, for a walk.

Rebecca was particularly happy that she and our young children were nearly 2,000 miles away from the cameras, breathing in some mountain air and surrounded by incredibly supportive colleagues at a work meeting in Colorado, when she saw the Reuters alert on her phone.

My wife, a former news producer, was appalled by what a once-respected news organization was trying to promote as "news." She called a couple of our neighbors to warn them before they headed home, and she checked on others to make sure that they were able to access their homes and maintain their privacy. But in her call to me, she simply joked, "I hope Reuters enjoys watching the weeds growing in our front yard!"

Twitter didn't chuckle like Rebecca. Many Republicans and Democrats cried foul on the Reuters stunt. Even some members of the press thought this was going too far, which I appreciated.

"Whatta town," tweeted Maggie Haberman of the *New York Times*.

"...creepy live broadcast," tweeted Jim Geraghty of *National Review*.

"This is not newsworthy. Spicer is at the White House, not at home.... and he has young kids," tweeted Yashar Ali, a freelance reporter.

The attitude among some in the media that a public official's personal life, even family life, is fair game is a view that unfortunately discourages some good people from public service. When I asked Jeff Mason, the White House Reuters reporter who had been the president of the White House Correspondents' Association, if he thought Reuters's stakeout of my house was appropriate, he informed me that he did not speak for the company.

The outrage against Reuters mounted to such a point that the live feed was taken down later that day.

Although the TV trucks left late that night, some print reporters and still photographers were still around our house the next day. The following morning, when I walked out of the house to take Bailey around the block, the paparazzi snapped away. Bailey, sporting her pink collar, managed to look great in her debut. Unfortunately, the media couldn't even get my dog's name right. In a photo caption, she had been renamed "Billy."

■   ■   ■

One of the most memorable aspects of the job was being able fly around the world on Air Force One with the president. Representing the United States in another country is an honor.

In May, we set off for a week-long tour of four countries (five, counting Vatican City). Of course, it wasn't a vacation for me or the president; it was President Trump's first big foreign trip. Our first stop was Saudi Arabia where—again, as a witness to history—I watched the president close a $350 billion arms deal with King Salman, which could mean hundreds of thousands of jobs for Americans. The president also facilitated a number of other commercial deals for American businesses.

President Trump was obviously in his element, wheeling and dealing, while amid a degree of pageantry I doubt even he had seen before.

Every trip abroad presents challenges because of the many ground rules that have to be negotiated with foreign governments. So, throughout this time, I was busy overseeing the press arrangements and dealing with disappointed reporters who, for whatever reason, could not get into one function or another.

Our next stop was Israel. In between meetings with the prime minister and members of the Knesset, the presidential party walked through Jerusalem. I watched the president approach the Wailing Wall, close his eyes, pray, and slip a prayer note into a notch in the wall. The presidential party also walked to the Church of the Holy Sepulchre, ascending the very incline that Jesus had walked to his crucifixion and seeing what may well have been his tomb. I felt a profound peace while walking through that dark and holy place, just as I was greatly moved by our brief visit to Yad Vashem, The World Holocaust Remembrance Center.

A powerful memorial to the victims of the Holocaust, Yad Vashem is dedicated to preserving the memory of the Holocaust victims and honoring Jews who fought against the Nazis. It was a very somber place.

After reading the stories of the victims and learning more about that horrific chapter in our world's history, I walked out quiet, reflective, and contemplative.

But the press was always with us. Coming out of Yad Vashem, the Israeli press yelled at me, "Hey, Mr. Spicer, what did you think? What did you think?"

Hope Hicks, who was between me and the president, whispered, "Just keep going."

"I think I need to talk to them," I whispered back.

I walked over to the press and spoke about what a profound impact Yad Vashem had on me. It was my second visit, but this visit was even more powerful than the first. I told them simply that it's nearly impossible to process the magnitude and scope of the horrors of the Holocaust. And then I kept walking, in silence for the rest of the way to our vehicle.

※　　　※　　　※

Our next stop was Vatican City where the president was scheduled to have an audience with the Holy Father, Pope Francis.

I was one of many Catholics on the senior staff—including Hope Hicks, Dan Scavino, Keith Schiller, John McEntee, and Joe Hagin—who wanted to attend. But the night before the trip, I scanned the manifest and saw I wasn't listed for the papal audience.

"Listen, the Vatican doesn't fool around with this stuff," Joe Hagin, the deputy chief of staff and a veteran of two previous White Houses, told me. "If someone's not on the manifest, they are not on the manifest."

"Okay, Joe, but what if I travel with the motorcade to the Vatican and take my chances?"

Joe did not like that idea, but he didn't say no.

The next day, I walked from our hotel to the motorcade only to be told very firmly that this would not work. Cars carrying people not listed on the manifest would not get through the Vatican gates. Climbing into one of the limos would be a ride to nowhere.

I was disappointed; being part of an audience with the pope in the Vatican would have been an honor and a dream come true. But I had another idea.

The night before, I went to Dan Scavino, who was on the manifest. I handed him a bag of ten olive-wood rosaries that I had purchased in Jerusalem.

"Let me ask you a favor," I said. "It doesn't look like I'm going to get in. Will you please take these with you?"

I told Dan that my mother had asked me to buy her a new rosary in either the Holy Land or Rome. I thought it would be great to take the rosary back to her *and* to have it blessed by the pope. I knew that the pope would bless everything in the room, and, while I might not be able to meet him, this would be a great way to connect with the Holy Father.

During the papal audience, one of the monsignors asked Dan, "What's in the bag?"

"I've got some rosary beads."

"Well, why don't we put them out on a tray?"

Pope Francis saw the silver tray, placed his hands over the beads, concentrated in earnest prayer, and blessed them. For those of us who trust that God has a plan, this was Him at work. I was reminded that this wasn't all about me and my getting a picture with the pope; it was very much about sharing God's grace—and, in my case, having blessed rosary beads for my mother.

The press inevitably discovered that I was not part of the papal audience, and they once again tried to make me a story. I got calls and emails—"Hey, how come you're not with the pope, Sean?"—and reporters trying to elicit a bitter comment from me. *Politico* ran a story about my disappointment, citing unnamed sources. While I would have loved to be part of that papal audience, I had not expressed disappointment to the media or anyone. In truth, I was incredibly humbled when Dan showed me a picture of the Holy Father laying hands on a silver tray of rosary beads.

I had learned not to share my personal thoughts—any thoughts I didn't want to see in print—with anyone but Rebecca, or perhaps in silent prayer. And I now found solace in the olive-wood rosary beads blessed by the pope.

When you truly believe that God has a plan, you have to live your life like that every day—not just for convenient headlines or the media's preferred narrative.

It is God who decides the "when" and "how" of our lives.

As we were off traveling the world, Christiaan Alting von Geusau, the leader of the International Catholic Legislators Network (ICLN), was meeting with Vice President Pence and Mick Mulvaney, director of the Office of Management and Budget, about the ICLN's upcoming, annual meeting near Rome. While Mick had attended the annual gathering of Catholic legislators in the past (as a member of Congress from South Carolina), he would not be able to attend this year. When Christiaan asked who could attend on behalf of the White House, Mick suggested me.

Rebecca and I looked at the meeting's schedule and saw that the ICLN gathering would take place the week before our children had to return to school for the fall. So, we decided to take them with us. And, fortunately, my mother was also able to join us.

The day we were scheduled to fly to Rome, Rebecca and I had lunch in the Navy Mess with Bishop Michael Burbidge, Father Edward Hathaway, Father Nicholas Barnes, Father Andrew Haissig, and Mrs. Janet Cantwell, the principal of our children's school. We prayed together for a safe and enjoyable trip, and we had a terrific lunch with great conversation that set the tone for our journey, which would begin at Dulles International Airport later that evening.

The next morning, we landed in Rome and visited a few of the famous historic landmarks in that majestic city. Then we drove forty-five minutes into the countryside to a quaint village called Frascati. At the top of a beautiful hill, up a winding road, sat an old monastery where the ICLN conference would take place.

It was a breathtaking location, and we could see the dome of St. Peter's Basilica from our dinner that evening. Throughout the conference, we had introspective and enlightening conversations with Catholic legislators from around the world, including Australia, Kenya, Argentina,

Thailand, Uganda, Ireland, Zimbabwe, the European Union, and the United Kingdom.

After Mass on Sunday, all of the ICLN attendees boarded buses that drove us to the Vatican. We walked past the Swiss Guard, up some gleaming marble stairs, and into a magnificent room with murals painted across the ceiling. We had to look twice to make sure it wasn't the Sistine Chapel. As we proceeded to our seats, we could hear, on a loud speaker, the voice of Pope Francis praying before a crowd.

A few minutes later, some large doors on the side of the room opened, and the Holy Father walked in, with a gentle smile across his face. He offered a blessing to all in attendance, and we joined in prayer. Then his representatives began motioning us up to the front of the room where we would meet the pontiff. When I introduced him to my mother, I mentioned that my father had recently passed away. I asked if he would pray for my father and his soul. He told me that he would do that. He also placed his holy hands on my children's heads, who were each carrying a rosary.

God indeed had a plan, and through faith *and* experience I have learned to trust in Him.

CHAPTER TEN

THE WAY FORWARD

Summer in Washington is known for being hot and humid. The summer of 2017 was no exception—in more ways than just the weather. Robert Mueller, who had been named special counsel by Deputy Attorney General Rod Rosenstein, was investigating Russian interference in the U.S. election. As a result, one word—"Russia"—had become a catchall not just for suspected collusion with a foreign power against a political opponent, but for almost any imagined personal or political misdeed of the administration.

President Trump became increasingly preoccupied with the daily developments of the investigation, speaking with his lawyers first thing every morning. His frustration with Attorney General Jeff Sessions (who had recused himself from the case) and Rosenstein (who had appointed Mueller) was boiling over into his tweets and public comments.

In my final weeks, I was determined to find ways to lower the temperature with members of the press. I thought it would help to focus more on the content of the briefings. I proposed doing more briefings without the drama of TV cameras and bright lights; I also suggested we bring subject-matter experts and Cabinet secretaries into the briefings to provide more complete information about and perspective into specific policy matters. I truly wanted to focus on the policy objectives of this administration, including national security, tax reform, and trade provisions.

I wanted the briefings to center on policies and proposals that could impact the daily livelihoods of families across America (many of whom voted for Donald Trump, looking for some economic relief) and that had great implications for the future of our country. But instead, the changes we implemented in the briefing room set off intense media speculation. Was a White House staff shake-up looming? What was the future of the communications shop? Was Reince's future as chief of staff on thin ice? When asked if there was any truth to the shake-up rumors, Sarah and I—in good faith—denied them. Until the president himself informed us that he was preparing to change the staff, we had no announcements to make. But we were hearing the same rumors as everyone else.

The game of gotcha continued, even in the off-camera briefings. The White House press corps complained that we had gone a dozen work days in July without an on-camera briefing—even though the president had been to Poland, Germany, and France and tradition held that no on-camera briefings would held while the president was traveling.

"This is *not* an accident," wrote CNN's Chris Cillizza. "What the White House is doing is working to kill off the daily press briefing—a ritual that has long functioned as the best (and often only) way for reporters to get the White House on record and on video about various issues affecting the country and the world."[1]

For the reasons I outlined in the previous chapter, I respectfully disagree. In today's multimedia, multi-channeled world, the on-camera daily press briefing was not only an anachronism—it was a source of more drama than illumination. We were finding that our off-camera briefings, "backgrounders," and one-on-one interviews were more productive, delivered greater detail and explanation, and ultimately yielded better insights for the media and the public.

Naturally, the White House press corps did not see it that way.

"Sanders and White House press secretary Sean Spicer appear to be working hard to be, at best, unhelpful and, at worst, openly misleading," wrote Cillizza who, by my recollection, never attended a briefing in the White House during my tenure, making his writing about the interactions of the press operation in the White House rather ironic. Cillizza took me to task for bucking a question a reporter (who was in the briefing room) had asked about how the administration's "Made in America" week (an effort to promote American products) might affect companies owned by the Trump family. As he should have known, I was prohibited from answering any legal questions about the president's personal business.

This constant wrestling with the media over words, terms, agreements, and understandings was getting old.

I gave considerable thought to how I could continue to serve while wearing a different hat. I questioned if I would be of greater service to the president if I became a full-time communications director or if I moved into a larger strategic role. Either course of action was better for me—and, frankly, better for the media—than to continue where I was.

And then came Anthony Scaramucci.

When Scaramucci joined the White House, he wanted to make sure that everyone knew he had the power to make changes he saw fit to implement. He was to report directly to the president and not, as is custom, to the chief of staff. So, for ten days, whether he was official or not, Anthony Scaramucci acted as a White House communications director and, in truth, as a deputy chief of staff. During those ten days, I kept my nose down, stayed busy keeping the White House tax reform meetings on pace, and met with a list of staff that had requested time with me. And I had to manage as best as possible the awkwardness of watching the White House communications staff grapple with the looming presence of this powerful, pungent personality.

My first and only interaction with Scaramucci at the White House was when he showed up in my office on his first day. I had called the entire communications staff—all forty of them—into my office to make sure they heard my news from me before they saw it on TV or their phones.

As I told them the news, I saw a lot of eyes with tears welling up in them. I felt as emotional as anyone. These were people I believed in, had fought for, and cared deeply about. I had worked in the trenches with many of them for several years, others for a few months. But we had worked through some tough times and shared some fun memories. We had slugged it out together during the 2016 presidential election when all the polls showed Trump losing, giving many media outlets license to write his political obituary long before election day. We had worked long hours, seven days a week, to rebuild the RNC and to launch first-rate digital media and rapid response teams. I was fortunate to work alongside such strong, intelligent, and dedicated people. I was going to miss them. And they were concerned about what the future held for them.

As I was in the middle of breaking my news to my colleagues, Scaramucci bounced in. Not realizing that he was interrupting something, he walked directly to me and gave me a faux "man hug." I am not much of a hugger, especially not with people I don't know well.

Other than that brief appearance, not once during the ten days of his tenure did Scaramucci ask to meet. And that was fine with me. Some of my staffers tried as best as they could to ingratiate themselves with Scaramucci. (Many reporters also tried ingratiating themselves with "the Mooch" by sending out flattering, congratulatory tweets in the hope of cultivating a friend on the inside.) Some tried to ignore him as best as they could. But ignoring him proved impossible because Anthony Scaramucci had made it clear that he was going to fire somebody. It wasn't that anybody in particular needed to be fired; it was that Anthony Scaramucci needed to fire someone to establish himself and express his dominance over the staff. He singled out one very competent and loyal staffer and compelled him to submit his resignation. He threatened and intimidated others.

Scaramucci did this because he had promised the president he would do what no one else had done—root out the leakers. There was no evidence that the man he sought to fire was a leaker, but perhaps the firing would intimidate those who did. I remained convinced that while there was some leaking coming from my shop, 90 percent of the White House leaks came from outside of the communications team. It was out of concern for this 10 percent that I had clumsily tried to check for messaging apps months earlier. But for the most part, the White House communications shop— which has to manage the fallout from leaks—was a place that got headaches from leaks. Still under pressure from his promise to the president, Scaramucci began to more loudly accuse his staff— women and men who worked tirelessly for the president—of being disloyal. Morale plummeted.

While Scaramucci began to publicly denigrate his own staff, I busied myself with trying to line up the external pieces Scaramucci would need to manage the orchestration of surrogates. The White House communications director must manage a wide field of surrogates in Congress, think tanks, and the lobbying industry. I wanted to make sure I continued giving everything I could to the White House and the country while I still had the honor and privilege of walking through those gates every day. I also wanted to ensure that no one would blame me for placing a banana peel in front of him should he trip and fall flat on his face.

The first slip up came one day into his job. Anthony Scaramucci called Ryan Lizza of the *New Yorker*. Because he believed they had similar backgrounds—supposedly, their fathers had been friends— Scaramucci assumed that he could vent to Lizza and that he would treat the call as an off-the-record, background conversation, without any attribution. The first rule of going off the record is to get an explicit agreement from the reporter. But Scaramucci didn't run the basic disclaimer.

Lizza, of course, immediately published the whole interview. In it, Scaramucci displayed the charming habit of referring to himself as "the Mooch." "Okay," he told Lizza, "the Mooch showed up a week ago. This is going to get cleaned up very shortly."

"This" being a communications shop that needed public humiliation and firing.

Scaramucci claimed, "What I'm going to do is, I will eliminate everyone in the comms team…" He also stated, "I'm going to fire every one of them, and then you haven't protected anybody, so the entire place will be fired over the next two weeks."

There are many ways to build morale in a team during a management change. Publicly declaring that you will fire everyone is not one of them.

Scaramucci reserved his greatest ire for the chief of staff. He continued to blame Reince Priebus for the release of his financial information, still not understanding that those documents were a matter of public record. In fact, he wanted the FBI to investigate the White House chief of staff.

"Reince Priebus—if you want to leak something—he'll be asked to resign very shortly."

There was more: "Reince is a f[***]ing paranoid schizophrenic, a paranoiac... 'Let me leak the f[***]ing thing and see if I can c[***]-block these people the way I c[***]-blocked Scaramucci for six months.'"

This was, of course, a very self-revealing comment. Reince had never blocked Scaramucci from the White House. He had respected the standards of financial disclosure and disinvestment that needed to be undertaken before someone—anyone—could assume a position as a top White House aide.

And paranoia? That answers itself.

So, here was a White House communications director telling a national reporter that the chief of staff was about to be fired for leaking.

Finally, Scaramucci took a turn to his trademark, wise-guy vulgarity: "I'm not Steve Bannon; I'm not trying to suck my own c[***]."

When the *New Yorker* broke the piece, Scaramucci accused Lizza of betraying him. Lizza told John Berman of CNN, "When the Communications Director for the White House calls you and tells you, on the record, that he's about to fire the entire communications staff, that he has called the FBI to investigate the Chief of Staff at the White House, and that the Chief Strategist is engaged in autofellatio, I think that is a fairly newsworthy set of comments."[2]

Even worse for Scaramucci was the release of the audio tape, a cleaned-up version of his conversation with Lizza that ran on every cable and major news channel.

In truth, if there was a betrayal, it was Scaramucci's betrayal of Donald Trump, Reince Priebus, and the good people who were to serve under him. What had originally stopped Scaramucci from getting a coveted White House job was the approval of a government office in the Department of the Treasury to sell his company to a Chinese conglomerate. Months after his brief stint, the Committee on Foreign Investment in the United States, the government organization that approves the sale of U.S. companies to foreign owners, still had not approved the sale, and the Chinese conglomerate pulled out of the deal.

■   ■   ■

Humiliated by his own words, Scaramucci was suddenly making nice with the staff and trying to give explanatory interviews in a desperate attempt to save his job. Everyone else knew that he was already a dead man walking.

While alternating currents of outrage and amusement flowed through the White House in the aftermath of Scaramucci's conversation with Lizza, I took great pains not to show any emotion and just keep doing my job. Some people asked me privately if I felt vindicated. I didn't need vindication.

I continued to meet with the president. While President Trump had appreciated the pugnacious side of Anthony Scaramucci, he was unpleasantly surprised—frankly, as shocked as anyone—by the recklessness with which Scaramucci approached his job. The president had thought he had hired an ace when, in fact, he had hired a kamikaze pilot. Even worse, the president had noticed that Anthony Scaramucci loved to give everyone the impression that he and the president were personally very tight. Now this presumed closeness had become a liability.

Scaramucci was, however, highly effective in his one main mission—taking out Reince Priebus as Donald Trump's chief of staff. It happened on a return flight from Long Island on Air Force One. Many people think that Air Force One is always the same plane, but Air Force One is the official military designation for whichever aircraft is flying the president.

On July 28, 2017, the president was scheduled to fly to Selden, a town on Long Island, to speak about gang violence and immigration. Because the local airport there has a shorter runway, it was decided that the president would fly on a smaller Boeing 737.

I had initially put myself on the manifest to take one last flight with the president.

One of my deputies stuck his head in my office.

"Did you hear who is on the manifest?" he said.

I shrugged my shoulders.

"Scaramucci."

I knew it was, of course, a desperate bid by Scaramucci to glue himself to the president. But it also clearly gave the Mooch an opportunity to get rid of the man he believed was his nemesis— Reince Priebus. I thought of the Boeing 737's tight quarters and the inevitable awkwardness of all of us sitting around a staff table, and I decided not to go. Besides, my team had the president covered. So, instead, I looked forward to some calm time back at the office. I especially wanted to catch up with Sarah, who was going to succeed me.

Back at the office, while I was working with the White House communications staff for the post-Spicer transition, a presidential tweet announced the appointment of General John Kelly, the Secretary of Homeland Security, as White House chief of staff. Several of us in the press office joined around a wall of televisions to watch live coverage of the transition. Reince later told me that he had given his resignation to the president earlier. Whatever happened on the plane, the optics were not good for my friend as he moved from the official motorcade to a car in front of the press, leaving the impression that he had been brusquely booted out.

Scaramucci's blistering and highly personal attacks in public had made Reince ripe for targeting, precipitating a move that was bound to happen sooner or later. From the very start, Reince had been in an untenable position, sharing authority with Kellyanne, Steve, and Jared.

When he accepted his new job, General Kelly, true to his military background, insisted that the chief of staff position would be a centralized control and filter between the commander in chief and his staff, with a traditional chain of command.

The most immediate loser under the new chief of staff would be Scaramucci, who was abruptly fired. He promptly sought to return to the Export-Import Bank of the United States, perhaps in hopes of downplaying the move as a transfer. Not soon after that, Steve Bannon was in the crosshairs. He had enjoyed great power as chief strategist under Reince Priebus—a cover that allowed him to operate in a nebulous and secretive way—but he would not last much longer either.

For those of us who had remained at the White house instead of traveling to New York on that day, a quiet day of planning had been upended. We were now handling one of the biggest news days we had seen.

With Scaramucci out, several people asked if I would consider staying on at the White House in a different role. Sarah was ready to be press secretary, so I would have the opportunity to play a role in strategy and planning on significant policy issues. I entertained the idea and then dismissed it. Over a drink, I mentioned the idea to Rebecca. She is a staunch believer in serving our country. So, I was curious about what her reaction would be.

"You made a decision. You need to stick to it," she said.

It was time to go.

■   ■   ■

In the weeks leading up to my resignation, I took a big personal risk and began a series of deep, background conversations with four reporters to help shape my own post-White House narrative. I had seen how quickly the media judged people during the campaign and transition into the White House. I did not know the end was as close as it was when I began my conversations with them, but the palace intrigue and interest in my future was escalating. If I wanted to shape my own story, I needed to loop some folks into the situation. I needed there to be some understanding of what I was thinking and why. Four outlets in particular would be crucial to converse with: Fox News, *Politico*, the *New York Times*, and CNN.

John Roberts of Fox News, a veteran reporter who had previous White House stints at CNN and CBS, was well respected, and I knew Fox's initial report of my departure would be critical.

Mark Preston of CNN was a long-time political reporter, whom I had gotten to know well during my time at the RNC. Mark and I had very candid conversations over the years. While I did not agree with all of his on-air analyses or published stories, he always listened to my points and engaged in a fair journalistic process. My relationship with many reporters at CNN had been strained, but Mark and I had kept lines of communication open and enjoyed constructive dialogue.

Next was one of the more unlikely suspects: Glenn Thrush of the *New York Times*. Glenn and I had had some rather epic exchanges in the Press Briefing Room. Even out of the public eye, Glenn and I also had some significant disagreements about the tone of his coverage and the accuracy of his reporting. Like it or not, though, at the time Glenn was a leader among the pack of White House reporters, and how he framed my departure would be very important.

The fourth reporter was Josh Dawsey, then of *Politico* and now of the *Washington Post*. My issues with *Politico*'s reporting could fill another book, but the publication's growing influence among reporters, political operatives, pundits, and talking heads could not be overlooked. As with Glenn, I had some well-known issues with aspects of Josh's reporting. I thought he placed too much focus on palace intrigue inside the White House instead of covering policy debates and achievements, but I felt Josh would try to understand my rationale. Months later, the White House Correspondents' Association presented the Merriman Smith Award for print reporting to Josh for his coverage of my resignation. The award read, "While the resignation story was widely covered, Dawsey reported details others simply did not have. Beautifully reported and written." No kidding—he had a great source.

When I talked with each of these four reporters—on deep background and far off the record— my goal was to show the human side of my thinking and to provide additional context. I cared about the president, the presidency, the GOP, and the country. But I also was increasingly concerned about the toll the job was taking on my ability to be effective and the toll it was taking on my family.

Despite the public profile that accompanies the press secretary's role, the job does not come with any physical security detail. While I was safe within the confines of the White House, I grew more and more concerned about the safety of my family. Rebecca had countless meetings and calls with members of the Secret Service and the Alexandria Police Department. She was on a first-name basis with several agents and officers, and she had their personal cell phone numbers plugged into her phone. We cut back on being outside or in public, but that didn't change much. The tweets and mail targeting my wife and kids were still getting old. (So were the reporters who started showing up at the front door of my mother's house.)

※　　　　※　　　　※

As I prepared to leave the White House, and in the months thereafter, I had plenty of time to reflect on the relationship between elected officials and the media—what is wrong with it and the best way forward.

Today's media is obsessed with palace intrigue instead of issues of substance, prioritizing the number of clicks, viewers, and subscriptions. The "always-on" nature of online news is driving journalists to prioritize being first over being right. The prospect of becoming a cable star is prompting previously obscure journalists to favor theatrics and outrage over insight. The inability of any journalist in the briefing room to call out the bad or misleading reporting or antics of another reporter for fear of retribution is a problem. And journalists, rather than critique and improve each other's reporting, are captives of a pack mentality—driven largely by the shrinking economics of the news business, a sector in which you'd better be nice to your peers because you might need their goodwill to get your next job.

There were other corrupting influences as well, such as the disappearing wall between news and opinion. The great journalists of the post-World War II era (at least most of them) were scrupulous about keeping their partisan views and opinions to themselves. Now, thanks to Twitter and cable news, many journalists tweet opinions and impressions that their job titles lend an aura of objectivity to. Because of this, one of the greatest journalists of our time privately confessed to me, "Sean, I can't tell you how disappointed I am in my profession."

Another journalist, Peter Hamby, formerly of CNN and now head of news at Snapchat, wrote a long, insightful paper at the Harvard Kennedy School's Shorenstein Center that diagnosed the problems social media is importing into media ethics.

He wrote, "With Instagram and Twitter-primed iPhones, an ever more youthful press corps, and a journalistic reward structure in Washington that often prizes speed and scoops over context, campaigns are increasingly fearful of the reporters who cover them. Any perceived gaffe or stumble can become a full-blown narrative in a matter of hours, if not minutes, thanks to the velocity of the Twitter conversation that now informs national reporters, editors and television producers."

Hamby concluded that "Twitter is the central news source for the Washington-based political news establishment."

The problem, and I suspect Hamby would agree, is that Twitter is not glue. It is a solvent. It is breaking us down and breaking us apart. (And yes, I see the irony of Donald Trump's former press secretary making this observation.) With Twitter at the center, substantive issues that require more than 280 characters get short shrift. Jaime Dimon, head of JPMorgan Chase & Co., expressed a sentiment common to many Americans in July 2017 when he said, "The United States of America has to start to focus on policy which is good for all Americans, and that is infrastructure, regulation, taxation, education. Why you guys don't write about it every day is completely beyond me."[3]

Twitter and other social media platforms let us say stuff we would never say to a person's face (at least most of us would not). We can keep pointing fingers or start calling out certain comments that are out of bounds. But that includes the media calling themselves out and holding themselves accountable. Politicians and citizens can get raked over the coals for non-private tweets, and so should journalists. We can't settle for just keeping up with the lowest common dominator on Twitter.

Many journalists see the president's attacks on "fake news" as an attack on them personally.

AP's Julie Pace told *Politico*, "The attacks on the media, the attempts to undermine our credibility, they see as very much part of the Trump agenda. I don't think it's a show in the sense that I do think that they see this as part of the agenda. This is something that they believe is central to Trump's success, is to try to undermine negative coverage about him. And I think they believe in that mission, I really do."

In making our case to the media, we should focus on highlighting the specific issues we have with certain stories as opposed to painting them all with a broad brush.

At the root of the media's behavior is a belief that the other side is playing dirty. When the president cracked down to catch leakers in the national security arena—including leaks of classified information, such as his conversations with national leaders—some in the intelligence world privately complained to the press that they were living in "a culture of fear."[4] President Trump would say that a person shouldn't have anything to fear as long as he or she is not breaking the law.

Last year, Senator Ron Johnson, chairman of the Senate Committee on Homeland Security and Governmental Affairs, said that serious leaks are "flowing at the rate of one a day." This statement is mostly not about the kind of insider leaks that come out of the White House about who's up and who's down or what the president had for dinner. The senator instead referred to serious leaks of classified information. His committee released a report revealing that the Trump administration is facing leaks at a rate that is "seven times higher than the same period during the two previous administrations." The committee's report also stated, "In short, the unauthorized disclosure of certain information can cost American lives, and our laws protecting this information provide for harsh punishments when violated."[5]

The leaks are bad enough. Compounding it from the president's point of view are the numerous errors of top news outlets. Jonathan

Easley of *The Hill* cataloged many "bombshell stories [about the president or his administration that] were either overcooked or included incorrect details."

For example, the Associated Press ran a story about how Environmental Protections Agency Administrator Scott Pruitt met privately with the CEO of a top chemical company and then decided to drop a ban on a widely used pesticide that has been shown to harm children's brains.

The meeting never happened. Easley listed similar embarrassments for CNN, the *New York Times*, and other major news organizations. Even worse—from the mainstream media's point of view—is the fact that many of these stories were corrected by Breitbart News.[6] If you have a jaundiced view of Breitbart, perhaps you might want to ask yourself the following question: what are we doing so wrong that we are susceptible to being corrected by Breitbart?

Is it any wonder that, faced with such a juggernaut of official and media opposition, the president lashes out? Or that so many nod their heads when the president attacks fake news and big news organizations?

If we are all believers in the First Amendment, then we should embrace the whole of it. The First Amendment is about more than the freedom of the press; it is about each of us being able to voice our views. While the media has the right to publish and broadcast what it chooses, the rest of us have an equal right to voice our beliefs and to criticize what the media writes and broadcasts. I have my differences with more than a few people in the media, but I still firmly believe that a healthy democracy must have a free and robust press corps. Our nation is the envy of the world because we all have the right to speak freely and are able to criticize our government and leaders. But with that awesome right should come a hefty responsibility.

Understanding that the First Amendment is for everybody is at the heart of establishing a better relationship between the White House and the press corps. Sometimes, the rhetoric stemming from this relationship has been overheated, and both parties were in need of the wisdom of Proverbs 15:18: "A hot-tempered person stirs up conflict, but the one who is patient calms a quarrel" (NIV). There have been tweets and statements from both sides that were intended to wound. But if we could all remain tough, critical, and in pursuit of the truth, we would be in a good place to start moving forward.

▓   ▓   ▓

During my last days in the White House in August 2017, I focused on tax reform. I worked closely with Marc Short of the legislative affairs team, Bill McGinley of the Office of Intergovernmental Affairs, George Sifakis of the Office of Public Liaison, experts from the Department of the Treasury, the team at the National Economic Council, and, of course, the White House communications team. All of us wanted to make sure that legislative, policy, and communications initiatives worked together like a symphony to advance the president's tax plan.

Planning the rollout of a big campaign was my wheelhouse. By the time my last day rolled around on September 1, I felt that we had a thorough, buttoned-down blueprint to get the tax reform across the finish line. After I returned to private life, it was a thrill to watch the plan unfold, Congress pass the tax bill in December 2017, and the president sign it into law as Americans across the country received economic relief unlike many have ever seen. This landmark tax package has been reviving the economy and getting Americans back to work.

It was also a pleasure to see Sarah take the podium. She is very adept at recognizing what works and what doesn't, the needs of the press corps, and the needs of the president. She hit the ground running because she is such a keen observer and quick learner.

As for myself, for the first time in my adult life, I was not working full-time for a campaign, a party, the military, or the government (save a small stint with my own firm in 2009). And that was by design. I now had an opportunity to make a living by speaking to business and political groups, to help well-selected clients, and, yes, to write a book.

I had talked long and hard with a number of people about the job of press secretary after election night—Reince, Hope, a couple of close friends and family members, especially Rebecca who expressed absolutely no hesitation about me taking the job. In fact, she encouraged me at every step. "It's an honor to be offered the opportunity to serve our country in any White House. It's also an awesome responsibility," she would say. Fewer than thirty Americans have had the privilege of serving as White House press secretary. I am honored to be part of that exclusive group.

I had sought out this job and fought for it. But it was a relief to finally be out of the hot seat— not just that of the press secretary, but of the RNC, the U.S. House of Representatives, congressional committees, congressional offices, and more campaigns than I can now remember.

Along with the daily pressure of being inside the White House, I was giving up the pressure of being a public figure of controversy. Rebecca and I could not go out to dinner without being mobbed—and often being told off or getting the finger, even in front of our young children. We found that the Army Navy Country Club—which we had joined when I was a junior Navy officer—was the only place we could go without being approached or recorded on a phone. There were times when we saw activists driving or walking by.

It had gotten to the point where I was even being accosted in places like Harris Teeter, where a woman lit into me while I was trying to buy frozen peas. She started while I was opening the freezer door. All the while I was hoping she wasn't recording our encounter in the frozen food section with her smartphone.

After she gave me an earful, I said, "Ma'am, I'm literally just trying to buy some frozen peas here."

"Really? You have kids? My kids like peas," she said.

"We have that in common. I hope you have a great night."

Shortly after I had announced my resignation, one of the White House operators, Joan Sass— another one of the countless, dedicated public servants who make the White House work so well— sent me an email with a quote from the late White House Press Secretary Tony Snow, who served under George W. Bush. "The White House, with all its pressures, intrigues, triumphs, betrayals, joys and disappointments, is the most special place you will ever work. Look out the gates at the people who slow their gait as they pass, trying to get a glimpse of someone— anyone. They know what you're likely to forget. You're blessed."

He was right.

On my last day in the office, the staff hosted a going-away party for me. I asked several of them to join me on the walk to the bar where the party was held. We walked out of the White House, past the Rose Garden, and on to the driveway by the South Lawn. A Secret Service officer opened the gates to the southeast driveway so that we could walk out as a group. After we passed through, I turned around, stopped, and watched those gates slowly close on my White House service for a last time.

Once I was outside the gates, there was an interesting change in how I was treated. Rebecca and I slowly started going to dinner with our children in public places. Once again, people would approach us, but the interaction was very different. Many people wanted to shake my hand and get a selfie. Some wanted to thank me for my service. And even liberal activists treated me like a notable person, instead of a cutout to harangue. "I may not agree with your politics, but I appreciate what you've done for our country," several have said to me.

I was determined to slow down, to be deliberate, and to explore my options while enjoying life with my family. I didn't expect that some of them would be a fleeting brush with the entertainment industry.

I got calls from several late-night TV shows, from Seth Meyers's to James Corden's. I thought it would be interesting to poke a little fun at myself, as long as it was good spirited and not mean. I made it clear to all of the shows that if they wanted me to denigrate the president, then I wasn't their guy. When Jimmy Kimmel's team reached out to me, I had some good conversations. I would later talk with Jimmy himself. I could sense that he was a truly decent guy, liberal but willing to be fair and funny. I also knew that President George W. Bush had been on Jimmy's show and had been treated with respect.

Soon after that call, I agreed to appear on his show. Rebecca and I flew out to Los Angeles the night before I was scheduled to appear. We made sure to make the most of our time and meet with as many people as possible. Chris Licht, Stephen Colbert's executive producer, asked me to meet him at the W Hotel, just a few blocks down Hollywood Boulevard from where we were staying. I had known Chris since his days as the executive producer of *Morning Joe*. I went to the meeting expecting Chris to ask me to be on *The Late Show with Stephen Colbert*. Instead, he had another gig in mind.

"Hey, I got an interesting question for you," Chris said. "How would you like to open the Emmys? Stephen and I were talking about this. We think it would be hysterical."

After a few seconds of stunned silence, I said, "Look, let me run it by my wife." Rebecca advised me to see the script before giving an answer. We agreed that I could have a little fun at my own expense, but I didn't want to do anything to anger either the president or the press.

I left Chris to join some high school classmates from Portsmouth Abbey School for dinner. After dinner, Rebecca and I met up with actor Rob Lowe who had famously played Sam Seaborn on *The West Wing*. Washington social maven Susanna Quinn had introduced us after I had been announced as press secretary, and I wanted to get his opinion on opening the Emmys.

"You have to do it," said Rob. After seeing the script, Rebecca agreed.

We flew back to Washington the day after I appeared on Kimmel's show, only to get ready to head back out to Los Angeles. Colbert's team wanted my appearance to be a surprise, so I did everything I could to make it known that I was back in Virginia. I even posted photos of myself doing television interviews from my front yard to establish that I was home.

Just two days later, we got back on a plane to Los Angeles. I was wearing a baseball cap and glasses, attempting to travel incognito. Once we arrived at the hotel, I had to stay in the room so that I wouldn't run the risk of someone seeing me. Rebecca could get us food (and a couple of drinks), and she could also answer the telephone when it rang in the room.

That afternoon, we were taken to the Microsoft Theater for a brief rehearsal with Stephen. I was whisked into the theater through a back entrance and blocked-off corridors. The stage and surrounding area had been cleared of all crew and guests to maintain the secrecy. My name was even kept out of the script.

So, on the evening of September 17, with butterflies in my stomach, I rolled a mock White House podium onto the stage to declare, "This will be the largest audience to witness an Emmys—period—both in person and around the world."

The gasps from the audience were audible.

Back stage, I had had a chance to meet LL Cool J, Dolly Parton, many Saturday Night Live cast members, and Alec Baldwin—who were all personable and charming. James Corden gave me a kiss on the cheek, and many other Hollywood A-listers talked to me as well. All of them said kind things about my willingness to poke fun at myself. I was actually shocked. I assumed our conversations would been contentious considering their stereotypical political leanings.

The warm feeling continued through several post-Emmy parties.

But it couldn't last, not in that environment. The next day, *Vanity Fair* and other Hollywood outlets began to report criticism of Stephen Colbert for inviting me. Many who had been nice to me were forced to recant and to virtually denounce me in the press and on Twitter. James Corden had to apologize three different ways.

Despite the bad aftertaste, I had enjoyed my Hollywood experience. I find it stimulating to talk with people who have different political viewpoints—and necessary. They might learn something from me. And, yes, I might learn from them, too.

■ ■ ■

I spent my career in service to powerful people, always in a supporting role to someone else who played the part of the principal—a member of Congress, an RNC chairman, a president of the United States.

Now I was my own principal. Now, at last, I was free to be my own man.

I will be forever grateful to the president, the First Lady, Reince, and my family for being able to have the honor and privilege of serving the country in this position. It is an amazing job, but it's a lonely job that very few people have had and even fewer can appreciate in the current environment.

The night I resigned, a White House reporter sent an email to my long-time friend Ron Bonjean that read, "One element of his legacy is this: he democratized the press room. By calling on those of us in the back of the room, he broke the grip that the front row had on the briefing. And I don't think it will go back any time soon. A lot more voices are heard now. So, from a guy at the back of the room, tell him thanks." I am professionally very proud of that accomplishment and do hope it lasts. We are a country of many opinions and voices, and they should be heard and respected.

It has been a long-standing tradition that the outgoing press secretary leaves a note to the incoming one. In his note to me, outgoing Obama Press Secretary Josh Earnest wrote, "Because your work is essential to the success of our democracy, it is not hard for me to set aside my political views and genuinely root for you to succeed in this role." Pure class.

I got notes and calls from many of my other predecessors. It's a small group from both parties who have shared in this truly unique role.

A few months after I left the White House, the rector of the Basilica of St. Mary in Old Town Alexandria, Father Edward Hathaway, distributed copies of the book *Perfectly Yourself: Discovering God's Dream for You* for Lenten reading. The author, Matthew Kelly, quotes political theorist and scholar Benjamin Barber:

> I divide the world into learners and non-learners. There are people who learn, who are open to what happens around them, who listen, who hear the lessons. When they do something stupid, they don't do it again. And when they do something that works a little bit, they do it even better and harder the next time. The question to ask is not whether you are a success or a failure, but whether you are a learner or a non-learner.[7]

Those words resonated with me.

So, would I do it again? Yes. I believe that God has a plan, and this was part of it. Some days, I was tested, but many days I got to be part of history, share my experience with family and friends, and help American citizens in some small way.

I hope to play a role in creating a more constructive dialogue and restoring civil discourse. I will strive to be less aggressive and accusatory, less judgmental, more patient, and more understanding. Will I be perfect? No. But will I try, and I will learn.

As I have traveled around the country, appearing at events and offering some ideas on how to repair our broken politics and our broken media, I have enjoyed having a platform that allows me to help find solutions that move our country forward in a constructive manner.

I have valued spending more time on causes I care about—caring for our veterans, curing cancer, and supporting adoption.

Spending time with my family, my mom, my wife, and my kids has been the best part. I now have time to attend—and enjoy—my kids' soccer, lacrosse, and baseball games, as well as their scout meetings and dance recitals.

And I also feel a deepening appreciation for the family and faith that makes me stronger. Through all the ups and downs that happened to me, the one thing that helped was knowing that I will always have this foundation of a family that is always going to support me.

I often wish my father could see me now. I wish that we could talk about all that has happened and share all that is yet to come. Not a day goes by that I don't think about him and how he looked at every day and every person. He lived his final days to his fullest, caring about others and focused on his family. I hope I can do the same.

Set a guard over my mouth, Lord;
keep watch over the door of my lips.

—Psalm 141:3, NIV

ACKNOWLEDGMENTS

This book—including my life stories and life lessons—couldn't have been possible without being surrounded by talented, supportive people who have shared their lives with me along the way.

My mom and dad. Thank you for all the sacrifices you made over the years…and for your never-ending patience, support, and love.

My wife, Rebecca—you have been my partner, my supporter-in-chief, my best friend, my editor, and a great mother to our amazing children, Rigby and Will. I couldn't have done any of this without you by my side.

My family: sister Shannon; brother Ryan and sister-in-law, Emma; nephews Harry and Bo; niece Josephine; mother-in-law Sally Miller; and Gabi Salas.

The Grossman, Martel, and Connelly families.

The President, Mrs. Trump, and the Trump family.

The Vice President and Mrs. Pence.

Reince Priebus. There is no question that had President Bush, Mrs. Bush, Vice President Cheney, and Reince not taken a chance on me in 2011, I would not have had the opportunity to serve in this White House.

John Sankovich, Elizabeth Manresa and Teddy Eynon, Jeff and Ginger Snyder, Ron and Sara Bonjean, Arthur Schwartz, Ben Waisbren, Jason Miller, Sean Hannity, Donald Trump Jr., Eric Trump, Lara Trump, Tommy Hicks, Brian Jones, Ted Kratovil, Ed Gillespie, Chris Swonger, Cliff Hobbins, Tim and Joy Csanadi, Karen and Stew Abramson, Laura Fogarty Nerney, Jennifer Boland Mayer, Karen Urbaniak Anderson, Sarah and Bryan Sanders, Newt Gingrich, Raj Shah, Lindsay Walters,

Vanessa Morrone, Kirsten Kukowski, Gretchen Reiter, Joe and Alyx Grogan, Mike Dubke, Jessica Ditto, and Ryan Mahoney.

My former colleagues from Capitol Hill and the Office of the United States Trade Representative, and my former bosses: U.S. Senator John Chafee, David Griswold, U.S. Representative Frank LoBiondo, Mary Annie Harper, U.S. Representative Mike Pappas, Jeffrey Krilla, U.S. Representative Mark Foley, Kirk Fordham, U.S. Representative Dan Burton, U.S. Representative Clay Shaw and Emily Shaw, Eric Eikenberg, U.S. Representative Tom Davis, John Hishta, U.S. Representative Jim McCrery, U.S. Representative Jim Nussle, Rich Meade, U.S. Representative Deborah Pryce, Andrew Shore, Ambassador Susan Schwab, Ambassador Karan Bhatia, Ambassador John Veroneau, Ambassador Peter Allgeier, and Tim Keeler.

The White House staff; the Residence staff; the White House operators; the military aides to the President; the White House Military Office; the White House stenographers; Rickie Niceta and the Office of the Social Secretary; the White House Visitors Office; Lindsey Reynolds and the First Lady's Office; the officers of the Secret Service; the public affairs office of the Secret Service; the special agents of the Secret Service; the Alexandria Police Department, especially Sergeant Wilbur Salas and Officer Francis Powers; the White House Medical Unit, especially Rear Admiral Ronny Jackson and the doctors and staff at Walter Reed National Military Medical Center; the White House Communications Agency; the team at the Navy Mess; White House Airlift Operations, especially the crew of Marine One, Colonel Bruce Ybarra, Colonel Alex Miravite, and the crew of Air Force One.

My colleagues at the RNC, the campaign staff, the transition staff, and the White House staff: Jeff Larson, Chris Carr, Billy Skelly, Bill Steiner, Sharon Day, Rick Wiley, John Phillipe, Dirk Eyman, Mike Gilding, Cara Mason, Angela Meyers, Tony Parker, Anna Epstein, Mark Isaacson (one of the most talented writers I have ever come across), the amazing, award-winning RNC video team (Josh Sharp, Matt Mazzone, and Lauren Hernandez), Annie LeHardy, Alexa Henning, Keith Schiller, Ashley Mocarski, Boris Epshteyn, Brad Rateike, Caroline Magyarits,

Carolina Hurley, Catherine Hicks, Clay Shoemaker, Dan Scavino, Elizabeth Oberg, Giovanna Coia, Helen Aguirre Ferre, Hope Hicks, Janet Montesi, Julia Hahn, Kaelan Dorr, Kate Karnes, Kelly Love, Kellyanne Conway, Lara Barger, Leah Le'Vell, Michael Short, Natalie Strom, Ninio Fetalvo, Ory Rinat, Sofia Boza, Stephanie Grisham, Steven Cheung, Jason Chung, Thomas Tsaveras, Marcia Kelly, Joanna Spicer, Marcus Tenenbaum, Jonathan Akhondi, Katie Gibson, Andrew Good, Chris Kitter, Betty Moore, Michael Anton, Michelle Meadows, Benjamin Weiser, Avi Berkowitz, Casey Finzer, Daniel Fisher, Andrew Bremberg, Ben Key, Mary Salvi, Cassie Smedlie, Steve Bannon, Ryan Mahoney, Rick Gorka, Jason Chung, Scott Parker, Lars Trautman, Colin Spence, Naji Filali, John Kashuba, Brett Federly, Kerry Rom, Mike Abboud, Zach Parkinson, Jeff Brownlee, Jim Fellinger, Duncan Braid, Richard Sant, Christina Vucci, Christine Callahan, Anthony Trecoci, Eric Schultz, Molly Harp, Macie Leach, Harry Fones, Mike Mears, Chad Connelly, Matt Pinnell, Justin Johnson, Lauren Hernandez, David Wilezol, Dennis Wright, Caroline Anderegg, Garren Shipley, Lani Short, Alex Stroman, Telly Lovelace, Ruth Guerra, Anna Sugg, Raffi Williams, Orlando Watson, Brittany Cover, James Hewitt, Marlon Bateman, Steve Guest, Sara Sendek, Johanna Persing, Lindsay Jancck, Matt Alonzana, Caroline Swan, Ben Key, Sara Armstrong, Sean Cairncross, Mike Shields, Liam O'Rourke, Connor McGuire, Brent Seaborn, Chris Young, Katie Walsh, Jon Black, Shealah Craighead, Myles Cullen, Andrea Hanks, Joyce Boghosian, Nick Ayers, Marc Lotter, Jarrod Agen, Josh Pitcock, John Whitbeck, Ron Kaufman, Brad Parscale, the RNC War Room, the 168, Tinna Jackson, Joe Hagin, Mike Ambrosini, Patrick Clifton, Stefan Passatino, Molly Donlin, Steve Duprey, Orlando Watson, Bettina Inclán, Raffi Williams, Dwayne Barrett, Tory MaGuire Sendek, Rebecca Helig, Mike White, Ken and Keith Nahigian, Danielle Hagen, Megan Badasch, Anna Stallmann, Anne Marie Hoffman, Rick Ahearn, George Gigicos, Casey Smith, Mick Mulvaney, Gary Cohn, Ashley Marquis, Ivanka Trump, Jared Kushner, Daniel Shanks, Special Agent Joel Heffernan, Eli Miller, Steven Mnuchin, Lewis Eisenberg, Ray Washburne, Ron Weiser, Ronna Romney McDaniel, Marc Short, Stephen Miller, Josh Raffel, H. R.

McMaster, Ricky Waddell, Rick Dearborn, Richard Grenell, Renee Hudson, Mallory Hunter, Cassidy Dumbauld, John DeStefano, Sean Doocey, Shahira Knight, Kirk Marshall, Elizabeth Steil, Rob Lockwood, Alex Angelson, Christine Toretti, Woody Johnson, Chris Applegate, Mike Vallente, Mike Omegna, Bob Carey, Chris Christie, Rudy Giuliani, Andrew Giuliani, and George Sifakis.

My Navy and military family: General Joseph Dunford, General Paul Selva, Vice Admiral John Cotton, Dana White, Brigadier General Edward Thomas, Rear Admiral James Carey, Captain Greg Hicks, Captain Paula Dunn, Captain Mike Dean, Captain John Lundberg, Colonel Pat Ryder, Colonel T. J. Rainsford, Colonel Jeffrey Dolsen, the Joint Staff Public Affairs Office, Lieutenant Commander Jason Laber, Lieutenant Commander Mike Peters, Lieutenant Commander Luke Riano, Lieutenant Kenyon Anderson, Commander Michael Husband, the Joint Staff North Unit, CHINFO, and the Navy PAO community.

The former press secretaries who reached out to offer their advice and counsel: Josh Earnest, Mike McCurry, Marlin Fitzwater, and Robert Gibbs. A very special thanks to Dana Perino and Ari Fleischer for the countless times you answered a call or sent an email to share your wisdom.

Dr. Howard Safran and the team at the Comprehensive Cancer Center at The Miriam Hospital for the care they provided to my father. We are also in debt to Kim Sierra, my father's physical therapist, who guided him to an early diagnosis.

The Basilica of St. Mary, its parishioners, and school—thank you for the prayers and support, especially the Very Reverend Edward Hathaway, the Reverend Andrew Haissig, the Reverend Nicholas Barnes, Janet Cantwell, Carmen Federle, and Elena Otero-Bigg. A special thanks to our former pastor, the Reverend Dennis Kleinmann, and Bishop Michael Burbidge.

Portsmouth Abbey School and its monastic community; the International Catholic Legislators Network and its leader, Christiaan Alting von Geusau; the staff of the Army Navy Country Club; and the board of directors and staff of the National Beer Wholesalers Association, especially CEO Craig Purser and CFO Kim McKinnish.

Virginia and Brian Norment, Sue Hensley and John Robusto, Christin and Martin Baker, Jeff and Michelle Solsby, Dawn and Jeremy Stump, Beth and John Ladd, Mandy and Adam Hayes, Maggie and Larry Hayward, and many other Alexandria neighbors.

Tony Oranato; Kay Foley; Susanna Quinn; Tammy Haddad; Sean Curran; Catherine Milhoan; Daphne Barak; the team at Worldwide Speakers Group, especially Bob Thomas and Dan Sims; Michael Gruen; Matt Zimmerman; Robin Goldman; Joy Deevy; Rob Lowe; the staff at Essex House in New York; Mickael Damelincourt; Daniel MahDavian; the staff at the Trump International Hotel Washington, D.C.; John Fredericks; Larry O'Connor; the team at EWTN; John Gizzi; Elaine Hackett; Brandon Bell; Allan Fung; Dr. Patrick Soon-Shiong and Michele Soon-Shiong; Alexandria Republicans; Chris Battle; Joe Zarbano at WEEI; the New England Patriots; and Robert and Jonathan Kraft.

Keith Kellogg; Peter Navarro; Marc Adelman; Jordan Karem; Madeleine Westerhout; Justin Clark; David Urban; Chris Marston; Mo Elleithee; David Axelrod; Gerrit Lansing; Gary Coby; and John McEntee.

Mel Berger and the team at William Morris Endeavor; Biteback Publishing; and the team at Regnery Publishing, including Marji Ross, Harry Crocker, Alyssa Cordova, Lauren McCue, Elizabeth Steger, Nicole Yeatman, Andres Taborda, and Chris Pascuzzo.

To the thousands of people who told us they were praying for us and the country.

And to God the Father, from whom all blessings flow. He has blessed me with having all of you in my life. Thank you.

NOTES

Chapter One: It's Over

1. Eliza Relman, "Scaramucci called Trump a 'hack' in 2015 and now says the president 'brings it up every 15 seconds,'" *Business Insider*, July 21, 2017, http://www.businessinsider.com/scaramucci-comments-about-trump-2015-hack-2017-7.
2. Brian Stelter, "Three journalists leaving CNN after retracted article," CNN, June 27, 2017, http://money.cnn.com/2017/06/26/media/cnn-announcement-retracted-article/index.html.
3. Heather Timmons, "What happens now to Scaramucci's $180 million SkyBridge Capital deal with China's HNA Group?" Quartz, July 31, 2017, https://qz.com/1042680/anthony-scaramucci-fired-what-happens-now-to-scaramuccis-180-million-skybridge-capital-deal-with-the-chinas-hna/.

Chapter Two: Against the Odds

1. Nate Silver, "Final Election Update: There's A Wide Range Of Outcomes, And Most Of Them Come Up Clinton," FiveThirtyEight, November 8, 2016, http://fivethirtyeight.com/features/final-election-update-theres-a-wide-range-of-outcomes-and-most-of-them-come-up-clinton/.
2. Josh Katz, "Who Will Be President?" *New York Times*, last updated November 8, 2016, https://www.nytimes.com/interactive/2016/upshot/presidential-polls-forecast.html.
3. Keith J. Kelly, "Newsweek prints 'Madam President' issue before election even happens," *New York Post*, last updated November 8, 2016, https://nypost.com/2016/11/08/newsweek-prints-madam-president-issue-before-election-even-happens/.

4.   Drew Magary, "Donald Trump Is Going To Get His Ass Kicked On Tuesday," *Deadspin*, November 6, 2016, https://theconcourse. deadspin.com/donald-trump-is-going-to-get-his-ass-kicked-on-tuesday-1788618628.

5.   "Our Final 2016 Picks," Sabato's Crystal Ball, UVA Center for Politics, November 7, 2016, http://www.centerforpolitics.org/crystalball/ articles/our-final-2016-picks/.

6.   James K. Glassman, "How to Sink an Industry and Not Soak the Rich," *Washington Post*, July 16, 1993, https://www.washingtonpost. com/archive/business/1993/07/16/how-to-sink-an-industry-and-not-soak-the-rich/08ea5310-4a4b-4674-ab88-fad8c42cf55b/?utm_term=. dd4ebdf3652c.

7.   Ibid.

Chapter Three: Lessons Learned

1.   Ewen MacAskill, "Donald Trump bows out of 2012 US presidential election race," *The Guardian*, May 16, 2011, https://www.theguardian. com/world/2011/may/16/donald-trump-us-presidential-race; Shannon Travis, "Was he ever serious? How Trump strung the country along, again," CNN, May 17, 2011, http://www.cnn.com/2011/POLITICS /05/16/trump.again/index.html.

2.   Shannon Travis, "Was he ever serious? How Trump strung the country along, again," CNN, May 17, 2011, http://www.cnn.com/2011/POLITICS /05/16/trump.again/index.html.

3.   Ibid.

4.   Sheryl Gay Stolberg, et al., "The 2006 Elections: The Voters; Rumsfeld Resigns; Bush Vows 'To Find Common Ground'; Focus Is on Virginia," *New York Times*, November 9, 2006, http://query.nytimes.com/gst/ fullpage.html?res=9E0CE7D61E3FF93AA35752C1A9609C8B63&page wanted=all.

5.   "Remarks at a White House Meeting With Business and Trade Leaders," The American Presidency Project, Gerhard Peters and John T. Woolley, accessed March 20, 2018, http://www.presidency.ucsb.edu/ ws/index.php?pid=39140.

6.   Becket Adams, "'Paid Democratic Hitman': Stephanopoulos' Bizarre Debate Question on Contraception Suddenly Makes Sense," *TheBlaze*, February 14, 2012, https://www.theblaze.com/news/2012/02/14/paid-democratic-hitman-stephanopoulos-bizarre-debate-question-suddenly-makes-much-more-sense.

Chapter Four: Meeting Trump

1.   "Full text: Donald Trump announces a presidential bid," *Washington Post*, June 16, 2015, https://www.washingtonpost.com/news/post-politics/wp/2015/06/16/full-text-donald-trump-announces a presidential-bid/?utm_term=.be5859d083a0.

2.   Steve Benen, "RNC: Trump's immigration rhetoric 'not helpful,'" MSNBC, June 17, 2015, http://www.msnbc.com/rachel-maddow-show/rnc-trumps-immigration-rhetoric-not-helpful.

3.   Linda Qiu, "Trump: I called McCain a 'hero' four times," PolitiFact, July 19, 2015, http://www.politifact.com/truth-o-meter/statements/2015/jul/19/donald-trump/trump-i-called-mccain-hero-four-times/.

4.   Ben Schreckinger, "Trump attacks McCain: 'I like people who weren't captured,'" *Politico*, July 18, 2015, https://www.politico.com/story/2015/07/trump attacks-mccain-i-like-people-who-werent-captured-120317.

5.   Russell Goldman, "Candy Crowley Defends Her Libya Comment During Presidential Debate," *ABC News*, October 17, 2012, http://abcnews.go.com/Politics/OTUS/candy-crowley-defends-libya-comment-presidential-debate/story?id=17500587.

6.   Patrick Howley, "Romney breaks silence on Candy Crowley's debate interference," *Daily Caller*, January 27, 2014, http://dailycaller.com/2014/01/27/romney-breaks-silence-on-candy-crowleys-debate-interference/.

7.   Ian Schwartz, "Trump: I Will Not Pledge To Endorse Republican Nominee, Not Run As Independent," RealClearPolitics, August 6, 2015, https://www.realclearpolitics.com/video/2015/08/06/trump_i_will_not_pledge_to_endorse_republican_nominee.html.

8.   MJ Lee, et al., "Donald Trump signs RNC loyalty pledge," CNN, last updated September 3, 2015, https://www.cnn.com/2015/ 09/03/politics/donald-trump-2016-rnc-pledge-meeting/index.html.

9.   Jonathan Easley, "Trump signs GOP loyalty pledge," *The Hill*, September 3, 2015, http://thehill.com/blogs/ballot-box/252685-trump-signs-gop-loyalty-pledge.

10.   Donald Trump, interview by Joe Scarborough and Mika Brzezinski, MSNBC, March 3, 2016, https://factba.se/transcript/donald-trump-interview-morning-joe-march-3-2016.

11.   Dana Milbank, "President Trump has finally released his comic book," *Washington Post*, February 12, 2018, https://www.washingtonpost. com/opinions/president-trump-has-finally-released-his-comic-book/2018/02/12/18cfb848-1045-11e8-9065-e55346f6de81_story. html?utm_term=.926b56226d1f.

12.   Colin Campbell, "The Republican Party suddenly canceled its NBC debate amid CNBC furor," *Business Insider*, October 30, 2015, http:// www.businessinsider.com/rnc-cancels-nbc-debate-reince-priebus-cnbc.

Chapter Five: The Never-Trump Convention That Never Was

1.   Ryan Teague Beckwith, "Read Hillary Clinton and Donald Trump's Remarks at a Military Forum," *Time*, last updated September 7, 2016, http://time.com/4483355/commander-chief-forum-clinton-trump-intrepid/.

Chapter Six: Upshifting the Downshifters

1.   "NCBC Planned to Use Trump Audio to Influence Debate, Election," TMZ, October 12, 2016, http://m.tmz.com/#article/2016/10/12/nbc-trump-tape-billy-bush-plan-election-debate/.

2.   David A. Graham, "Donald Trump's Disastrous Debate," *The Atlantic*, October 9, 2016, https://www.theatlantic.com/liveblogs/2016/10/ second-presidential-debate-clinton-trump/503495/.

3.   Zach Carter, "Karl Rove: Donald Trump Can't Win," *HuffPost*, October 23, 2016, https://www.huffingtonpost.com/entry/karl-rove-donald-trump-cant-win_us_580cb4c1e4b000d0b15727dc.

4.   Matt Apuzzo, et al., "Emails Warrant No New Action Against Hillary Clinton, F.B.I. Director Says," *New York Times*, November 6, 2016, https://www.nytimes.com/2016/11/07/us/politics/hilary-clinton-male-voters-donald-trump.html.

5.   Rachel VanGilder, "Trump holds final rally in Grand Rapids: 'The election is now,'" WOOD-TV, November 7, 2016, http://woodtv.com/2016/11/07/donald-trump-at-devos-place-in-grand-rapids/.

6.   "Relive the Trump's stunning win in under 2 minutes," CNN, November 9, 2016, video, 1:42, https://www.youtube.com/watch?v=9mYVi7WHyiU.

7.   Andrew Prokop, "A top Trump staffer just promised to post video of Hillary Clinton's election night concession call," *Vox*, May 9, 2017, https://www.vox.com/policy-and-politics/2017/5/9/15596276/trump-scavino-hillary-clinton-concession-call.

Chapter Seven: Baptism by Fire

1.   Brett Edkins, "Record 6.8 Million Watched Trump's Inauguration On Twitter's Live Stream," *Forbes*, January 24, 2017, https://www.forbes.com/sites/brettedkins/2017/01/24/record-6-8-million-watched-trumps-inauguration-on-twitters-live-stream/#37ce0292a296.

2.   "CNN Dominates MSNBC During the 45th Presidential Inauguration," CNN, January 21, 2017, http://cnnpressroom.blogs.cnn.com/2017/01/21/cnn-dominates-msnbc-during-the-45th-presidential-inauguration/.

3.   Charles Savage, et al., "Trump's First Week: Misfires, Crossed Wires, and a Satisfied Smile," *New York Times*, January 27, 2017, https://www.nytimes.com/2017/01/27/us/politics/president-donald-trump-first-week.html.

4.   Valerie Richardson, "Outraged critics assume RNC meant Trump, not Jesus, in Christmas reference to 'new King,'" *Washington Times*, December 26, 2016, https://www.washingtontimes.com/news/2016/dec/26/outraged-critics-assume-rnc-meant-trump-not-jesus-/.

5.   Rich Noyes, "Even As Media Whine About Trump, Their Hostile Coverage Shows No Let Up," NewsBusters, December 12, 2017, https://www.newsbusters.org/blogs/nb/rich-noyes/2017/12/12/even-media-whine-about-trump-their-hostile-coverage-shows-no-let.

6.   "News Coverage of Donald Trump's First 100 Days," Shorenstein Center on Media, Politics and Public Policy, Harvard Kennedy School, May 18, 2017, https://shorensteincenter.org/news-coverage-donald-trumps-first-100-days/.

7.   "Press Briefing by Press Secretary Sean Spicer, February 1, 2017," The American Presidency Project, Gerhard Peters and John T. Woolley, accessed April 10, 2018, http://www.presidency.ucsb.edu/ws/index.php?pid=123146.

8.   Ben Schreckinger, "'Real News' Joins the White House Briefing Room," *Politico*, February 15, 2017, https://www.politico.com/magazine/story/2017/02/fake-news-gateway-pundit-white-house-trump-briefing-room-214781.

9.   Brian Montopoli, "Obama's 'Enchanted' Answer," CBS News, April 29, 2009, https://www.cbsnews.com/news/obamas-enchanted-answer/.

10.   Zeeshan Aleem, "Trump's assault on CNN and BuzzFeed, explained," *Vox*, January 12, 2017, https://www.vox.com/policy-and-politics/2017/1/12/14240264/trumps-cnn-buzzfeed-dossier.

11.   Amy B. Wang, "ABC News apologizes for 'serious error' in Trump report and suspends Brian Ross for four weeks," *Washington Post*, December 3, 2017, https://www.washingtonpost.com/news/arts-and-entertainment/wp/2017/12/03/abc-news-apologizes-for-serious-error-in-trump-report-suspends-brian-ross-for-four-weeks/?utm_term=.24f9f449588b.

12.   "Exclusive: Trump presser convinced NSC candidate Harward to decline," MSNBC, February 17, 2017, video, 2:03, https://www.msnbc.com/all-in/watch/exclusive-trump-presser-convinced-nsc-candidate-harward-to-decline-879994947802.

13.   "Press Briefing by Press Secretary Sean Spicer, February 21, 2017," The American Presidency Project, Gerhard Peters and John T. Woolley, accessed May 18, 2018, http://www.presidency.ucsb.edu/ws/index.php?pid=123397.

14.   Philip Rucker, et al., "After testy call with Trump over border wall, Mexican president shelves plan to visit White House," *Washington Post*, February 24, 2018, https://www.washingtonpost.com/politics/after-testy-call-with-trump-over-border-wall-mexicos-president-shelves-plan-to-visit-white-house/2018/02/24/c7ffe9e8-199e-11e8-8b08-027a6ccb38eb_story.html?utm_term=.b6d7acd68ec3.

15.   "Press Briefing by Press Secretary Sean Spicer, January 31, 2017," The American Presidency Project, Gerhard Peters and John T. Woolley, accessed April 10, 2018, http://www.presidency.ucsb.edu/ws/index.php?pid=123150.

16.   Barbara Starr and Ryan Browne, "US tries to ID hundreds of al Qaeda contacts thanks to Yemen raid," CNN, March 2, 2017, https://www.cnn.com/2017/03/02/politics/yemen-raid-al-qaeda-intelligence-contacts/index.html.

Chapte Eight: Turbulence, Inside and Out

1.   Paul Bedard, "53% drop in arrests of illegals at Southwest border crossings, 6-year low," *Washington Examiner,* July 7, 2017, https://www.washington examiner.com/53-drop-in-arrests-of-illegals-at-southwest-border-crossings-6-year-low.

2.   "Times presents 'news' that's just propaganda for Bam," *New York Post*, February 27, 2017, https://nypost.com/2017/02/27/times-presents-news-thats-just-propaganda-for-bam/.

3.   Liam Stack, "Trump, Mika Brzezinski and Joe Scarborough: A Roller-Coaster Relationship," *New York Times*, June 29, 2017, https://www.nytimes.com/2017/06/29/business/trump-tweets-mika-brzezinski-joe-scarborough.html.

4.   Nicole Lewis, "Pence's claim that 'more Americans are working today than ever before in American history,'" *Washington Post*, November 28, 2017, https://www.washingtonpost.com/news/fact-checker/wp/2017/11/28/pences-claim-that-more-americans-are-working-today-than-ever-before-in-american-history/?utm_term=.31ef7ef06ff1.

5.   David Harsanyi, "This Is Why We Can't Trust Factcheckers, Part Infinity," *The Federalist*, November 28, 2017, http://thefederalist.com/2017/11/28/cant-trust-factcheckers-part-infinity/.

6.   Jim Drinkard, et al., "AP Fact Check: The audacity of hype," AP News, February 18, 2017, https://apnews.com/85d259aa4d4e4892be3b225f7b108c39.

7.   Scott Wong, et al., "Trump, GOP lawmakers struggle with messaging," *The Hill*, July 1, 2017, http://thehill.com/homenews/house/340320-trump-gop-lawmakers-struggle-with-messaging.

8.   Tim Hains, "MSNBC's Chris Matthews Jokes About Wanting Trump To Kill Jared Kushner: 'One Good Thing Mussolini Did Was Execute His Son-in-Law,'" RealClearPolitics, June 30, 2017, https://www.realclearpolitics.com/video/2017/06/30/msnbcs_chris_matthews_jokes_about_wanting_trump_to_kill_jared_kushner_mussolini_executed_son-in-law.html.

9.   Philip Rucker, et al., "Why some inside the White House see Trump's media feud as 'winning,'" *Washington Post*, June 30, 2017, https://www.washingtonpost.com/politics/why-some-inside-the-white-house-see-trumps-media-feud-as-winning/2017/06/30/3ee9ec72-5da5-11e7-a9f6-7c3296387341_story.html?utm_term=.25f1a0530db7.

10.   Annie Karni, et al., "Sean Spicer targets own staff in leak crackdown," *Politico*, February 26, 2017, https://www.politico.com/story/2017/02/sean-spicer-targets-own-staff-in-leak-crackdown-235413.

11.   Michael S. Schmidt, et al., "Trump Campaign Aides Had Repeated Contacts With Russian Intelligence," *New York Times*, February 14, 2017, https://www.nytimes.com/2017/02/14/us/politics/russia-intelligence-communications-trump.html.

12.   Peter Baker, "Citing Recusal, Trump Says He Wouldn't Have Hired Sessions," *New York Times*, July 19, 2017, https://www.nytimes.com/2017/07/19/us/politics/trump-interview-sessions-russia.html.

Chapter Nine: Memorable Moments, Memes, and Mistakes

1.   "Full interview: Sean Spicer's apology," CNN, April 11, 2017, video, 7:36, https://www.cnn.com/videos/politics/2017/04/11/sean-spicer-entire-hitler-holocaust-apology-wolf-blitzer-tsr.cnn.

2.   "I Was Going to Fire Comey Anyway, Trump Tells Lester Holt in Interview," NBC News, May 11, 2017, video, 2:34, https://www.nbcnews.com/nightly-news/video/i-was-going-to-fire-comey-anyway-trump-tells-lester-holt-in-interview-941538371971.

3.   Glenn Thrush, et al., "'Looking Like a Liar or a Fool': What It Means to Work for Trump," *New York Times*, May 12, 2017, https://www.nytimes.com/2017/05/12/us/politics/trump-sean-spicer-sarah-huckabee-sanders.html.

4.   David Ferguson, "Why does Steve Bannon make less per year than Omarosa?: White House publishes list of employee salaries," *RawStory*, June 30, 2017, https://www.rawstory.com/2017/06/why-does-steve-bannon-make-less-per-year-than-omarosa-white-house-publishes-list-of-employee-salaries/.

5.   Joe Concha, "Maddow's Trump's tax return reveal delivers 4.1 million viewers for MSNBC," *The Hill*, March 16, 2017, http://thehill.com/homenews/media/324417-maddows-trumps-tax-return-reveal-delivers-41-million-viewers-for-msnbc.

6.   David Rutz, "Spicer Fires Back at Reporter Over Georgia Runoff Result: 'It's a Loss' for Democrats," *Washington Free Beacon*, April 19, 2017, http://freebeacon.com/politics/spicer-fires-back-at-reporter-over-congressional-runoff-race-its-a-loss-for-the-democrats/.

7.   John Bowden, "Former WH press secretaries: End live daily press briefings," *The Hill*, June 28, 2017, http://thehill.com/homenews/news/339836-arl-fleischer-embargo-white-house-briefing-video-for-use-later.

8.   Mike McCurry, et al., "Advice for media and Trump from two former presidential press secretaries," *Columbia Journalism Review*, January 5, 2017, https://www.cjr.org/covering_trump/white_house_press_corps_trump.php.

9.   Melissa Chan, "'I'm Not Sorry.' Indian-American Woman on Why She Confronted Sean Spicer in an Apple Store," *Time*, March 15, 2017, http://time.com/4699621/sean-spicer-woman-apple-store/.

10.   Paul Crookston, "Sean Spicer Encounters Courageous Anti-Fascism at the Mall," *National Review*, March 13, 2017, https://www.nationalreview.com/corner/sean-spicer-questioned-harassed-trump-critic-shree-chauhan/.

Chapter Ten: The Way Forward

1.   Chris Cillizza, "The White House is trying to kill the daily press briefing," CNN, July 17, 2017, https://www.cnn.com/2017/07/17/politics/press-briefings/index.html.

2.   Lisa de Moraes, "Ryan Lizza Punches Back At Anthony Scaramucci Claims About Profane Interview," *Deadline Hollywood*, July 28, 2017, http://deadline.com/2017/07/anthony-scaramucci-interview-reporter-defends-ryan-lizza-cnn-1202138057/.

3.   Hugh Son, "Dimon Says Being an American Abroad Is 'Almost an Embarrassment,'" Bloomberg, July 14, 2017, https://www.bloomberg.com/news/articles/2017-07-14/dimon-says-being-an-american-abroad-is-almost-an-embarrassment.

4.   Ali Watkins, et al., "Trump's leaks crackdown sends chills through national security world," *Politico*, July 7, 2017, https://www.politico.com/story/2017/07/07/trumps-leak-vendetta-sends-chills-240274.

5.   Todd Shepherd, "Senate Republicans say Trump fighting an 'avalanche' of leaks," *Washington Examiner*, July 6, 2017, https://www.washingtonexaminer.com/senate-republicans-say-trump-fighting-an-avalanche-of-leaks.

6.   Jonathan Easley, "Media errors give Trump fresh ammunition," *The Hill*, July 4, 2017, http://thehill.com/homenews/media/340564-media-errors-fuel-trump-attacks.

7.   Matthew Kelly, *Perfectly Yourself: Discovering God's Dream for You* (North Palm Beach, FL: Beacon Publishing, 2017).

INDEX